EDIBLE
ITALY

A Traveller's Guide

EDIBLE ITALY

VALENTINA HARRIS

EBURY PRESS
LONDON

Published by Ebury Press
Division of The National Magazine Company Ltd
Colquhoun House
27–37 Broadwick Street
London W1V 1FR

First impression 1988
Copyright © 1988 Valentina Harris

ISBN 0 85223 678 6

Edited by Sue Wason
Designed by Harry Green
Maps and illustrations by Tony Garrett

Computerset by MFK Typesetting Ltd, Hitchin, Herts
Printed and bound in Great Britain by Butler &
Tanner Ltd, Frome and London

Dedication

Per P, perche senza di lei, non avreste mai
letto una mia parola – con tutto il mio
profondo rispetto e tanto affetto.

Contents

How to use this book

The aim of this book is to encourage, aid and abet the visitor to Italy to explore and discover aspects of local cooking methods and traditions from one end of the country to the other – region by region.

We have set it out in a logical order, travelling from the north to the most southern tips, so that, wherever you are, you can look it up and find out what is actually worth eating and drinking in your area. Each region also has a *Worth Taking Home* section, which gives you advice on what is easy to take home to remind you of your stay.

I hope, that if you are in Bologna, Torino, Taranto or Roma, EDIBLE ITALY will help to make you feel much more at home and much less of a *turista* than you did on your last visit. And even if you're not in Italy at all, I hope this book will bring the country alive for you, and entice you to come and taste its pleasures soon.

The Regions

We have set the book out into 14 regions, which are then subdivided into provinces, because that is how the system works in Italy. If, for example, you are in the region of Lombardia, you will be travelling through one of the region's 9 provinces and the signs will tell you you're in the province of Mantova, in the town of Ròdigo, *not* in Ròdigo in the region of Lombardia. A very few provinces have been left out if they have no bearing on the food of the region. In some cases, for reasons of space (eg Umbria and Le Marche), 2 regions have been grouped together in the same chapter.

I do hope you will find EDIBLE ITALY useful and interesting, and in some cases, surprising, for such was my intention. For example, not many people think of Italy as a cake- and sweet-eating nation, yet there are so many cakes, puddings and pastries for each region that it is really hard to choose what to have. In each region I have provided a long list of the local *pasticcerie* and descriptions of what they are like. So often I have watched friends on holiday with me in Italy floundering in difficulties – when all they wanted to do was buy some *prosciutto* and figs! So often I have had to help out a terrified tourist who forgot to get his *scontrino* at the *cassa* before ordering his *caffè*, which then turned out not to be the pale milky cup he was expecting anyhow!

What to eat

You will find here a general view of why certain foods are to be found in each region – the climate, landscape, economy and so on – what the specialities of each area are and how best to enjoy

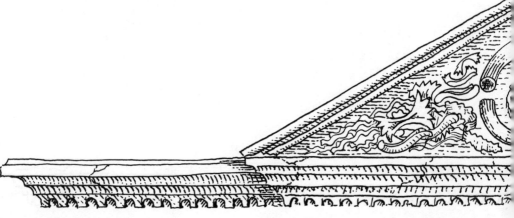

them. In each region, depending on local conditions, you will find detailed information about one or all of the following specialities: *salumi* salami, sausages and cured meats; pasta; *pesce e frutti di mare* fish and seafood; *carne e caccia* meat and game; *formaggio* cheese; *frutta e verdura* fruit and vegetables; *pasticceria* cakes, biscuits and puddings; *vino* wine; *bevande* drinks.

There are some customs and import regulations that must be observed, so please check up with customs before you try to bring home a stuffed wild boar or something extraordinary. As there are sometimes restrictions on meats, I have not suggested you bring home any *salumi*, unless it's vacuum packed. However, if you find it's not restricted to bring home loose salame, *prosciutto*, *speck* or *zampone*, then go ahead and fill your bags!

Sagre e Feste: Feast Days and Festivals

I have tried to include just some of the local festivals which relate directly to food. Of course, in certain areas almost every village celebrates its own feast days and saints' days, and while not necessarily devoted to edible matters, there will nearly always be some kind of local speciality, a biscuit or cake, perhaps, which is made specially for the occasion.

Where to eat

In all parts of the country, where I have found good regional restaurants, concentrating on their own local dishes without resorting to the *menu turistico*, I have mentioned them and what I ate there.

A good book to help you find many of the regional restaurants I have mentioned is published in Italian by Rizzoli and is entitled *Guida ai ristoranti tipici regionali*. Seek them out to get to know the local produce and how it is cooked best, and so discover more about the area you are in.

Mineral water and mud baths

Something else I also mention here and there are the *stazioni termali*. These are the thermal spas which are having a huge current revival in popularity. You would be hard pushed to miss the advertising campaigns, and unwise, if you have the time, not to visit at least one. There are many of them all over the country, set around the natural mineral water springs where you can drink the waters, swim in them or, in some cases, have warm mud baths.

Going to a spa can be an extremely cheap and relaxing holiday, with fairly basic food, but usually very good local wine, and a range of accommodation.

It was time to write this book, so that everyone can enjoy the food and drink of Italy to its fullest extent, and thus get an inkling into what 'being Italian' is all about.

The food of Italy is an enormous subject that I have covered to the best of my ability in the space available. I am certain there are things that have been forgotten or left out, but I hope nobody will be offended – such a huge amount of information is hard to condense and cover totally.

Meanwhile, I urge you to seek out the very best that my Italy has to offer you so that nobody need ever return and say they 'ate better Italian meals at home than I did over there. . . .'

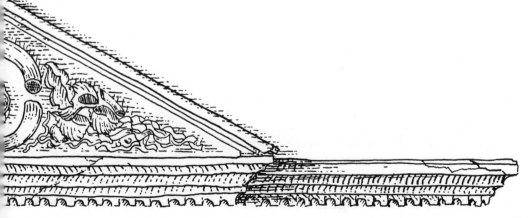

Introduction

In Italy, those who like to eat well (and they are many!) are finally waking up to the fact that it is time to re-evoke the best of her food, the traditional regional dishes that have lasted the test of time, born out of Italy's exciting history and changing pattern. A small handful of restaurateurs and food writers have gradually begun to write and talk about the glories of Italian regional cuisine and it is slowly becoming better known and properly appreciated – this book gives me a chance to help this crusade and encourage my readers to seek out the very best food available. So often visitors to Italy are confronted with the endlessly boring *Menu Turistico*. Pinned up in the window, its endlessly repetitive list of dishes is exactly the same whether you are in Trieste, Rome or Palermo. For far too long the Italian restaurateurs have played safe, offering those same dishes that they know will always sell: *spaghetti alla Bolognese, pizza, fritto misto,* and so on. The traditional regional dishes that are so much a part of *where* you are get forgotten and lost.

With this book you will know where you are and can begin to enjoy the true essence of the local gastronomy. If it's *spaghetti alla Bolognese* you're after, for instance, you must try it in Emilia Romagna, its birthplace, to get a taste of the real thing. If you want to eat *pizza,* I promise you that nothing you have ever tasted will be anything like the true *pizza* of Naples. And so to Piedmont for superb, creamy, truffle-scented pasta, to the Veneto for the smoothest, tastiest risotto you have ever eaten, to Sardinia for tender suckling pig cooked in an underground oven, to Puglia for succulent handmade pasta ears *Orecchiette,* served with juicy lamb sauces, to Sicily for remarkable ice cream flavoured with jasmine or lemons, and so on. Each corner of the boot has its own specialities, its own delicacies, its distinctions – and although many similarities do exist from one region to another, the differences far outweigh them.

Eating out

Officially a restaurant must display its menu outside, but in practice this doesn't always happen. Even if there is only a tourist menu outside, don't be afraid to go in and ask if they've got anything else. Often good local restaurants offer no written menu, so you must make a point of seeing what the locals are eating, and decide what looks good. With this book, you'll know what should be available, and will be able to ask for it. If you don't know what to ask for, you simply won't be offered it.

My hope is that, armed with a little knowledge, you'll dare to try dishes you've never heard of, and make a point of sampling unfamiliar local specialities, because no other medium so clearly represents the character of a place than the food which is eaten there.

For those who are self-catering the same rule applies – how can you successfully shop if you can't recognise or don't know what to do with the produce on sale? What is worth buying? What is it called? What do you do with it? Is it worth taking home with you? To my mind, the answers to these questions are vital, and will help people avoid ending up on holiday in, for example, Calabria, eating badly or plumping only for what they can recognise. Why eat fish fingers in Calabria when there's fresh swordfish?

Somebody actually said to me the other day 'All Italian food has got tomatoes in it, that's the essence of it.' It happened to be someone I especially didn't want to offend, and so kept my cool, but it made me wonder how many other people think that way. As a statement, it couldn't be less accurate or more misplaced, yet the Italians have thus far done such an appalling international public relations job with their vast range and variety of dishes that it isn't really surprising that people end up with that sort of impression. In a country that can't settle on a government for more than a fleeting moment – so great are all its different needs that what suits the Lombard industrialist is guaranteed to rub the Lucanian peasant up the wrong way – you are guaranteed to have major differences on the cooking front, not only in terms of the ingredients used, but also the methods of cooking and the quantities consumed. Pasta ties the whole country together, of that there is little doubt – spaghetti and tagliatelle are wrapped around it like ribbons on a parcel. Yet the pasta you'll be served in Friuli, in a thick soup with beans, will be totally different from the plate of hand-made, coarse *fusilli* you'll get down south, dressed with the very brightest tomatoes, the shiniest oil and shimmering silver fish. Italian food means variety above everything else – and you are just about to discover just how much variety there really is.

This book gives me the chance to write about the country that will always be my home. It is the country where I learned to cook, and developed my undying love for the authenticity of the delicious local dishes and became interested in their origins. It goes without saying that one of the main influences on food anywhere is the country's historical background – but surely it would be hard to find as much of a tangled web of history woven into food anywhere else in the world. So many have fought over *la Bella Italia*, so many races and nations and creeds have passed through and left a little of themselves behind and so much of it all is still so obviously here – you really are almost eating historical fact!

A brief look at ancient Italy

There is little doubt that Italy's past has a bearing on what people eat in the present. The Etruscans seem to me to be the least obscure of the early civilizations. In approximately 616-509 BC parts of Italy were inhabited by these nature-loving, happy people, who fished, danced and hunted. They lived in wooden houses, but their temples were made of stone. Fervently religious, a portion of their food and a great deal of wine were presented daily to their household gods. Their way of life derived from the Greeks, and their diet seems to have consisted of what they hunted or fished, and what grew wild or in their fields. They ate simple food such as roast meat, fish, vegetables, bread and fruit. Some say they invented a form of pasta – there are paintings which show them eating something that looks a lot like tagliatelle, but this hasn't been proven.

Then came the Romans, and things began to change a little – the meals prepared and eaten between the third century BC and the fourth century AD were much more similar to the ones enjoyed in this century. Antipasti were a very important part of the meal – lots of little bits and pieces laid out on the table for people to pick at, followed by a main course and then a dessert. Fish, meat or game would usually be cooked quite simply, but with a sauce served separately. Sauces played a large part in Roman cuisine, they were extremely popular and many of the ancient recipes still exist. They also used mustard and drank beer – things we take so much for granted today. In keeping with the carnal, lusty and sometimes downright repulsive habits of the times, the tables of upper class Rome must have been a real cornucopia of delights with delicious dishes of roast fish, meat baked in pastry, pies with cheese and chicken livers, velvety soups and purées, pea or asparagus soufflés, even Lucanica sausage was available, and then all the wonderful fruit and vegetables that still flourish in *la campagna Romana*.

Following the Triumph of Rome, various foreign influences began to invade and eventually destroyed the Empire, but all the various forces that brought about the tragedy were to some extent influential on the cuisine of the country. Under Constantine the Great (c. 274-337) the more sophisticated Byzantine eating habits (they were using forks) began to pervade the Roman kitchens, and other ingredients from far-flung

INTRODUCTION

places like Macedonia, Persia and so on began to take their place in local kitchens, but the long bloody battles and misery can't have been very conducive to the enjoyment of good food or the creation of interesting dishes.

The following centuries began to provide the beginnings of the changes in the eating habits between one end of the country and the other. With the death of Charlemagne in 814 and the kingdom of Italy established anything but firmly, it was King Berengar who was elected to rule over what had previously been part of Lombardy, but the conditions were not favourable for Italy's independence just yet. The Arabs still successfully occupied Sicily, the Byzantines lingered on in the south, the Pope hung on to the realm of St Peter and the Huns continued to raid whatever was left up north, so it is no wonder that the marvellous patchwork of differences in traditions, races and customs continued to develop – certainly as far as food goes – and Byzantine and Arab eating habits are still very much a part of the cuisine of southern Italy and Sicily.

The tomato arrives

Came the Renaissance and the artistic genius of the Florentines could not help but influence the art of food along with the art of everything else. Sweet and sour flavour combinations became very fashionable, with dishes like tagliatelle boiled in rose water, then flavoured with cinnamon and sugar appearing at Renaissance banquets. Further north in Venice, the spice traders were flooding the kitchens with all manner of exotic delights like caviare from the Black Sea, spices from Arabia, and sherry wine from Cyprus. Doubtless this was the most interesting period for the development of Italy's cuisine. It was crowned by the arrival in the sixteenth century of the tomato from Peru. Tomatoes were first used by the reckless Neapolitans (everybody else thought it was the evil apple of the Garden of Eden) who still cherish it above all other ingredients. Its arrival certainly brought about the most important change in the way food looked and tasted. Rice had reached Venice, and the Doges' cooks concocted marvellous creamy risottos and desserts with them, adding the newly discovered flavours from the East, raisins and spices, while Caterina de' Medici, great gourmet that she was, did her utmost to take the best of Italian cuisine into France and brought back with her the best of French cuisine as wife of Francis I. Thus her greatest passion – ice cream – was known throughout Europe by the 16th century, and dishes like *lepre dolce forte* have never been finally established as being either French or Italian in origin.

The Spanish Gloom

During one of the worst periods of Italian history, the Spanish Gloom (1534-1601), most of the fun and enjoyment went out of Italian life as the Spaniards imposed their own brand of austerity and puritanism on the proceedings. Some Spanish dishes came into the picture at around this time which have stayed – the Lombard *caseula* is a typical example, but on the whole the food turned as staid and boring as the rest of life, with little colour or sensual pleasure. But the disappearance of the joys of eating were only temporary.

In the peaceful 18th century, Austria ruled the country from Vienna and Italy flourished artistically – painters, poets, opera singers and composers from Italy were adored and admired all over Europe and the great food specialities also began to be known in every European capital, with Italian cafés and restaurants proving their success. Rich Europeans came to Italy for antiques and to visit the newly discovered ruins of Rome and Pompeii. The food scene became fairly cosmopolitan, with the more acceptable Renaissance oddities surviving and the best of all the foreign food from Greece, the Orient, Arabia and Austria, France and Spain adding itself to the native tradition.

During the Napoleonic wars and the French Revolution (1791 to 1815) there is no doubt that the great cooks of Italy were as much influenced by the French culinary expertise as everybody else was influenced by the other aspects of French style. However, as Caterina and Maria de' Medici had taken so many of the Italian cooking secrets into France with them centuries earlier, it makes me wonder just how much of what Napoleon brought back to us was actually original. In any case, until the unification in 1870, it hadn't appeared obvious how different the food of each region actually was. It was only when the Italians suddenly all became Italian that they discovered their very different cultural and gastronomic habits; even though there was a common theme running through the question. 'We have made

Italy,' said Massimo d' Azeglio, the great Piedmontese statesman, 'and now we must make the Italians.' Sardinian food now had a strong Spanish influence – they used and still use to some extent the letter B instead of V and their menus are filled with dishes with names like *coietas* and *culigiones*. The south, struggling against poverty and wretched soil conditions, was still feeling the influence of the Greeks, Byzantines and Arabs quite strongly. The central area seemed to be the area least affected, at least in terms of food, whereas in the north there were Austrian and Yugoslavian dishes jostling for position among French and Oriental concoctions. That is how it still is to a great extent, although the road system, railway link and modern communications have largely closed the gaps up. A century or so later on, after the briefest flirtations with *haute* and *nouvelle cuisine*, the Italians are going back to the good old dependables – dishes like polenta and pasta, wholesome food with no frills or fuss and plenty of raw vegetables and fresh fruit. In fact, barring the rude excesses, they eat more like the ancient Romans now than they ever did, although another course between the antipasto and the main course has crept in as an optional extra. The current trend reflects that elsewhere and leans towards less red meat, more fish and poultry, more fibre and a revival in mineral water and good wines. Italians are more health conscious about their food now than in recent decades, though sadly this will probably mean the loss of some really special delicacies – I'm sure it will only be temporary.

'Dimmi come mangi e ti dirò chi sei'

'Tell me what you eat and I'll tell you who you are' goes the proverb. And really nothing else needs to be said, because the history of the country has made it so. What a Calabrian puts into his mouth is very different from the choice of the Piedmontese, and it is just this fabulous, multi-coloured, multi-layered patchwork of flavours and ingredients, customs and preferences that make Italian cuisine into the incredible pageant of remarkable variations and extraordinary names and traditions that I love and am still discovering.

SHOPPING FOR FOOD

Just to point you in the right direction, these are the various names of Italian food shops.

● *MACELLERIA* The butcher's shop. What you need to know for basic meat buying is that *manzo* is beef, *maiale* is pork, *agnello* is lamb, *montone* is mutton, *vitello* is veal, *vitellone* is slightly older veal. *Vitello da latte* is very young unweaned veal – it will be the most tender and expensive. *Capretto* is kid. *Bistecca* is steak. *Spezzatino* is stew. *Arrosto* is roast. *Fettine* are thin slivers of meat suitable for *scaloppine*, *cotolette* or other quick meat dishes. *Tacchino* is turkey and you can buy it in *fettine* also – thin slices of breast. *Pollo* is chicken and *petti di pollo* – skinless breast

of chicken, is a very good buy. Game is called *selvaggina*.

● *DROGHERIA* General grocery shop. Will stock all dry groceries from flour and biscuits, jam, coffee, spices, etc. to pasta, and often bread, too. Can also be called *ALIMENTARI*, which is less refined and more like a general store which also sells cheese and *salumi*.

● *FRUTTERIA* or *FRUTTA E VERDURA* will be the sign outside greengrocers' shops where all fruit and vegetables will be bought by the kilogramme (just over 2lb). The smallest weight you are likely to be able to buy is half a kilo, the prices are easily visible and refer to the kilo price. Most fruit and vegetable shops allow you to feel, smell and touch the produce before choosing. When buying a watermelon, knock it sharply with your knuckles – it should make a lovely booming noise – this tells you it will be sweet and juicy. Always smell melons, peaches and tomatoes before buying them. Tomatoes in particular will have a very distinctive smell at the top under the stalk which will tell you if they are fresh or not. As with everything else, practice makes perfect when buying, but it is useful to know what fruit and vegetables are at their best in various parts of the country.

Every Italian housewife has her own favourite place to buy greengroceries, and having bought her kilo of oranges, onions and whatever else, before leaving the stall or shop, she'll ask for *'un mazzetto d'odori'* a bunch of herbs. The seller will deftly snap off a leafy celery stalk, a sprig of basil, parsley, thyme, marjoram or anything he may have, screw them into a rough bunch tied up with a rubber band and tuck them into the shopping bag.

• *PASTICCERIA* is a cake and pastry shop where you can buy all kinds of biscuits and pastries and cakes, often ice cream too. Pastries vary so much from one place to another so it is worth knowing what to look for.

• *PANETTERIA* is a bread shop which will sell a huge variety of bread. These are currently very fashionable and there are many of them in large and small Italian towns all over the country which vie with one another for having the largest number of different kinds of bread in all kinds of shapes and sizes.

• *PIZZA A TAGLIO* A shop which sells pizza by the slice, wrapped in a sheet of paper and which can be consumed as you walk along, or wrapped up and taken home, or to a picnic.

• *VINI E OLII* This is a shop which sells olive oil and wines of all kinds. A more sophisticated wine shop is called an *ENOTECA*. In some of them you can taste the wine before buying, particularly if it is *vino sfuso* – wine in a barrel which is decanted for you into an unlabelled bottle.

• *PESCHERIA* A fish shop. All the fish will be on display with the prices again visibly displayed and referring to the kilo price. Here you can buy less than half a kilo in some cases – for example with very small fish or shellfish. Don't be afraid to ask for advice. *MERCATO ITTICO* indicates a fish market.

• *SALUMERIA* A shop that sells *salumi*. It can also be called a *SALSAMENTERIA*. It will sell *salame, mortadella, prosciutto cotto* and *prosciutto crudo* (cooked and raw ham) and other similar preserved meats. Here you ask for a minimum of *mezz'etto* half an *etto* of whatever you've got your eye on. It will all be on display. The price is usually visible and refers to the price per *etto* (100g/4oz or a tenth of a kilo). To give you

an idea, two ettos (*due etti*) of *salame* amply feeds up to about 6 people.

• *CASEIFICIO* is a cheese shop. It will normally sell locally produced cheeses, so if you are in a *CASEIFICIO* in Rome don't expect to find *parmigiano*. Cheese can also be bought in an *ALIMENTARI*, as can a limited amount of *salumi*, and for cheese the minimum amount you should be able to buy is about one *etto*. About 3 *etti* of *parmigiano* will last a family of four about a week to grate over pasta, using it daily.

• *LATTERIA* A milk shop which will often be part of a bar. Here you will also be able to buy yogurt and cream (but not cheese) and possibly eggs, though you are more likely to find them at the *ALIMENTARI*. Eggs are bought singly or in any number – you don't need to have either a half dozen or a dozen. *Uova da bere* means an egg that is fresh enough to drink raw – which Italians frequently do.

• *PASTIFICIO/PASTA FRESCA* A fresh pasta shop. Here you buy by weight or you can explain to an assistant how many people you need the pasta for and let them advise you.

Generally you can allow one *etto* of pasta per person. *Fettuccine, tagliatelle, ravioli* or *tortellini* with spinach or meat filling, *cannelloni, gnocchi* and many others will be on sale here with distinct regional variations. Naturally in a region such as Emilia Romagna you will have the widest selection of all. Prices are per *etto*, and are usually visible.

• *GELATERIA* is an ice cream shop with all the flavours usually on view. You can buy just a cornet or individual serving in a *coppetta* tub or buy some in weight – half or a whole kilo or more – and take it home with you. Freshly whipped sweetened cream – *panna montata* – can also be bought here to take away and use at home.

• *TORREFAZIONE* is a place where coffee is freshly ground and sold. This, too, can be part of a *LATTERIA* or *GELATERIA* or a bar.

PLACES TO EAT OR DRINK

• *BAR* Here they serve coffee, alcoholic or soft drinks, and usually sandwiches, buns, pastries or other snacks. In a bar you go to the till first and tell the cashier what you want and pay for it. You will be given a till receipt which you then give to whoever is serving behind the counter as proof that you have paid for what you order.

While Italian beer is nothing very special, it is a good thirst quencher. The most popular of all the Italian brands is *Birra Peroni,* the *Nastro Azzurro* version being the most special of the two. In the North, where they do take their beer drinking seriously, the beer is mostly imported from Austria and Germany.

If it's an aperitif you're after, have a *vermut* vermouth, *dolce* or *secco* sweet or dry, or a *Negroni, Campari,* or *Punt e Mes.*

After a meal, pop into a bar for a coffee and a digestif *amaro.*

• *RISTORANTE* is a smart restaurant (or one that has pretensions to being a smart restaurant) with a varied menu. In a *ristorante* you are more likely to be served a complimentary drink as you are shown to your table and the service is usually by white-coated waiters.

• *TRATTORIA* is the next step down from the *ristorante.* The food and service will be generally more in the family style although the menu will still be fairly extensive. It does not always follow that a *trattoria* will be cheaper than a *ristorante* although that ought to be the principle.

• *OSTERIA or LOCANDA* This ought to be the cheapest kind of place to eat, but to confuse the issue there are many very upmarket and elegant restaurants who have simply stuck the word *Osteria* or *Locanda* in front of their name to give themselves some sort of kitsch appeal. The way a place looks and a careful look at the menu before you actually sit down will give you a much better idea of what you are in for.

• *TAVOLA CALDA / GIRRAROSTO / TAVOLA FREDDA* Fast disappearing, which is a shame as they are very good value for *lira,* these small establishments that sell a selection of cheap and cheerful dishes like salads, cold meats, chickens roasted on the spit and sandwiches. In this case you order and pay at the counter, then find

So You Thought You'd Just Have a Cup of Coffee?

There is such a wide range of types of coffee available in a bar that it can be quite bewildering – so here is a helpful direction.

• *Un caffè* – means an *espresso* coffee – a very tiny quantity of rich, dark strong coffee. Served in a little thick cup or a small glass.

• *Caffè ristretto* – means an even smaller and stronger cup of *espresso,* the amount of water in relation to the coffee grounds used is substantially reduced.

• *Caffè lungo* – means same amount of coffee grounds as for an *espresso* but with more water to dilute it. You can have the water cold or hot or tepid: *un caffè lungo freddo, caldo, tiepido.*

• *Caffè macchiato* – means an *espresso* with the surface stained with just a tiny drop of milk to 'stain it'. The reverse is also available. *Un latte macchiato* is a glass of milk with a stain of coffee on the surface. *Latte macchiato freddo* is a cold stained glass of milk. *Latte macchiato tiepido* is a tepid stained glass of milk.

• *Caffèlatte* is a milky coffee without the foamy surface.

• *Cappuccino* is a milky coffee with a foamy surface – sometimes you can order a *Cappuccino con panna* which will have a topping of whipped cream.

• *Caffè coretto* means it will be an espresso 'corrected' with an addition of spirits. A generous glug of your favourite tipple is poured into the tiny cup of coffee. You can order a *caffè coretto con grappa, con whisky, con cognac, con Sambuca* and so on.

• *Caffè decaffeinizzato* means decaffeinated coffee (such as *Hag* – which is simpler to say!)

At home you make coffee in a *caffettiera.* There are two kinds, which function in much the same way by allowing the boiling water to trickle up through a funnel, through the ground coffee and into the empty section of the machine out of which you pour the coffee. The technique is simple and they are inexpensive to buy. The more old fashioned and slightly more finicky one is called a *Napoletana,* the modern version is a *caffettiera moka.*

somewhere to sit down and eat. They also serve soft drinks and beer, sometimes wine but no spirits.

• *PANINOTECHE* These are quick snack places to eat, making the best of delicious Italian bread. Basically they sell sandwiches *panini* with every imaginable filling made with all sorts of bread. It's the sort of place to grab a bite to eat before the theatre or movies and is very popular with young people as they're cheap and cheerful. Beer and soft drinks and sometimes wine are on sale to wash down your *panino*.

• *BAR/PASTICCERIA/GELATERIA/SNACK BAR* will indicate a large establishment, usually with tables scattered on the pavement outside or even a *sala da thè* tearoom inside, where you can savour all kinds of delights from a simple cup of coffee or tea to a Scotch on the rocks, a sandwich or ice cream. Here you can sit down at the table and order from the waiter as you would in a restaurant. In a *ristorante, trattoria* or *osteria/locanda* you will ask and pay for the bill at the end of the meal. At a bar your till ticket will be carefully placed on your table along with your order. You can then either leave the money on the table – plus tip – or pay the waiter directly and then leave the tip on the table.

Tipping

12½% is the normal amount to tip. If it's not enough, you'll soon find out!

National Holidays

Local Feast days are held in honour of town Patron Saints generally without closure of shops or offices. Contact local Tourist Boards for dates. Offices, banks and shops closed:

1 January	15 August
6 January	1 November
Easter Monday	8 December
25 April	25 December
1 May	26 December

Chiuso per Ferie

In July and August you may very well find this notice on shuttered shop windows or firmly closed restaurant doors. The big cities like Rome, Milan and Turin empty during these months as their inhabitants head for the coast, the hills or different climes. So as not to be disappointed, avoid the big cities in these months, or be prepared to find many places closed.

Official shop opening hours

8.30/9.00 a.m.–12.30/1.00 p.m. and 3.30–7.30/8.00 p.m. Though in northern cities like Milan, Turin and Venice, you will find the lunch break shorter. There are variations depending on where you are.

By law, every shop has to close on one day each week, and this will be stated on the door – eg *Chiuso Martedi*. However, you will find that in the summer, shops in resorts will open every day.

THE BEST ITALIAN INGREDIENTS

One thing is certain, wherever you are, pasta will be on offer in some form or another for it is as much a part of Italy as the vine.

Like all good things in life, to be enjoyed properly it must be respected and there are basic rules that must be followed. Firstly, it is important to recognize the relationship between the basic shape of pasta and the sauce it is dressed with. The shape of the pasta is designed to absorb and collect more or less of the sauce depending upon its consistency. Therefore a naturally clingy sauce will have no trouble sticking to *fettuccine* or *spaghetti*, whereas shells or *fusilli* have indentations where the more rough textured sauces can be gathered efficiently. Generally, chubby, short pasta goes best with thick, rich, meaty, fishy or vegetable sauces whereas fine, delicate shapes go best of all with smooth, refined sauces. For example, a fresh tomato and basil sauce marries perfectly with fine *spaghettini* but doesn't suit *maccheroni*. *Penne* sit well with a sauce of peas and ham and cream whereas they instantly divorce *pesto*. Largely it is a question of common sense and trial and error, but no self-respecting Italian (whether they can cook or not) has any doubts about which pasta shape goes best with which sauce.

Pasta, *basta* pasta!

There are about 656 different pasta shapes on the market. Each year the manufacturers remove one and design a new one (or bring back an old one). All kinds of hype are fair in this battle – Barilla even got the great designer, Trussardi himself to design their shape called *marille*. But spaghetti is still the favourite, even after all the innovations. Pasta must always be properly hot, and must never be overcooked – it becomes totally indigestible if it reaches your stomach in a glutinous mass. Never serve cheese with fish pasta dishes. When eating or serving stuffed pasta, consider the relationship of the dressing with the stuffing inside – there is no joy in eating meat-stuffed ravioli with a tuna fish sauce!

You can buy pasta in a packet as factory-made durum wheat pasta – *pasta asciutta* (*spaghetti, maccheroni, penne, eliche*, etc.) or as factory-made egg and flour pasta – *pasta all'uovo* (*tagliatelle, fettuccine, paglia e fieno*, etc.) or you can buy fresh hand-made *pasta all'uovo* from a shop. Or, make *pasta all'uovo* yourself at home with a good rolling pin and some energy – or buy a pasta-making machine, electric or hand-turned. *Pasta all'uovo* is sometimes green or red – this means spinach or tomato has been added to the dough. Since you can't taste the flavour of colouring vegetables such as carrot or beetroot, to my mind other coloured pastas are simply a waste of time – though to some they are pleasing to the eye. Stuffed, baked, in a soup or *in brodo* (added to a really good chicken or meat broth) pasta is good for you, doesn't have to be fattening unless you go mad with the sauce, and almost everybody likes it in some form or another.

Its origins are somewhat obscure: there is a small amount of evidence to show that the Etruscans ate it (they seemed to know a good thing when they saw it), but it is certain that the Romans did. They made a kind of gruel with flour and water, fried it into little pancakes and then cut the pancakes into strips. These were then dressed with a sauce or mixed with chick peas to create *laganum et ciceris* – the ancestor of present-day *pasta e ceci* (pasta with chick peas) as eaten by Romans and all Italians today. In Sicily, the Arabs were busy making *Ittryia* – a kind of early *fusilli*, while the Greeks brought a kind of *maccheroni* (*makrios*) to southern Italy. Marco Polo may have brought the idea of spaghetti back from China, but pasta was around for a long time before that voyage.

Olio d'Oliva – Olive Oil

In very broad terms, production of olive oil begins in earnest in Liguria, and develops its way south. Some very good olive oil is available in extremely small quantities further north, but it's quite hard to get hold of. The further south you travel, the richer and stronger tasting the oil will become.

Some private olive groves will sell you their produce in an unlabelled bottle and a few restaurants have their own olive groves and presses attached to the premises, and are happy to sell you some of their oil.

All olive oils are best enjoyed while very fresh, preferably within a year of pressing. Unless vast amounts of additives have been added to your oil, it should be consumed quite quickly once opened.

The choice of oil is a matter of personal taste and what you want to use it for.

Extra Vergine means there is no addition of other types of oil.

Vergine means there is a small addition of other oil, perhaps corn oil or vegetable oil, permissible by law.

If the bottle has neither written on it, you can be sure there is rather a lot of other oils mixed in with the olive oil.

Extra vergine is the most expensive, *vergine* less expensive. Then there is *olio di frantoio* which is almost completely unrefined, and has a thick sludgy deposit at the bottom, and looks opaque. There is a wide variety of oils made specifically for babies and young children, *olio d'oliva per bambini* available from chemists.

When I buy olive oil to bring home on a plane I make a point of buying it in a can rather than a bottle. Can you imagine having a bottle break in your luggage? *Olio extra vergine Sasso* and *olio extra vergine d'oliva şagra* both come in cans and are excellent.

Here is a list of my favourites in order of preference. Most you can buy anywhere, but the very best may only be found in high-quality delicatessens like *CASTRONI* in Rome, or the shops on via Monte Napoleone in Milan.

● *S.P. Pallanca* is a much sought after and delicious olive oil from the Ligurian riviera. It is produced in limited amounts so each bottle is numbered as one would find on a rare bottle of wine. Only olives of the *gentile* variety are used for this excellent oil. Three types are available on the open market. One is *mosto* which has an odd opaque quality about it as small particles of olive have been allowed to filter through with the oil.

● *Riserva F.M.* uses only olives which reach the right stage of ripeness in February and March (hence F.M.). This is a very fine and delicate oil.

● *Primavera* is a shiny, transparent oil made with olives picked during the spring, then filtered very carefully. If you can get hold of a bottle of *this* oil, then you'll know what good olive oil is all about.

• *Badia a coltibuono* From the Lucca area comes this dense, green, rich oil in its lovely oblong bottle. It is blessed with all the excellent qualities of a pure *extra vergine* but is a little strong tasting for some people. It is quite expensive, but well worth it.

• *Monini* One of the most popular and purest olive oils. It's rich, thick and greeny golden without being too overpowering. Available as *extra vergine* and *vergine*.

• *Sagra* An excellent oil with an added bonus – it is available in cans.

• *Sasso* The *extra vergine* version comes in a very attractive gold can. A very well-known, tried and tested oil.

• *Dante* Another old-fashioned brand, very good and not too full-bodied.

• *Carapelli* This is an oil with a nice mild flavour which makes it good for cooking.

• *Bertolli* Again, a very well-known brand of excellent oil which is available everywhere.

• *San Giorgio* The cheapest I have come across, not very pure but actually rather good, especially for cooking.

Gelati – Ice Cream

The ice cream theme is one with many fascinating variations.

• *Gelato* is basic ice cream and comes flavoured with fruit or ingredients such as chocolate, coffee, *torrone* etc.

• *Semi-freddo* is an ice cream that is softer and richer and less 'frozen' than ice cream.

• *Torta gelata* is a cake made of layers of ice cream in different flavours.

• *Granita* is crushed ice to which a flavouring such as fruit syrup or fruit juice or coffee has been added.

• *Sorbetto* is also crushed ice with flavouring, but in this case the ice and flavouring have been turned into a smooth, slushy consistency.

SICILIAN SORBET

Ice cream was first introduced in Sicily by the Arabs who had first thought of the idea of cooling themselves down by adding wine, fruit or vegetable juice to ice and thus creating a delectable dessert. The name for this ancestor of ice cream was *sorbet* and the name and the idea took firm root in Sicily where they are still passionate about their cold concoctions. In 1660 the first Sicilian café was opened in Paris – Le Café Procope was run by its owner Procopio Coltelli, and soon became famous throughout Europe for its fantastic iced desserts. Shortly after a rival café – Le Café Napolitaine was opened nearby by the famous Tortoni whose delicious Bisquit Tortoni is still famous as a really self-indulgent, calorie-packed ice cream speciality. Caterina de' Medici was mad about ice cream, so it wasn't long before the art of creating it spread as far as Florence.

In those days, making ice cream meant achieving low enough temperatures with no refrigerators or freezers. By adding ammonia and potassium nitrate to water, the ensuing chemical reaction was enough to lower the temperature to freezing point – enough to make the basic ice. To lower the temperature still further, all that was required was to mix ice and rock salt together in $\frac{2}{3}$ and $\frac{1}{3}$ proportions for a temperature of $-18°C$ ($0°F$). This was then cold enough for making small quantities of ice cream and sorbets. These days, cream and a custard are used to make the basis of ice cream to which an enormous amount of flavouring is added to make up for the generally poor quality of the cream – Italian cream is generally rather thin and weak. It is the addition of excellent fruit or chocolate or whatever the flavouring is to be that gives it its perfection, along with hours of careful mixing at controlled temperatures.

Polenta

This is maize meal – either white or yellow, boiled with water to make a very thick porridge. When it has amalgamated into the right texture, the polenta is finally turned out on to a wooden board or table top and smoothed into a sort of cake shape. It is then sliced into wedges and served with a juicy stew of game, meat or fish, or with milk and butter, or with cheese. In Friuli the texture is more sloppy and the polenta is less easily sliced. In this case a portion will be spooned on to the plate with the accompaniment spooned over it. It has a fairly bland flavour and its purpose is to fill hungry bellies. Its origins go back to a time when poverty was rife and there was little to eat. It's a starch alternative to rice, bread, potatoes or pasta and I assure you is a deliciously filling meal, particularly on freezing cold days. Like *grappa* (see page 18), it crops up most frequently in areas where it gets very cold. The leftovers can be fried in oil, or grilled or the polenta can be thinly sliced and layered in a dish like lasagne with mozzarella and tomato and baked in a hot oven until gooey inside and crisp on the top.

Parma Ham – *Prosciutto Crudo*

This seems to have become the generic term for ham which has been cured and is still basically raw (as opposed to *prosciutto cotto*, which is ham that has been cooked by boiling it or sometimes baking it). The most popular version is still *prosciutto di Parma*, produced in and around the city in the region of Emilia Romagna, where the excellent strain of pigs bred specifically for the production of *salumi* (preserved meats of all kinds) enjoy good pasture lands and expert farming. But to my mind the very best prosciutto is *San Daniele*, produced in that little town high up in the north. *San Daniele* is pale pink, delicately flavoured and with a remarkably tender texture. If you want the very best, *San Daniele* is generally considered to be the king of prosciutto, although there are lots of different kinds of *prosciutto di Parma* and some are considerably better than others.

If prosciutto is not good it will be over-salty and have a stringy, fibrous, unpleasant texture or be too fat and greasy. Good prosciutto is sweet and succulent with a smooth tender texture. Unfortunately it is a case of paying a bit more for getting the best on offer.

Parmigiano

Real *parmigiano* comes from the region of Emilia Romagna and is instantly recognizable because it's got *parmigiano Reggiano* branded on to the outside crust. These cheeses are huge, round cartwheels – a whole cheese is so valuable that they are kept in safes under specific conditions to preserve freshness and quality. If the crust has *grana padano* printed on it then the cheese you are grating is *formaggio grana* from the Padano province of Lombardy. *Grana Padano* is just as expensive and just as valuable – in fact frankly I can't honestly tell the difference between one and the other. Depending upon the quality and maturity of the cheese it will be used either exclusively as a grating cheese on pasta or rice dishes, or eaten by the wedge as a cheese course on its own, or as a combination of the two. It is a wonderful, marvellous cheese – almost completely fat-free because it's made with the discarded whey of other cheese. It is essential to

many Italian dishes and a valuable source of protein.

The younger the cheese, the more moist it will be; older cheese will have a chalky appearance and be drier.

Mozzarella

The best kind of mozzarella is made with buffalo milk. White water buffalos are fairly common in central and southern parts of Italy. *Mozzarella di bufala* is bigger and less starkly white than cows' milk mozzarella – it has a slightly greyish tinge. The cheese is kept in whey to keep it fresh, once home a mixture of half water and half milk does the same job. The fresher it is the better it will taste. On no account must it be just wrapped up or left without a liquid bath to sit in – otherwise it will go hard and yellow. This is the cheese that goes soft and stringy when heated, it is used a great deal on pizza, in pasta dishes and many other specialities. *Fior di latte* is ordinary cows' milk mozzarella, *ciliegine* are very small round mozzarellas and *treccia* is a mozzarella in long strips that have been braided together into a plait.

Stoccafisso and Baccalà

All over Italy different names are given to the same basic food. Local spellings are different, and sometimes different things are given the same name. In the case of dried cod, the names given are either of the above. I think that in general *stoccafisso* is dry salt cod, whereas *baccalà* is just dried. But I have discovered that in some places the two names are swopped around. In any case, before cooking the fish has to be soaked in cold water for a very long time to reconstitute itself, and it is then usually cooked in a stew of some kind.

ITALIAN WINES AND WINE LABELS

Despite the fact that Italy produces more wine than any other European country, involving almost 2 million producers of various degrees of size and importance, as recently as 1963 there was still no official classification for Italian wines. This is extraordinary, when you consider that France had set up her own method of controlled classification over a century beforehand. However, the D.O.C. system has improved the status of Italian wine all over the world.

Labelling on Italian wine is divided into three categories:

• *Denominazione di origine semplice (D.O.S.)* A label used very little, meaning just that the wine is made with traditional methods and in the vineyards of its place of origin.

• *Denominazione di origine controllata (D.O.C.)* The most used of the three categories, D.O.C. wines represent about 10 per cent of wines produced in Italy. They are the best of the wines, though many producers of wine good enough for this accolade still prefer to sell it *sfuso* – unbottled, by the carafe or barrel, saving themselves expense.

D.O.C. lettering means that the wine has been scrupulously checked and passed as being what the label says:

• That it comes from where it says it comes from,
• That the conditions in which it has been produced have been rigorously checked,
• That the correct amount of wine according to the size of the vineyard is being produced,
• That the alcoholic and acidity levels of the wine are correct,
• That the local traditions and customs have been adhered to wherever possible to retain the essential character of the wine.

• *Denominazione di origine controllata e garantita (D.O.C.G.)* denotes that the wine is of particular value. It guarantees the authenticity of the wine and the label must contain the producer's or bottler's name and the place of bottling, as well as the producer's trademark and a vintage date. It will also have a state stamp on it, and be numbered and serialised.

MOSTO

Mosto is the must, the wine that has just begun to turn from grape juice into wine. It is very light and agreeable as a wine to drink easily, but it doesn't keep for very long, as fermentation has only just begun. It's usually quite cloudy, and too much can cause stomach upsets. You will probably only come across it in a vineyard, especially around harvest time, when the young wine is tasted to see how it will turn out next year.

GRAPPA

This clear gin-coloured drink is made from the leftover squashed grapes after the wine has been made. Distilled many many times to create a pure, fiery spirit it is particularly popular in northern parts, where it gets very cold and snows heavily. I haven't ever liked it very much, but no one can say I haven't tried to! At our home in Tuscany there is a marvellous *grappa* still, hidden in the washhouse behind the hen house. Here our dear Venetian friend and caretaker Beppino used to distil his own firewater, with regular tastings, for anybody who popped in whatever their age! Whenever it's been time to go back home in recent years, he has pressed a bottle of the stuff upon my protesting hands and sent me packing with his usual wicked grin. I will now confess that over all those years I have ended up using his lethal potion to light rebellious fires with on damp, dank winter days. He would be horrified if he knew, but I hope he'll be comforted to know that it wasn't especially *his* grappa I don't like – it's all kinds of grappa, except for the most mild and those tasting most strongly of added ingredients such as herbs or fruit.

If this *is* your tipple, you will be spoiled for choice all over the north of Italy.

MINERAL WATER AND SOFT DRINKS

Water is quite safe to drink in most parts of Italy, but in restaurants it is usual to drink *acqua minerale*.

• *Sangemini* is the most expensive one available on the market and is readily available at the chemist. It is a very pure and light mineral water whether it is in fizzy (*frizzante*) or still versions (*naturale*). This is the mineral water that newborn babies, nursing mothers and old people will be given to drink.

• *Claudia* This mineral water comes from Anguillara, near Rome, and is guaranteed to rid the body of impurities and aid digestion. It comes in both still and fizzy versions and has a fairly high calcium content.

• *Fiuggi* is also quite expensive and is recommended for anybody suffering from kidney problems of any kind or similar urinary troubles. It's very pure, quite sweet and is usually sold still.

• *Appia* I went to school on the via Appia Antica and when we went swimming the pool water was unrefined spring water from this source. It's naturally slightly fizzy, although a more sparkling version is available – this means it has gas added to it.

The Appia spring water is also used to make Appia soft drinks such as *limonata* lemonade and *aranciata* orangeade.

- *Panna* One of the most popular still drinking waters, it comes in a very handy plastic bottle.
- *Ferrarelle* 'bottled as it comes out of the spring' says the advertising slogan, the result being a very fizzy, quite sharp tasting, diuretic water which is recommended for digestive problems.
- *Boario* Extensively exported, this is another of the most popular mineral waters, both in still and fizzy versions.
- *Uliveto* A very under-advertised but really quite excellent mineral water with many of the qualities of Fiuggi water for cleansing and refreshing the system.
- *Levissima* Very light and easily digestible water – another one that is good for invalids.
- *San Pellegrino* Quite a bitter taste and so fizzy it stings the nose. A very well-known mineral water, it also goes into soft drinks such as *bitter San Pellegrino*.

When you order mineral water in a restaurant the waiter will ask you if you want *naturale* or *gassata* – do you want still or fizzy water? This is entirely a matter of taste – I don't honestly feel it is much to do with what you're eating.

SOFT DRINKS

It's interesting to note that Italy's restrictions on food additives and colourings are very tight, and soft drinks are therefore healthier than you might think.

- *Spremute* – freshly squeezed fruit juice, usually lemon, orange or grapefruit (*spremuta di limone, arancia, pompelmo*).
- *Succhi di Frutta* – fruit juices, more like pulp: *Pera* pear, *mela* apple, *albicocca* apricot, *pesca* peach, *prugna* plum.
- *Limonata* – fizzy lemonade.
- *Aranciata* – fizzy orange.
- *Chinotto* – dark brown fizzy drink flavoured with quinine.
- *Bitter* – bright red soft drink which tastes like Campari.
- *Crodino* – made by the Crodo mineral water organisation, this is an orange tinted drink with a herby flavour.
- *Gassosa* – clear lemonade.
- *Spuma* – very cheap soft drink, basically sugar and water with a little added flavouring.

FESTIVALS, FEASTS AND PICNICS

Carnevale is the period immediately before the rigours of Lent set in – such as they are in these liberated times. It lasts approximately a fortnight, the 2 highlights being the Thursday and Tuesday before Ash Wednesday – *giovedì grasso* and *martedì grasso* (Fat Thursday and Fat Tuesday). All over the country, *carnevale* is celebrated by fancy dress parties, parades and practical jokes. It is a time for laughter and fun, with plenty of delectable pastries and biscuits cooked specially for the occasion and washed down with wine (see separate regions). Particularly popular are deep fried pastries, as these can be prepared outdoors in enormous frying pans and eaten by the revellers. Carnival in Venice is especially famous and here the costumes are more exciting and adventurous than in any other city and where everybody has at least one joke played upon them. Carnival is like a vast street party. The fancy dress parade of Viareggio is famous throughout the country and is always filmed on the national news. Everywhere there are children and grownups throwing confetti *coriandoli* or streamers at the passers-by.

Christmas/Natale

The traditional cakes and pastries arriving in the shops are the first indication that Santa Claus or the *Befana* the witch are on their way. *Panettone, pandoro, torrone,* chocolates, *panforte, ricciarelli, panpepato* – all are an intrinsic part of Italian Christmas and are available all over the country. More local regional specialities will only be available in those areas (see separate regions). Christmas Eve is celebrated in most parts of Italy with a fish-based meal (no meat is permitted but fish, cheese and vegetables feature very strongly). After that the presents are opened, and then the family goes to midnight mass.

On New Year's Eve, family and friends gather together, stay up until midnight and then eat a huge meal with several courses – not being a religious festivity just about anything goes from turkey to pasta or roast beef and baked fish, with plenty to drink. On Twelfth Night the old witch Befana comes down the chimney bringing presents for good children and coal for bad children. Among the presents there will inevitably be sticks of *torrone* and chocolates.

Easter/Pasqua

Easter Sunday morning is the time to go to Church, preferably on an empty stomach, carrying with you the joint of meat or the eggs you are going to consume at the lunchtime feast. At the end of mass the congregation gathers around the altar with their food and the priest sprinkles holy water all over it and them. You can then go home and cook your lunch knowing it is properly blessed. Lamb is popular as an Easter Sunday roast, as is kid in certain areas, but virtually every province or region has its own Easter speciality.

Nationwide you will see *la colomba* on sale. This dove-shaped cake is covered with sugar crystals and toasted almonds and has more or less the same texture and flavour as *panettone*.

Picnics

Italy is a country made for having picnics, wherever you happen to be. There is a vast amount of food ideally suited for picnics, like *salumi*, cheeses and all the fresh fruit and vegetables, as well as superb bread in all its forms. Many *alimentari* and *tavola calda* establishments also sell things like pies or *focaccia* (plain pizza dough with no topping, just a good dousing of olive oil and salt). An Italian preparing food for a picnic will probably include a huge bowlful of hot pasta, dressed and ready, transported in marvellously inventive ways to preserve as much heat as possible. Cooking meat on an open fire is also permissible in some places and very popular.

WHAT THE CLEVER COOK BRINGS HOME

In order to reproduce good Italian food successfully at home you need at least some of the tools of the trade. To my mind, nothing is more vital than a proper metal colander (*scolapasta*) with solid handles and sturdy legs to stand on, such as you can buy cheaply and easily through the country. It is rather bulky if you haven't got a helpful car boot to stow it in, but you will find it remarkably useful once you've got it home with you. It takes large amounts of pasta without any difficulty and it doubles as an excellent steamer over a pot of boiling water, and it also allows you to wash and clean large amounts of vegetables.

A proper parmesan grater *grattugia da formaggio* is another absolute must. The holes are smaller than on a standard cheese grater and the grating blades very sharp – please mind your fingers. You can buy them with a handy under-dish to catch the cheese in or even a detachable, deep bowl underneath – big enough to keep an average sized wedge of cheese in.

A *mezzaluna* is a half-moon-shaped wide blade with two tough handles – usually wooden – on either end. It is very useful for chopping onions, herbs, garlic and the like, but you do need a little practice in order to get the technique quite right (use a rocking movement). These are available in many sizes depending on how much you are ready to spend. The rather bulky handles of a *mezzaluna* make it hard to store it in a drawer so you might want it hanging on the wall.

Terracotta is always a popular and safe buy; you can buy jugs, plates – including oven-proof pizza plates, bowls of all sizes and other objects. The colours and texture of the finished items varies depending upon where you are. The further south you go the more likely you are to find really cheap terracotta.

China and glass make good presents – everybody knows how beautifully Italians make both china and glass things. Large salad bowls make a particularly useful and interesting present, but so do huge cups for breakfast coffee, glasses for wine with coloured rims or made of heavy green glass, serving platters and half-moon-shaped side salad plates. Markets are often a good place for crockery and glass, otherwise look out for specialised shops that will probably also sell other local souvenir-type items such as rugs or basketware.

If you want to make fresh pasta at home and save yourself some of the arm strain – you can buy a hand-turned aluminium and steel machine made by a firm called *Imperia*. It is great fun and really does make superb pasta.

Small oil cans are another good investment. They are usually made of steel with a long narrow spout, a lid and a handle. They enable you to pour out oil carefully without wasting it – simply decant from the large can or bottle into the little jug.

Pure Pesto Magic

It is immediately obvious that it is the sea that gives Liguria her life blood. This is a territory of mountains and hills, remote and almost unpopulated, next to a rich and green coastal strip – densely populated, chaotic and busy, where gardens, sumptuous villas, bustling resorts, hotels, factories and busy cargo ports follow quickly one on top of the other. There seems to be a struggle to squeeze things into no longer existent space along the coast. Houses are built on terraces into the cliff faces and the fields are also terraced, giving the impression of giant steps leading down to the sea.

The famous Ligurian riviera divides into two – on the one hand is the Riviera di Levante, east of Genoa, which includes Portofino, Rapallo, Portovenere, La Spezia and Chiavari. On the western side is the Riviera di Ponte, which includes Capo Mele, Capo Mortola, Alassio, Sanremo, Ventimiglia and then you're over the border and into Monaco and France.

Perfect climate

The region has an almost perfect climate, completely influenced by the sea and protected by its mountains. The temperature is mild even in midwinter, similar to what you'd find south of Naples, and in summer you are cooled by the sea breezes. Snow and ice are rare, even in the mountains. Along the coastline, climate and soil are perfect for traditional Mediterranean plants like myrtle, juniper, bay trees and the lovely arbutus, with its delectable fruits – and herbs, herbs grow all over Liguria. Today's building and the more economical considerations of vineyards, olive groves and citrus plants have begun to change the natural greenery of the area.

Love for the sea

Although the region is almost all mountainous, this is not a land of mountain people. They are fishermen and sailors – after all, Columbus was born here – and they have a very good money sense to boot. The thousands of tiny ancient churches like those in Portofino and the many abbeys and monasteries of the Benedictines and Cistercians scattered everywhere are a testimony to the long years of defence of the people's religious beliefs; the splendid palaces tell of Baroque and Renaissance glories, of Genoa as a great city. Nowadays Liguria allows her cities to sprawl untidily, lets commercial interests take over from culture and beauty, but at the root of it all is a great love for the sea, a deep respect for the land so patiently moulded into terraces to prevent it slipping down the cliff faces into the water, and a keen sense of good food and how best to prepare and enjoy it.

Whatever doesn't grow or can't be caught in Liguria simply doesn't figure in the cuisine. There are, for example, no *salumi* here which are genuinely local. With no pasturelands little stock is raised, so meat and dairy products are not used much, and when they are, they seem to be viewed with a touch of suspicion. But everything that *is* available is used to its best advantage. In fact, the Ligurians are thought to be rather mean, but it is only a matter of making the most of what they've got. The ubiquitous *pesto* is the best example of this. Basil, nuts, olives, sheep's cheese and garlic were freely available. On the face of it, this might seem an unlikely combination, but the Ligurians grind and pound them all together to create one of the perfect sauces for pasta.

The Ligurian cuisine emerges as a clear, concise tradition, with definite flavours and precise textures, accompanied by cleansing, refreshing wines.

GENOVA & PROVINCE

Genoa, like Venice, was always destined to become a maritime state because of her location at the junction of the Via Aurelia, the main coast road into France, and she was in a strong position to connect this area with the ports of the Levant. Genoa grew wealthy by exporting Crusaders to the Holy Land in the 12th and 13th centuries, and was a powerful maritime republic in the Middle Ages, pitted in opposition against Pisa and Venice. Today she is Italy's biggest port and one of Europe's major ports too.

The city surrounds the port like an amphitheatre, with the sea in front and the hills providing the backdrop, its buildings erected in steps and its streets all on slopes. The old town centre is a labyrinth of stairways and steep narrow lanes, squeezed in between tall houses. Around this central core are the Renaissance and Baroque palaces with their ageless beauty, and round them begins the enormous sprawl of modern building spreading beyond the city itself until it reaches the industrial zone.

This is a busy, lively, rich city, where trading and commerce are dear to everyone's hearts – the Genovese friend, in showing you a new dress, will first tell you how much she spent, then go on to ask if you like it. . . .

I like Genoa, despite its many obvious faults. I like the odd cosmopolitan mix of its language, with many Turkish, Arabic, French and Yiddish words invading the Italian. Above all I like the food of this city, especially the slightly grubby, scruffy portside or 'old city' haunts, where you get some of the atmosphere of the city's spirit along with authentic local cooking. I particularly

recommend *PIRO*, on top of the hill known as San Siro di Struppa, right next to a very lovely ancient church of the same name. From here you will get a fabulous view and eat food that could not be more Genovese if it tried. Fish, of course, features strongly, and the taste of wonderful herbs pervades many of the dishes. I had *baccalà e totani fritti*, mixed fried octopus and chunks of *baccalà* in batter, *lattughe ripiene in brodo*, lettuce leaves stuffed with herbs, minced veal and breadcrumbs and boiled in broth, or you could try *tomaxelle*, veal olives, stuffed with hard-boiled eggs, breadcrumbs, more herbs and minced veal. All the best local specialities are on the menu, and your host will help you choose.

Down by the port, eat at the *TRATTORIA DEL MARIO*, for more fish dishes, or *minestrone alla Genovese*, with its large ladleful of *pesto*, the most Genovese taste of all. Here you'll rub shoulders with men who work with ships and sea water and come here on a regular basis. Be prepared for some rough behaviour and raising of voices – it's all part of the scene.

LA SPEZIA & PROVINCE

Right at the heart of the gulf bearing the same name, La Spezia is a modern energetic town spreading out over the neighbouring hills. Its development has been a bit messy thanks to the decision to build round the military base of the town in the first years after Unification. The result is a city with an odd military feel about it. The harbour is filled with armed ships, not cargo boats, and the streets are filled with young men in squeaky-clean white sailor uniforms.

This province is one of the three smallest in the entire country, yet the little resorts along this stretch of coast are famous the world over and hard to beat for unspoilt beauty. Sarzana is the only important inland town, a delightful market town with an easy, relaxed atmosphere.

The Magical Cinqueterre

Portovenere remains one of my favourite places to go. Here there are lots of very good restaurants and trattorie, but the best for really authentic local food is *AL GAVITELLO*, on the Salita Doria. (Park as soon as you reach the town as it is a pedestrian area – you can walk from one end to the other in about ten minutes.) Here we had fritters made with sultanas and *baccalà* and a wonderful seafood soup along with superb walnut *pansoti* and properly-made *pesto*. As Portovenere gets very crowded, your best bet in high season is to hire a boat in the tiny harbour and get the boatman to take you to Cinqueterre. (There is also a ferry service but then you're limited to its return times.) Cinqueterre is a collection of five fishermen's villages constructed out of the cliff face. They are difficult to reach by land, and not all that easy by sea, especially if it's rough. The villages are famous for the wonderful wine they produce here on steep terraces and for the general prettiness of the scenery. In the village of Vernazza, my husband insisted that we ate at the restaurant at the top of the castle right on the port – there are a lot of steps to get up there, but once on the terrace the breeze is blissfully cooling and the food is all delicious. We had enormous potato *gnocchi*, smothered in *pesto*, *datteri di mare*, the wonderful local sea dates, and *torta di ricotta*.

However, Cinqueterre wine is strong, so be very careful on your way down all those stone steps – with hindsight, I think I was really quite lucky not to have broken my neck on the way back.

Lerici is the perfect resort for sitting in cafés and eating superb ice cream. There is a gelateria called *LA MAGIA DEL GELATO*, where they make all kinds of wonderful creamy, cooling concoctions with marvellous names like *orgasmo, sospiro d'amore, delirio, estasi* (orgasm, sigh of love, delirium, ecstasy). It's a great place to spend a lazy afternoon with plenty to do and see. This bay is where the great English poet Shelley met his untimely death while on a boat trip with Byron and friends. His villa can be seen on the opposite shore from the portside cafés. Every year in the month of August the townspeople commemorate the sad occasion with lanterns, boats and candles, moving out to the spot and singing, praying and tossing flowers on the water.

SAVONA & PROVINCE

Savona used to be Genoa's rival and it has several lovely old buildings and an elegant architectural plan which makes it clear that this is a proud and beautiful city with a heritage of its own. The long arched porticoes remind one of towns in Piedmont or Emilia Romagna, but unfortunately it is surrounded by an important commercial port serving many of the major industries of Piedmont

and all that this entails. This is not my kind of town, yet to sit a little while beneath the porticoes in the town centre, and sip a cup of espresso – it *is* possible to forget the ugliness.

Inland you'll find Albenga, an ancient Roman and medieval settlement which is an important fruit and vegetable market centre for all the local produce, especially peaches, apricots, tomatoes and artichokes.

IMPERIA & PROVINCE

This is the centre of the region's olive oil production, which, along with tourism and flower cultivation, represents the basis of the province's existence. There is no proper industry here of any sort – just miles and miles of flower-filled coastline, greenhouses, olive groves and seaside resorts. The most important centres are Sanremo and Bordighera, Taggia (which is one of the most important flower-producing towns) and Ventimiglia, the border town between Italy and France. This stretch of coastline is known as the Riviera dei Fiori – the Riviera of Flowers.

PASTA

As with most Ligurian cooking, the herbs are the most important ingredient and they are used not only in the sauces, but in the pasta dough as well. Ligurian dough is very white, because of the fine

Powerful Pesto

This is the most well known of all the local specialities, and although it is easy to make, it requires an experienced hand to get it just as it should be. The principal element is the basil, which in these parts is cultivated in every available corner. Traditionally the basil is pounded (nowadays more often than not it will be put in a food processor) and mixed with olive oil. In this region where the sun is almost always shining and the temperature rarely varies, this is an oil which is fine and delicate. Adding pinenuts, or walnuts, garlic and Parmesan cheese, you end up with a deliciously smooth, green sauce which is used to flavour minestrone, but above all as a dressing for pasta. Purists amongst the Ligurians say you should only make pesto when basil is in flower.

Local Specialities

- *Pansoti* are like *ravioli*, filled with *ricotta* and local herbs, generally dressed with a walnut sauce, or *tocco*, the juices of a joint of roasted meat.
- *Trofie* are little light-as-a-feather *gnocchi*, usually dressed with *pesto*, but which also marry perfectly with a sauce of mushrooms.

flour used, and when the chopped herbs are mixed in, a lovely speckled effect is created. The pasta is sliced finely into ribbons to make the superb *trenette verdi* traditionally served with *pesto*, as indeed is most pasta in this region.

Ravioli is reputed to have been born in Liguria, and here it is stuffed with borage, minced meat, brains and chard, or often with fish.

Pasta dressed with *pesto* is sometimes combined with other ingredients to give a dish of, for example, diced potatoes and pasta *al pesto*, or green beans and pasta *al pesto*, or cannellini beans with pasta *al pesto*. This makes for a very different texture and a delightful combination of flavours.

PESCE E FRUTTI DI MARE

Fish and Seafood

Strangely enough this is a region poor in local fish. The sea here is not deep enough in most places for there to be any fishing of any relevance,

while in some parts it suddenly drops to great depths, which is again unfortunately no good for the local fishermen. The most commonly caught local fish destined for use within the region are sardines *sardelle*, mackerel *sgombro* and anchovies *acciughe*. What fish there is will be used to its best advantage – the reputed parsimony of the Ligurians will see to that – so you will get *Ciuppin* fish soup and *Buridda* fish stew, using various different fish together in one dish.

In the course of their travels, Ligurians of the past discovered salt cod in the far-flung northern parts and brought it home to cook it in their own inimitable way – with tomatoes, potatoes, pinenuts, garlic and sultanas. Here it is called *stoccafisso in umido* or *stoccafisso accomoda*.

CARNE E CACCIA

Meat and Game

Meat does not really figure in the local cuisine. There is only one meat dish that can be counted as a real speciality of any note and this is *cima alla Genovese*. It's a piece of veal, usually stuffed with lots of delicious ingredients including minced veal, offal, Parmesan cheese and peas, though the filling varies enormously depending on where it's made. It is then boiled in broth and served cold in thick slices.

Otherwise, since there are no pastures for cattle to graze, the alternative to fish is usually rabbit *coniglio*, which is often cooked very simply with sage and olive oil; chicken *pollo*, lamb *agnello* or snails *lumache*.

Local Specialities

- *Buridda* Liguria's renowned fish stew, a bequest of the Saracens, which is a mixture of fish cooked with fried onions, carrots, celery, parsley, anchovies, pinenuts and tomatoes.
- *Cappon magro* (a joke title meaning literally 'lean capon') is a triumphant fish dish for very special occasions. It's a bit like Russian salad, consisting of layers of cooked vegetables and fish on a bed of dried slices of bread rubbed with garlic. The whole dish is doused with a marvellous green sauce *salsa verde* made with

chopped and pounded parsley, capers and gherkins mixed with olive oil, and then decorated with lobster.
- *Ciuppin* Fish soup consisting of a variety of fresh fish caught locally flavoured with celery, garlic, onions and parsley, sieved to give a delicious smooth soup.
- *Musciame* or *mosciamme*, the traditional food of sailors, is tuna fish or dolphin meat dried in the sun. The sailors used to keep it hanging from the masts of their ships for long voyages.

FORMAGGIO
Cheese

Though there are few local cheeses (for the same reasons as there is little meat), what there is is well worth seeking out and trying. Most of the local cheeses are made with sheep's milk and turned into various forms of *pecorino*. Cheese made here has a delightful 'wild herb' flavour from the herb-strewn rocky pastures.

FRUTTA E VERDURA
Fruit and Vegetables

The mountainous nature of the region is not favourable for a great number of crops – what cultivable surfaces are available have, to a great extent, been swamped by industrial and tourist

grown – followed by tomatoes, asparagus and artichokes, peaches and apricots, particularly in the Albenga area.

The enormous importance of herbs in the food must not be overlooked. Basil *basilico* grows profusely everywhere and is used especially for making *pesto*. But rosemary *rosmarino*, oregano *origano* and marjoram *maggiorana* as well as thyme *timo* and sage *salvia* are grown a great deal.

Olive oil is produced principally in Oneglia and the groves close to Imperia. Some citrus fruits are also grown here, particularly tangerines in and around Sanremo.

PASTICCERIA
Cakes, Biscuits and Puddings

- *Castagnaccio* A rich, thick cake made with chestnut flour, pine nuts, sultanas, olive oil and caraway seeds.
- *Latte dolce fritto* A thick egg custard, spread on a plate and left to cool, then dipped in egg white and breadcrumbs and deep fried in strips.
- *Pandolce Genovese* or *Pan di Natale* A delicious spicy, nutty Christmas cake, a bread dough enriched with sultanas, candied pumpkin, pine nuts and sugar.
- *Panettone Genovese* The Genovese version of the classic Christmas cake. This one is less sophisticated and a bit heavier than the traditional Lombard version.
- *Pasta Genovese* The original light and airy Genoese sponge.
- *Pizza dolce* A very simple crisp cake, golden brown and delicious – perfect for eating with cold white wine.
- *Ravioli dolci* Deep-fried *ravioli* with a filling of candied fruit blended with bone marrow.
- *Sacripantina* A sort of trifle made with sponge cake in layers with liqueurs and creamy custard of various flavours.
- *Sciummette* Light-as-a-feather egg white fritters, covered in a cream of milk, eggs and pistachios.
- *Torta di mandorle* A very strong-tasting almond cake that has a delightfully delicate texture.
- *Torta di pasta Frolla alla Genovese* Delicious fruit tart with the cherry jam filling enclosed in an envelope of shortcrust pastry.

Local Specialities

- *Condiggion* A salad of peppers, cucumbers, tomatoes, garlic, basil, lettuce and so on, traditionally served on a bed of sliced dried bread, soaked in oil, vinegar and water.
- *Mesciua* A 'poor' soup, made with chickpeas, beans, grain and celery, with rosemary, garlic, onion and carrot to flavour it. The name means 'mixture'.
- *Minestrone alla Genovese* The classic soup made from lots of fresh vegetables, finished with a generous helping of *pesto* to give it that unmistakably Genovese flavour.
- *Torta Pasqualina* A savoury cake which requires a long and dedicated preparation. It's a cake of layers (there should be 33) with chard, *ricotta*, Parmesan cheese and marjoram, decorated on top with hard-boiled eggs. Eaten traditionally at Easter time, in particular on Easter Monday, which is the day for having a picnic.

---

development: olive groves have been sacrificed for yet more hotels. On the other hand the delightfully mild climate on the coast favours the cultivation of many specialised crops. Flowers come top – carnations being the most widely

VINO

Wine

RED WINE

• *Barbarossa* Produced in the province of Savona, this is a light-coloured red wine, perfect for everyday drinking at table. It has a light, pleasant flavour and a delicate bouquet.

• *Rossese di Dolceacqua* Fine ruby red wine produced in limited quantity in the Imperia province. A soft, rounded flavour and an unmistakable bouquet of wild roses.

WHITE WINE

• *Coronata* A fresh, light, crisp wine with an unmistakable bouquet of lemons.

• *Pigato* A bouquet of almonds characterises this light dry wine, which is perfect to accompany fish.

• *Polcevera* The best Ligurian wine for drinking with cold seafood or delicate fish dishes. A light, delicately flavoured and delicious wine.

• *Campochiesa* A fairly rare and specialist wine, delicate and fresh. Considered a fine table wine.

• *Verici* This is the wine traditionally drunk with *ciuppin*, the local fish stew. It's fruitier than many of the local whites, with a heady bouquet and rounded flavour.

Wines Of The Five Worlds

The extraordinary wines produced in the tiny area of Cinqueterre provide us with two superb D.O.C. wines. These are *Cinqueterre bianco secco*, very dry and clean tasting, perfect with all seafood, egg dishes, calves' liver and fish soups. The other one is the extremely rare *Cinqueterre Sciacchetra* made with grapes that have just begun to dry out in the sun. Amber gold in colour it varies from being sweet and velvety to an almost dry flavour.

All the Cinqueterre wines are worth a special mention, and well worth trying, but do remember some of them can be quite strong! The better ones are *Vermentino*, *Albarola* and *Trebbianco*. They remain the best known of all the Ligurian wines.

WORTH TAKING HOME

All the locally grown herbs are fragrant and delicious, though the king of them all is basil. Ligurian olive oil is considered the best, so you're certainly in the right place to stock up. Locally made *pesto* is very good and in jars will keep for a good long time. Otherwise, try bringing home a plant, some pinenuts, walnuts and a nice big piece of parmigiano and of course the olive oil, then you can make your own.

Tangerines grow well along the riviera near Sanremo, and you can easily bring some back with you. Keen gardeners should bring back local seeds and bulbs of the flowers and plants that grow so abundantly in this stunningly lovely region, but check regulations first.

SAGRE E FESTE

Festivals

On the second Sunday in May the town of Camogli has a wonderful fish festival. Tons of fish are fried in a massively wide frying pan with a huge handle. The festival commemorates a night during World War II when the village fishing boats returned safely and laden with fish through a mine-ridden part of the sea. It was decided to offer the catch of one day and one night to the guests of Camogli every year, in homage to St. Fortunato.

Elegance, Truffles and Rustic Cheeses

Often these two regions are considered as one. Although geographically part of Piemonte, Valle d'Aosta is an independent region, where the people speak a patois, and where it is officially recognised to be bilingual in French and Italian.

PIEMONTE the leader

This region has for the most part a proud history, and she has always led the way for the rest of the country, showing a spirit of unity and a strength and an ability in the people that few other Italians have been capable of. In fact the unification of Italy came about largely thanks to the efforts of this region and its people. Cavour, a fervent Piedmontese, was the country's first prime minister, and his parliament proclaimed the first king of Italy to be Vittorio Emanuele, king of Piedmont. French was the official court language until the middle of the 19th century, and in most of the region the local dialects are halfway between French and old Tuscan Italian to this day. The influence of Savoy and the French is also evident in the food.

Elegance

This is a region of high mountains and soft hills, of rich opulent cities, sophisticated, elegant and smart, and gentle farmers and quiet vineyards.

The landscape spreads out like a fan, with steep snowy mountains to the north, sloping down abruptly into the rich plains, where cities sprawl in every direction, stealing the space available for the intensely cultivated rich and fertile countryside. Rice fields lie like mirrors, villages dotted among them like little islands. Rivers run fast, channelled into a very efficient irrigation system. The Colline del Po and the Monferrato hills roll peacefully into the distance, sprinkled with small-holdings, tiny villages and ancient castles amongst the neat rows of vines and the fruit trees.

The climate of this landlocked region is typically continental, with cold, dry winters, hot summers, and rain in spring and autumn. In the winter months, the snowfalls are heavy, and the temperatures fall a long way below zero. On the plains and along the rivers, fog is a common problem. A particularly mild climate can be enjoyed on the shores of Lake Maggiore.

Awe-inspiring

How glad I am that I chose the autumn to come here, when all the flavours and colours of this glorious region are at their peak. I discovered a cuisine with two definite sides to it – the elegant city food and the humble, simple peasant food. It is a fairly rich and not madly healthy way of eating; there is an awful lot of butter, cream and rich cheese involved, a lot of red meat too. But the overriding impression is the strength of the flavours – it all tastes very strong – garlic is lavishly plonked into everything, truffles are shaved over everything that happens to pass them by, and the wines leave me tasting them still hours after I've drunk my fill. Yet as this is a region that draws you to the great outdoors, to ramble the soft hillsides or to trek or ski on its fabulous mountain slopes, in the invigorating air, it certainly gives you the appetite for the richness of the food. I found myself awed by the place, awed by the incredible heights of the snow-capped mountains, awed by the elegance of the cities, awed by the strong silence of the people, so definite and positive in their attitude towards all aspects of their society, and so protective of their land, cities, dishes and wines. It isn't surprising to me that this region should have given us the first capital city of the country, that it should have so strongly led the way – with Piedmontese food and wine in their bellies and their tough personality how could they not be leaders at a time when leaders of any repute were hard to find?

The industrial development of the region and the healthy economy have brought many immigrants to Piedmont from southern regions like Calabria, Puglia or Sicily. The general tendency is to leave the countryside for the big cities like Turin and many of the thriving farms are actually being run by immigrants from the south. The first impact that this southern influx had was on the open markets, suddenly flooded with peppers, tomatoes, aubergines and olives, brilliant colours and pungent smells that were completely alien to the rigid, stoic, Piedmontese society. And it brought with it a much more healthy way of eating. The two worlds – the north and south – are gradually integrating within the big cities to create a new Piedmont. But the mountain people, the people living off the land, and the city people will always be separate.

TORINO & PROVINCE

Piemonte is divided into six provinces, with Turin by far the most densely inhabited, and very much its centre, a natural point on the route across the mountains. The city is like the drawing room of the region, reflecting the elegance of its people. It is the second most important industrial centre in the country after Milan, with FIAT and other car manufacturers heading the list.

Its straight, wide roads, crossing at perfect right angles, the wide tree-lined avenues, the airy piazzas with porticoes lining the sides of the squares, all combine to give Turin a somewhat severe air, a modern, neat look that makes it very different from other Italian cities. Somehow you can't forget that this was Italy's first capital city. Renowned for its marvellous libraries and university, museums, theatres and art exhibitions, it is a lively cultural centre on a par with any European city. In Corso Casale I found a delightful restaurant, the *RISTORANTE CAMPAGNOLO,* where the menu is prepared day by day according to what is best of fresh local produce in the market. The pasta, *taglierini* and *agnolotti,* is home-made twice a day and I had a superb *Spaghetti al prezzemolo e funghi porcini,* spaghetti with parsley and *porcini* wild mushrooms. The *antipasti* were especially good – hot local vegetables in winter, raw in summer, and *carne di bue affumicata* smoked beef.

From here it is easy to walk into Piazza Gran Madre, where there is a delightful delicatessen called *VERRUA* selling local cheeses and *salami. PEIRANO,* the renowned chocolate shop is in Corso Moncalieri.

Hot dipping

In the *TRATTORIA OSTU BACU* there were hot *antipasti* which were part of a menu which could not have been more traditionally local. I had *bagna cauda,* chunks of fried beef and raw vegetables to dip into a wonderful sauce. This was followed by *Tajarin,* thin pasta like *tagliatelle,* with truffles, snails and frogs' legs in a delicious fricassee, and to end it all a delicious *zabaione.* The wine selection was a revelation, and I learned a great deal about the local wines thanks to the care and consideration of the sommelier called Claudio, who turned out to be the adored son of the cook Maria. A visit to *GARESIO* at Via Stradella 237 will reward you with some bent and uneven hand-made *grissini* breadsticks, which are a speciality of these parts. In the province lies the valley of snow resorts called Val di Susa, with the ski centres of Sestriere and Bardonecchia. I visited Pinerolo because it was once so famous for its riding school, but there was an air of times now long gone around the stables. It did, however, have a marvellous market for local agricultural products.

VERCELLI & PROVINCE

Vercelli is a very pretty old town, once an ancient Celtic settlement, sitting on the plain on the right-hand bank of the Sesia river. The surrounding plains are ideal for growing rice and Vercelli is in fact the major European rice centre. There are experimental rice-growing establishments here, and various kinds are exported all over the world. Rice was introduced into Italy by the Aragonese in the 15th century. Since then, the developments of its culture have been truly amazing – there are even turbines which heat the water for the growing grains should it get too cold for them!

The fields are flooded so that the rice can grow (in 1859 the flooded rice fields stopped the advance of the Austrian troops as they marched on Turin), but by spring the plants have grown and the water has disappeared. The *modine,* women who used to wade through the fields to pick out the weeds by hand, have vanished, weedkillers in a bottle are now considered better value for money.

The main centre of this province is Biella, situated in a richly cultivated area, which produces a great deal of cheese. The town, famous for wool, is in two distinct halves, Biella Piano below and, on a hill a little way above, Biella Piazza. In Prato Sesia a shop called *PALTRINIERI* will provide a wide selection of the local cheeses.

IL BARACCA, in Bottaline near Biella, provided a real Piedmontese lunch, though the owners insisted this was Biellese cooking rather than Piedmontese – who's splitting hairs? The food was perfect, and particularly good was the dish of raw fillet of beef, thinly sliced and dressed with olive oil and lemon juice – which I had thought to be a dish originating from Alba....

The province of Novara, too, is richly agricultural – more rice fields, more wonderful cheese.

ALESSANDRIA & PROVINCE

Medieval Italians, united against Barbarossa, built a fortified city not far from where the Tanaro river flows into the Bormida. It was named in honour of Pope Alexander III. The medieval aspect persists in the historical centre, but this is surrounded by a collection of green and airy streets, houses with gardens, wrapped around by a busy industrial suburban band. Alessandria is famous the world over for being the birthplace of the famous Borsalino hat!

Alessandria is also surrounded by rice fields, and rich fields of wheat and corn, peaches, apples and hazelnuts, and there are poplar woods which are cultivated for furniture making.

Casale Monferrato is at the centre of the province's wine production, and still in the Monferrato area is the spa town of Acqui Terme where you can go for a marvellously relaxing 'hydromineral' cure.

ASTI & PROVINCE

Right in the middle of the wine production area of Monferrato is Asti, a medieval town with many perfectly preserved buildings within the old town walls. It is also a modern, happy, thriving city with plenty of greenery and a lively atmosphere. Asti, nicknamed 'the capital of wine', is surrounded by excellent wine vineyards and eating-grape vineyards too, with the famous Asti Spumante as its flagship. Wine is the most active industry here. At Canelli they make vermouth, *spumante,* various wines and liqueurs. Agliano, on the hills amongst the vineyards, is especially famous for its excellent Barbera wine, and for curative mineral waters too.

CUNEO & PROVINCE

Here the industrial explosion has been contained. The province, largest in Piedmont, is mostly mountainous or at best hilly, its sound economy based on growing peaches, apples, strawberries and raising beef and veal. Cuneo is a lovely city in a beautiful position, which has been the scene of many a battle in times gone by, including one which lasted thirty years in the early 15th century. There were apparently thirty cheeses representing the point of contention, and the battle fought between the Marchesato of Saluzzo and the city of Cuneo was counted as a year for each cheese. Why they came to blows over the cheese is no longer known.

The mountain people have always been poorer than those from the plains in Piedmont, but recently they have begun to establish their own identity, by means of their superb cheese, made here in exactly the same way now as it has been for centuries. In spring and summer the milk is taken directly from the pastures and turned into cheese on the spot. The most important of the provincial towns is Alba – where not only is the sublime white truffle hunted in the surrounding woods but also strawberries grow juicy and sweet. Wine and sweets are also produced here. Bra is also a wine centre, and Fossano the most important animal market in the area.

SALUMI

Salami Sausages and Cured Meats

The *salame* of Piedmont is called *salame d'la duja*, and is preserved in jars of lard to keep it soft and moist.

Prosciutto di capriolo Roebuck prosciutto is a memorable alternative to the pork variety with a much stronger flavour. *Zampone* stuffed pig's trotter and *cotechino* stuffed savoury sausage are part of that great Piedmontese work of art, the *Bollito*, where many different kinds of meat are boiled together and served with a rich selection of sauces. Then there is a selection of raw *salami, salame crudo,* and cooked *salami, salame cotto.* Tiny little tender soft sausages *salsiccine* and the delicious liver pâté *pâté di fegato,* with truffles, of course.

PASTA

In this region, where the influence of French cooking is so strongly felt, the most traditional pasta shape is the elegant fine *tagliolini* served with deliciously creamy white truffle sauces, *salse di tartufi bianchi.*

Finanziera (see Local Specialities), often used

Local Specialities

- *Tajarin* Piedmont's very own pasta. Thin light *tagliatelle,* either dressed with the juices from roast meat, or with butter and truffles. No wider than ½ cm.
- *Gnocchi alla bava* Light potato *gnocchi* dressed with butter and melted *fontina* cheese and white wine.

as an accompaniment to soufflés, can also be blended with pasta such as *maccheroni* and is then baked in a pastry case in *Pasticcio di Maccheroni alla Finanziera.*

PESCE E FRUTTI DI MARE

Fish and Seafood

Piedmontese cooking does not really include fish. Being a landlocked region it naturally doesn't have sea food, and being a cuisine ruled by its traditions and local produce, it refuses to import what doesn't belong. If it can be said to use fish, I would say it has to be the humble anchovy – used to flavour other dishes rather than eaten on its own. I found a few recipes locally that did use lake and river fish to some extent. Pike *luccio* stewed in the oven with a bottle of white wine poured over it; eel *anguilla* cooked with truffles; tench *tinca* fried or roasted with garlic and herbs and trout *trota* cooked in various ways, the best ones from the River Sesia.

CARNE E CACCIA

Meat and Game

Veal *vitello,* the most sophisticated of all meats, is widely used. Tender, pink and juicy, it goes into one of the region's most famous dishes, *vitel tonné* (see local specialities).

Here the beef *manzo* is excellent, and famous throughout the country for its consistently good quality and the skill with which it is butchered and prepared.

A lot of offal is eaten – tongue *lingua* (of veal) is extremely popular, and cooked in many delicious ways. Spleen *milza* (beef or veal) is used a great deal both in mixed offal dishes – *fricia* – or on its own to make *cima del povero* where it is stuffed with chopped leftover meat, herbs and vegetables, boiled and served sliced with butter-glazed vegetables.

Pork *maiale* is not nearly as popular as beef or veal, or poultry, and appears only rarely on the menu. However, the traditional dish made with fresh pig's blood that crops up all over the country under different names and recipes is also prepared here where it's called *marzapani novaresi* and is like a sausage, *not* like marzipan.

Goose *oca* is very much used on the Piedmon-

Local Specialities

● *Bollito* The wonderfully triumphant dish of various boiled meats – *zampone*, *cotechino*, chicken, beef, veal and so on, cooked with pungent herbs and served steaming hot with the famous green sauce, *bagnet vert*. There is also a red version of the sauce called *bagnet ross*. In the Langhe, *bollito* consists of only boiled veal, and is served with a different sauce, called *cogna*, made of pickled fruit, mainly grapes, prepared at harvest time and kept in jars.

● *Brasato al Barolo* A dish of braised beef, marinated in a bottle of the best Barolo. Usually served with rice, or polenta.

● *Finanziera* A delicious mixture of chicken livers, peas, cream, mushrooms and minced veal, used as an accompaniment to soufflés. The name derives from when Turin was filled with bankers and financiers who wore a costume called *Finanziera* and who were apparently particularly fond of this dish. It was easy to move the name from the clothing to the dish.

● *Grive* In French it means thrush, but it is actually a peasant dish of meatballs made with pork liver and pork meat with bread-crumbs, egg, juniper berries and cheese, all fried in a pan.

● *Lepre in Civet* The Piedmontese equivalent of jugged hare – a hare cooked slowly in its own blood. The same method is used for chamois *camoscio*.

● *Vitel tonné* The classic dish of roast veal sliced on a dish, covered with a rich mayonnaise mixed with shredded tuna fish. Served cold, garnished with capers and gherkins, and anchovies for extra flavour.

tese plains, and chicken *pollo* is popular all over the region, but the moorhen is peculiar to the Vercelli and Novara areas, where it is known as *pulotti* and is cooked as a traditional September dish.

Autumnal flavours

In cooking that is so reminiscent of the flavours of autumn – mushrooms, truffles, chestnuts, hazelnuts and grapes – it was only natural that game should make its appearance on the menu once the hunting season begins in earnest. Partridge *pernici* are available, as are pheasant *fagiani*. Quail *quaglie* are popular too, and duck *anatre* are prepared in many ways in the Novara area.

Once off the plains, chamois *camoscio*, happy in the high rocky crags of the northern part of Piedmont, are delicious when cooked *alla Piemontese* – in a rich stew, and roebuck *capriolo* also appears on the table, usually cooked in a red wine casserole. Rabbit *coniglio* is very popular and is cooked imaginatively and with great care, as is hare *lepre*.

Frogs *rane* are cooked in all sorts of ways. These little creatures constituted an important part of the peasant's diet in areas where rice grows, and the damp marshy atmosphere gave them an ideal habitat. But, since the introduction of weedkillers, most of the frogs have not survived, and traditional dishes using frogs are becoming scarcer. They may be stuffed and baked, deep fried in batter or cooked with garlic and oil. Snails *lumache* are extremely popular here, as they are in Lombardy, and are served with plenty of garlic and butter, or with walnuts and tomato, stewed in Barbera, or fried with onions.

Embattled Chicken

There are two very different stories attached to the origins of *pollo al Marengo*, the chicken dish named after the famous battle. According to one, Napoleon turned up at an inn on the eve of the battle of Marengo and the cook had nothing but chicken to cook. Knowing he hated roasts she quickly invented this dish of stewed chicken with tomatoes, onions, mushrooms, garlic and white wine. The other version is that it was prepared on the Marengo battlefield by the only surviving cook, using what he could find after the gunfire had destroyed practically everything.

FORMAGGIO
Cheese

The delicious *fontina* is used to make the wonderful fondue *fondua* which is a wonderfully warming meal for cold snowy days. It is sold as *piccante* mature or *dolce* mild – both kinds are superb, soft and slightly chewy, with an appetising golden colour like butter.

Castelmagno is reputed to have started the war which lasted 30 years. Produced in the tiny village of Pradlèves (pop. 170, cattle 2,000), this noble cheese was served to Charlemagne and the popes of Avignon. Each cheese weighs 5 kg (over 10 lb), and 200 tonnes are produced every year. Like *fontina*, this and most local cheeses melt very easily and blend well with cream and butter and truffles to make many of the superb sauces used so much here.

Local Speciality

• *Fonduta* The local version of fondue made with melted *Fontina* cheese and white wine.

FRUTTA E VERDURA
Fruit and Vegetables

Many varieties of apples *mele* and pears *pere* are grown all over the hilly districts. The very small, crisp and crunchy summer pear, *perette di San Pietro*, is worth finding. Strawberries *fragole* are grown mostly in the Cuneo area, and are usually available from late spring onwards. There are several varieties, including the baby ones called *fragoline*. Delicious peaches *pesche*, juicy yellow cling and white are used for making stuffed baked peaches. The hazelnuts *nocciole* are famous throughout the country for their excellent quality.

While over half the national rice production comes from this region, there is little room on the remaining sloping land for many other vegetables. But there are several types of beans *fagioli* which thrive in the climate and the remaining available soil. Celery *sedano* and cardoons *cardi* also grow well. But of course the white truffle of Alba is the supreme vegetable of the region.

PASTICCERIA
Cakes, Biscuits and Puddings

This is a rustic region but with an elegant, chic and sophisticated side, with expensively dressed ladies gathering for a chat, and aristocratic drawing rooms where once the future of the country was planned. It was inevitable that a wide selection of frivolous, neat *pasticcini* like *lingue di gatto, baci di dama* and others would be produced – all of which were consumed by the trayload during political discussions or over a gossipy afternoon tea. At the court of Savoy the cooks invented an infinite variety of puddings and creamy desserts using the riches of the countryside, that have resisted the test of time.
• *Amaretti* Delicious macaroons, far removed from the classic *amaretti* from Saronno which are available all over the country.
• *Baci di dama* Superb almond pastries covered in melted chocolate.

Local Specialities

• *Insalata di ovoli alla Piemontese* Antipasto made of wild mushrooms dressed with a sauce of egg yolks and lemon juice mixed with olive oil and covered with shavings of fresh truffles.
• *Puccia* A winter dish of cabbage and pork mixed into polenta, coated with Parmesan cheese.
• *Trofeja* An extremely tasty and rich bean soup traditionally cooked in a terracotta pot with four handles from which it takes its name. It contains bits of pork – like the head, tail, or trotters.

• *Martin Sech al Barolo* Pears stewed in Barolo, one of the most ancient and traditional of all the Piedmontese desserts. For the recipe to be absolutely authentic, it's important that the pears should be the russet-skinned variety 'Martin Sech', but this is currently suffering a blight of unidentified cause.
• *Pesche ripiene* Dessert made with fresh peaches stuffed with almonds and crushed *amaretti* and baked in the oven. Best made with white peaches.

- *Budino Piemontese* A wonderfully biscuity pudding, flavoured with liqueur.
- *Confortini* Light, crisp *lingue di gatto* (langues de chat).
- *Krumiri* Tea-time or breakfast biscuits, fragrant, crisp and crumbly, sold in traditional red tins.
- *Salame del Papa* The traditional Easter cake of the town of Alessandria, consisting of crushed biscuits, cocoa, butter, rum, Marsala and sugar, shaped into a sausage and chilled until firm, then sliced like a real *salame*.
- *Savoiardi* Taking their name from the ancient kingdom of Savoy, these biscuits are as light and fluffy as a feather, pale yellow and absolutely melt-in-the-mouth.
- *Spumone Piemontese* Made with *mascarpone* cheese, this is a rich, creamy mousse flavoured with rum.
- *Torta alla Monferrina di zucca e mele* Superb apple and pumpkin cake with chocolate. Generally considered a family cake, as it isn't really attractive enough to serve to guests!
- *Torta alle nocciole* A light, rich and buttery hazelnut cake, very popular all over the region.
- *Torta gianduia* A complicated-to-make layered chocolate and hazelnut cake, traditionally served with the word *GIANDUIA* written across the top.
- *Gianduiotti* Wonderfully rich and smooth long triangular chocolates made with milk chocolate flavoured with crushed hazelnuts. The most famous of all Italian chocolates.
- *Zabaione* The oldest of all the regional desserts – one egg yolk, one tablespoon of Marsala, one tablespoon of sugar, and one tablespoon of water per person, beaten with a whisk in a copper bowl over hot water until foaming, light and pale yellow – served hot or cold.

VINO
Wine

Although the region produces a very limited quantity of wine compared with other parts of the country, what it does produce is truly superb and very special. In recent times the output has increased considerably, which has brought the prices down, but fortunately not the quality of the wines. It is still the region with the most D.O.C. wines and one of the very few with D.O.G.C. wines.

There are 35 D.O.C. areas, spread all over the countryside. The most noble and best-known vineyard is the Nebbiolo, from which all the great Piedmontese wines descend. The region also produces the grape called moscato di Canelli, from which Asti Spumante is made – after champagne, the most famous sparkling wine in the world.

On the whole, this is a region of red wine drinkers, although efforts are being made to bring white wines into the limelight too. I do urge you not to miss the experience of tasting for yourself, at least once in your life, the perfection and delight of the incredible wines from this region.

RED WINE

- *Barbera* Different kinds exist, their price varying according to quality and vintage. A rich, heady, strong-flavoured wine for drinking with the excellent local beef dishes.
- *Dolcetto* Again, there are various different types, but the best is *Dolcetto d'Alba*, a sharp-tasting, garnet red wine, with a lingering aftertaste.
- *Gattinara* My favourite, rounded, full-bodied and smooth.
- *Grignolino* A valuable and very much respected and sought-after wine – like all the reds, full-bodied and strong.
- *Nebbiolo d'Alba* A pure tasting wine with a multi-layered flavour that goes perfectly with all the local truffle dishes.

WHITE WINE

- *Cortese di Gavi* Famous, and rightly so. A deliciously dry wine with a light golden colour, perfect for drinking with trout.
- *Erbaluce di Caluso* Dry and fresh-tasting, is also available in a sweet version.

ROSÉ WINE

- *Malvasia di Casorzo d'Asti* A fairly dark rosé wine, very good with veal dishes. Dry and fairly full-bodied. Also available as a sweet sparkling dessert wine.

SPUMANTI

- *Asti Spumante* It can be dry or sweet, produced with Moscato d'Asti grapes and made with the Charmat method. Other sparkling wines are also produced locally using the Champenois method, but they generally use imported grapes from Lombardy.

Fabulous Funghi

Here truffles are the white variety not the black ones found in Umbria. Available from October to the end of November in the Alba region, they are sniffed out by trained dogs at night, so the dogs must be white, or they can be lost. The industry of truffle hunting is so lucrative that the dogs become extremely valuable, and it is sadly common practice in this competitive world for rival *trifolau* to poison a rival's beast.

Truffles are always eaten raw, never cooked, and, maybe because of their price, are always grated on to food.

These truffles have a powerful distinctive aroma and a far more delicate flavour than their black cousins, and as the local cuisine is more sophisticated than that of Umbria, they are used in more delicate dishes with ingredients like butter and cream, to enhance the mild flavoured meats like chicken, or on fine tagliatelle.

All truffles have a unique and delicious flavour and perfume, hard to beat, and indeed to describe. Very expensive, the price will make you pale, but you do only need a little bit to achieve the stunning effect of their flavour.

DESSERT WINE

• *Barolo Chinato* A sweet version of the rich red wine. Drunk as a digestif or with desserts.
• *Malvasia di Castelnuovo Don Bosco* Named after the famous saint, this is a golden, rich and lingering dessert wine.

BEVANDE
Drinks

• *Vermouth* The famous brands like Martini, Cinzano, Punt e Mes, have their home in and around Turin. Martini and Cinzano are available dry, red, white, sweet and rosé. They are made with wines, herbs, flowers and secret ingredients to age-old recipes and are enjoyed all over the world in cocktails or on their own. Punt e Mes has a more distinctive and deep, spicy flavour of its own, bitter sweet with a hint of sharpness. It is a dark red colour and makes a delicious aperitif.

SAGRE E FESTE
Festivals

In the village square of Castiglione in the province of Asti they celebrate *La Fagiolata* on 2 January. Huge great pots of beans are stewed in the open air and then distributed to everyone with plenty of wine and laughter.

Also in the province of Asti, in Nizza Monfer-
rato, they celebrate the auction of the cardoon and the truffle in the first week of November, culminating on the first Sunday. The festa is in honour of San Carlo, with music, stalls and the auction to round things off.

In Asti itself, the main regional festival is on the second Sunday of September. There is plenty of traditional food and samples of peasant customs like cheese-making, grappa-distilling and so on.

There is also the yearly wine festival in Asti, lasting a week at the main Expo Salon in the city, towards the end of September. The wines shown are also for sale, and you can do plenty of tasting.

WORTH TAKING HOME

Need I say truffles, if you go at the right time of year (October to March). The fresh ones are very expensive, and must be used quite quickly, so it might be better to buy them canned or in a tube of delicious purée. Don't miss taking a good sized wedge of *fontina* cheese, some dried local mushrooms and a few bottles of Barolo – even if you don't buy any other kind of wine.

I do recommend you buy yourself a *trofeja*, the terracotta pot which gives its name to the soup traditionally cooked in it. It's a lovely pot which can be used for anything. Be sure to take home as big a bag of *gianuiotti* (buying them loose by weight is cheaper than a box) as you can carry!

VALLE D'AOSTA –
Valley of the Cheeses

It is in this the tiniest of all the regions of Italy, that the highest mountains have gathered together to form the dramatic icy peaks of Europe's tallest Alpine range. The Matterhorn (*Il Cervino* to Italians), Mont Blanc, Monte Rosa and Gran Paradiso are all in this area.

The heavy snowfalls that are part of the scenery from October to March make most of the mountain roads and the two major passes into France and Switzerland impassable for most of the year, but they also attract thousands of holiday makers to the many ski resorts and hotels nestling among the mountains. This is a rich and lucky region, popular with tourists, who provide jobs and incomes for almost everyone. The Casino of Saint Vincent also contributes to the region's commercial success.

A sixth of the territory is taken up by the National Park of Gran Paradiso. This was a royal hunting reserve until 1922 when it became a national park for the preservation of local flora and fauna. Here there are many species that are in danger of extinction elsewhere – marmots, wild goats, chamois, foxes, mountain pheasants, golden eagles and many more, all living in a fabulous environment surrounded by rhododendrons, pine forests, gentians and other rare wild flowers.

Valle d'Aosta is so small it has no internal provinces. Aosta, the capital, is a commercial, industrial and tourism-rich city, its importance lying in its link between Italy, Switzerland and France. Of the historical monuments, don't miss the Roman theatre, the Arco d'Augusto, and the medieval church of San Orso.

Best Restaurant

Also, don't miss the wonders of *IL CAVALLO BIANCO* in via Aubert 15. This restaurant is one of the oldest and best established in the whole country. Over four centuries ago passing travellers would stop here to exchange their horses, and sample the same delicious food which is on offer today, but which has been lovingly brought up to the haute cuisine standard of the restaurant. Your meal will not be cheap, but you will remember it all your life, and it is not just my opinion that *IL CAVALLO BIANCO* is the most important re-

gional restaurant in the country. Nothing is out of character, every detail is absolutely authentic to the region and the food is exceptional. After a meal here you really will be aware of the French influence on the cuisine of the Val d'Aosta.

Look out for the fantastic *terrine di coniglio* rabbit terrine, *carbonada con polenta* beef carbonnade with polenta, *intingolo di cosce di rana disossata* boned and casseroled frogs' legs, *faraona* guinea fowl, *capretto* kid, and a fabulous selection of home-made desserts and cakes. Also on the menu is the region's most famous dish, *fonduta Valdostana*, fondue made with the most delectable local cheese – *fontina*. All rounded off with a really amazing wine list with the very best of the region's wines.

Wherever you eat in this region, you will notice many French names on the menu – *boudin, caillettes, blanc manger* – the gastronomic currents of France flow through every mouthful. But you'll also be aware of the excellent beef, dairy produce, and wide selection of game and fish that is available.

Conservation

This is a region where the people are very much tuned in to their environment, where they care passionately about their wildlife and their scenery and defend them wholeheartedly – a feeling unfortunately hard to find in other parts of Italy. Alongside this strong conservationist feeling is a pride in the traditions of the region – you'll see local costumes worn with elegance and ease, and the food you'll eat may not be the healthiest in these modern calorie- and cholesterol-conscious times, but it will be delicious, and perfectly cooked. These local specialities and wines are guaranteed to feed the spirit and the stomach, leaving you comforted and satisfied.

SALUMI
Salami, Sausages, and Cured Meats

The most famous of all the local *salumi* is *mocetta*. This is a leg of chamois which is dried with spices rubbed into it, then very thinly sliced to be served as an antipasto. *Lardo salato* also crops up frequently – a highly salted and flavoured lard, also served as an *antipasto*, though not to everyone's liking. *Boudin* is the local form of black pudding, almost identical to the French blood sausage of the same name. A soft, squashy, highly flavoured sausage – and to my mind, also an acquired taste. *Carne sottosale* is meat which has been preserved in salt, rather like salt beef. There are various kinds of sausages *salsicce* in varying sizes and shapes, usually a mixture of beef and pork. Often cooked in delicious casseroles with red wine, or more simply grilled on a wood fire.

PASTA

The pasta eaten in this region tends to be the big, rich, filling, stuffed varieties like *ravioli*, *agnolotti* and *crespelle*. These come with a wide variety of meat or vegetable fillings and are usually simply dressed with butter and grated Parmesan. *Tagliatelle* are also quite popular, though this is not the region to find brilliant red tomato sauces on your pasta – you're much too far north to expect that, unless you're in a restaurant that doesn't serve authentic local specialities. *Gnocchi* are also very popular, especially if smothered in a huge helping of *fonduta*.

Local Specialities

- *Polenta alla Valdostana* The polenta is cut into small discs and placed in an ovenproof dish, covered with *fontina* and a mild tomato sauce, then baked in the oven.
- *Polenta Concia* While the polenta is cooking, *fontina* is added to the mix and allowed to melt into the polenta until smooth and evenly distributed. Just before serving it receives a dressing of butter and Parmesan. The same recipe is also prepared in Piedmont, but there milk is boiled with the polenta. It's delicious but extremely rich.

PESCE E FRUTTI DI MARE
Fish and Seafood

Delicious trout are caught in the clear rivers and streams. Although often simply grilled or fried, you will be more likely to come across trout dishes where the fish has been enhanced by delicious sauces with a cream base and the additions of herbs, wine or almonds.

CARNE E CACCIA
Meat and Game

Beef *manzo* is the main meat used here. It is of excellent quality and is used imaginatively and expertly to make superb stews and warming casseroles as well as roasts.

Local Specialities

- *Costolette di vitello alla Valdostana* Little veal chops stuffed with *fontina* and *prosciutto* and fried in butter.

Many of the older recipes for cooking meat use methods of preserving it in salt to keep it as a standby during the freezing winter months – *Carbonada* used to be preserved in this way.

Venison *capriolo* is popular, the subject of many superb recipes, including one I came across, using a sauce of myrtle berries covering a roast haunch.

Pigeon *piccione*, pheasant *fagiano*, chamois *camoscio*, rabbit *coniglio*, and other game is available in season.

FORMAGGIO
Cheese

Fontina is the only really important cheese of the region, a fatty cheese with a semi-soft texture and a lovely buttery colour. It can be fairly sweet or peppery, depending on the variety, and there are a great number of varieties! It's used a lot in cooking, especially for *Fonduta*, and in many other dishes throughout the entire country. Try it melted on toast.

FRUTTA E VERDURA
Fruit and Vegetables

The agricultural activity of this region is typical of a mountainous region, with no great wide spaces where crops can abundantly spread. Rye, potatoes, apples and pears are the only important crops, and even these are limited by the climate and landscape.

PASTICCERIA

Cakes, Biscuits and Puddings

• *Ciambelline d'Aosta* Little doughnut-shaped biscuits made with equal parts of white and yellow cornmeal flour. Traditionally given to friends and relatives as gifts by the bride and groom at old-fashioned mountain weddings in place of the sugared almonds customary almost everywhere else these days.

• *Dolce Savoiardo* A very simple and incredibly light cake made with stiff egg whites and cornflour, flavoured with grated lemon zest and vanilla.

• *Torcetti di Saint Vincent* The favourite little pastries of Queen Margherita of Savoy, who would often visit Saint Vincent, and frequented the town's most famous *pasticceria* (now closed) to buy these delicious buttery pastries twisted into semi-circles and eaten with tea, milk or wine.

• *Panna cotta* With the superb cream available, a great many cream-based desserts appear. This one is almost identical to crème brûlée – cream and eggs, baked in a bain-marie and topped with caramel.

• *Tegole* Almond pastries named 'roof tiles' because of the way they look.

In a restaurant called *DA PIERRE* in Verres I tasted the very best ice cream I had come across in ages. With such wonderful cream it is only logical that is should be made well. But up here ice cream will not be flavoured with a thousand flavours of fruit and sunshine. What I had was a really excellent vanilla ice cream *crema*, served with a pool of hot *zabaione* and deliciously crisp and fragrant biscuits.

Soufflés also form a part of the local cuisine,

again with a very strong French slant. Particularly delicious are those flavoured with fresh berries – raspberries *lamponi* or myrtleberries *mirtilli*.

VINO

Wine

The vineyards of the smallest Italian region are situated on the highest vine terraces in Europe, in the Dora Baltea valley. The grapes are native to France and Piedmont, and many of the wines that appear elsewhere in Italy with Italian names crop up here with French names – *pino nero* is quite correctly called pinot noir, *pino grigio*, pinot gris, and so on.

RED WINE

• *Donnaz* Made with Nebbiolo (Picoutener) grapes, transplanted to the region, with small additions of other grapes like Freisa, Neyret and Vein de Nus. It has a delicious bouquet of raspberries and a slightly bitter, very dry flavour. It is a brilliant red colour and is the perfect companion for all the superb cheese-based dishes, and with white meat and game. It must be aged for at least three years.

• *Enfer d'Arvier* Called *enfer* (hell) because of the so-called Hells – the narrow vineyards strategically placed amongst the rocks at 800m above sea level. It's a very strong wine – 18° – with a lovely shiny colour and delicate bouquet. Perfect with the local antipasti, especially *mocetta*.

• *Rosso di Chambave* This is the best wine to drink with *Carbonada*. It has a smooth rounded flavour, and a very strong winey bouquet. A fine table wine produced in Chambave and Champlon.

• *Torretta* Produced in St. Pierre, where the vine is particularly well cultivated. A ruby red wine with a dry, slightly bitter flavour especially good with poultry, roasts and game.

WHITE WINE

• *Blanc de Morgex* This is made with grapes cultivated at 1000m, the highest in Europe. A very light, pale wine with a slightly herby bouquet and flavour. To me it tastes like the freshest mountain air. Perfect with antipasti and soups.

DESSERT WINE

• *Malvasia de Nus* A sweet wine with a slightly sour taste too, rather hard to find, but well worth buying if you do come across it. It's a golden colour, with an intense bouquet and a delicate flavour. This is a wine to be drunk on its own as an aperitif, or after dinner, but it is also the essential drink to sip while eating *tegole* or *torcettini de Saint Vincent*.

• *Montouvert* This is a really delicious dessert wine with a sweet, refined flavour, of a lovely golden colour.

• *Moscato di Chambave* A very bright yellow wine that marries especially well with fruit. Very small quantities of this wine are produced, so look out for it in the area of Chambave and in Saint Denis and Varrayes. It has the unmistakable flavour of moscato and a delicate bouquet.

• *Enfer d'Arvier* A very small quantity of this delicious red wine is also produced as a sweet dessert wine, using partially wilted grapes. It's syrupy and thick, with a typically liqueurish texture.

WORTH TAKING HOME

Fontina is hard to get hold of outside Italy, and as this region is where you'll find the best available, do take some home. Ask to taste the various kinds on sale and choose the one you like the best. It will keep for as long as a normal hard cheese.

Take one of the *grolla* coffee holders and prepare the traditional coffee, by adding a glass of red wine, 4 tablespoons (60 ml) of grappa, a 2-inch piece of lemon rind and sugar to taste, to a demitasse of espresso per person. Heat it in a bain-marie, transfer it to the *grolla* and impress everyone at your next dinner party!

Really attractive fondue sets for making *fonduta* are on sale all over the region. If you haven't got one, here is your chance to buy a really pretty one that will be made by experts.

Any of the local wines mentioned will be well worth taking home with you, especially those which improve with age such as *Donnaz* and *Enfer d'Arvier*.

The Holy Grail

It is unlikely that the locals will drink coffee on its own! Up here they like to mix it with wine, grappa and sugar. This is called *Caffè Valdostano nella grolla* – the *grolla* is the traditional cup from which it is drunk. The *grolla* is a large wooden vessel with a lid and usually about four spouts from which the coffee is drunk directly. It is a symbol of the region – the essential local souvenir! It's always intricately carved with vine leaves, bunches of grapes and other decorations. It can also be just a single *grolla* with one spout. It is descended from the ancient Graal (grail), the cup from which knights of old would drink a toast, using one graal with lots of spouts from which they would all drink in turn. It looks very much like an altar cup.

3

Eat, Drink and Make Money

Lombardy's size is not her only imposing feature. Over the centuries she has been the site of bloody battles, religious fervour and power struggles. Named after the Longobards, the particularly wild long-bearded West German tribe who occupied the area in the 6th century, Lombardy emerges today as a wealthy, prosperous region whose people have a staunch, efficient and independently aware approach to life which ensures the region's continuous success.

The industrial explosion here has been very fast. As early as the beginning of this century people here survived off the land, sheer human muscle power aided by water buffalo, oxen and donkeys. The streets of the cities were walked by street sellers from the countryside, *la campagna,* hauling baskets of garden produce, snails, fish and frogs. The canals which flow through Milan were still clean enough for women to do their washing in them. But ever since the first factories began to spring up on the plains, huge steel and concrete monstrosities, nothing has stopped the region's programme of expansion and it has provided salvation for the train-loads of

southern immigrants who come north to fill the factory vacancies.

It must be the success of the region which causes everyone from Florence south to be so rude about Lombardy and its people. Yet surely the remarks about the pushiness of the Lombards is nothing more than a few kilos of good vinegar grapes? Because, say what you will, life on a day to day basis *works* up here: the public transport system, in fact all communications, function as they should, and the tourist would find it genuinely difficult to get lost, or to eat badly.

High class fast food

Lombardy's food seems to be a result of the demands of this successful commercial life. It is said that the local specialities spring from a need to combine two courses in one, in order that the Lombard can rush through his meal to get on with making more money.

Osso buco with risotto, *casseula* and several other dishes are certainly combinations, but the Lombards are just as capable of sitting down and enjoying a meal at leisure as any other Italian. In fact they make consistently good use of all the high quality local produce – the beef, veal, vegetables and dairy produce.

No other region of Italy has such wide expanses of varied territory. The landscape will never bore you for long. Lombardy is situated between the Alps in the north, and the Po in the south. The mountains become alpine foothills, falling away into *colline*, soft hills, which cross the centre of the region. The water from the mountain rivers is distributed to the areas where it is needed by a network of canals crossing the interminable plains. Many of these *navigli* are easily navigable, providing a very pleasant and simple way to travel around and see the region from a different viewpoint. In particular, the *Naviglio di Pavia* is a worthwhile trip to take, a leisurely voyage with plenty of fabulous villas to admire and bridges to sail under.

The plains seem to just stretch out for ever, a fertile landscape alternating with the terrifyingly vast industrial complexes. If it's beauty one seeks in Lombardy, the lakes are there to provide it. Tiny mountain lakes are scattered about the slopes and valleys, but the major five: Maggiore, Como, Iseo, Lugano and Garda are the ones providing oases of green peace and tranquillity for the city weekender and tourists. Garda in particular has a very Mediterranean feel about it, with a temperate climate, olive groves, palm trees and oleanders.

Lombardy's major river is the Po, meandering across the plains, with many old traditions attached to it. There are five more rivers, yet with all this water, they still say they want the sea!

A curious balance is kept between the aspects of this landscape – they may be quick to expand or erect another chemical factory and pour tons of unsavoury goo into their rivers and lakes, yet every year they celebrate *La Festa degli Alberi*, where everybody plants a sapling and tends it with love and care. There is so much natural beauty here, quite apart from the artistic heritage – I hope the balance remains intact and that things that matter won't be obliterated by *il progresso* for the sake of a few more Lire.

The climate, however, leaves quite a lot to be desired! It is unbearably hot in the summer, and in winter fog and snow bring nothing but misery, unless of course you're heading for a skiing holiday at Bormio (fog permitting). The winter climate isolates villages and farming communities

from one another – perhaps the reigning spirit of independence is partly historical and partly forced on the people by sheer weather power. Certainly, the huge *cascine* farms, which were constructed to house 50 families or more, all carefully arranged in rank and status, all living a protected communal existence within the high turreted and barricaded walls, were also built to be weatherproof. Cool in summer, warm in winter, life inside was a world within a world. This natural isolation must surely be part of the reason for the enormous differences in the way people eat in Lombardy, the variations of the same dish from one village to the next.

The one common denominator for all the variations however, is the superb quality of everything, from the bread to the wine. While fast food has become popular in the cities, so long and leisurely meals still take place in the countryside, especially among the hunters of the Bergamasco or the Bresciano. Wherever you are in Lombardy, the food will be exceptional.

MILANO

After a couple of days in this elegant and hectically paced city, I was staggered by the consistently good quality of the food and drink on offer at every level, from fast foods to smart restaurants. Gualtiero Marchesi's restaurant is enchanting, his concept of nouvelle cuisine *all'Italiana* is refreshing, but I cannot help feeling that only the snobbish Milanese would put up with being so shamelessly conned by what amounts to plate decorations at exorbitant prices. I savoured better and more original delights in a backstreet haunt – risotto with cherries and deep-fried sage at reasonable prices.

Le vetrine alla Milanese

The window displays of the expensive and specialist food shops are breathtakingly lovely – *IL PECK* is astonishing, for cheeses by the hundred, but for everyday meals we go to the covered markets for enjoyable shopping. Here all the various shopkeepers lay out their wares tastefully, and the atmosphere is as friendly and easygoing as that in my tiny village shop at home. The superclean efficiency does not prevent the stallholders from flirting with the elderly spinster and her order for two veal cutlets.

I was keen to secure myself a piece of genuine

grana while in Milan. This is the Lombard counterpart to Emilia's *parmigiano Reggiano*, and the arguments as to the merits of the two cheeses would take us to the end of the book. Twenty minutes after embarking upon my quest I was wishing I'd never bothered to ask. Rosy-cheeked and cheery as a dairy farmer, the expert behind the counter was giving me a run-down on which type to use with which dish, the various ages and textures he had available and which is the best for grating, and which should be eaten as it is. I finally headed back out into the traffic, clutching a selection of wedges, and longing for the open countryside.

PAVIA & PROVINCE

Pavia, an ancient Roman city, capital of Lombardia under the Goths, Franks and Longobards. It can boast stunning examples of Renaissance architecture – the Duomo, the Visconti castle and the amazing Certosa, which combines one of Italy's loveliest churches with courtyards and cloisters grouped around it. There is a cheese, *certosa*, presumably named after the building, which has a delightful sour-yet-creamy quality about it. Much used in cooking, it is also considered digestible enough for babies and small children.

The province itself takes in the Lomellina plain, where from the green damp gloom *cascine* rise and watch over the square water fields where the rice grains swell. At the foot of the Apennines lies Voghera, the centre of the Oltrepò Pavese, which is mostly given over to the vast vineyards providing many excellent wines such as Barbera as it has done throughout history.

Zuppa support

A local speciality is the delicious *zuppa pavese*, a perfect bowl of hot broth with its farm-fresh egg floating on a secure raft of toast. This was given to Francesco I to fortify him on the eve of the battle of Pavia in 1525 – but, despite the backing of Pope Clement VII and the many bowlfuls of soup, the French were defeated and the Spanish domination of Italy was set to begin.

A good point of reference for wine lovers – the Lombard wine distribution and promotion centre is called *Enoteca Regionale di Lombardia*, and is in via al Monumento 5, in Certosa di Pavia. It forms part of the excellent restaurant *VECCHIO*

MULINO, and is worth a visit for the immense collection of bottles and information.

If you decide to visit Vigevano, on the east bank of the Ticino, a must for gastronomic and visual pleasures, don't attempt it on a *festivo* non-working day, as you'll discover all the people involved in the local footwear industry are there with you. But for a truly memorable meal, go on an ordinary weekday, and after lunch, go forth and discover Parona where the pastries called *offelle* come from. They are almond and nougat sandwiched between rice paper, and must have the *Pro Loco Parona* mark on them to be authentic.

VARESE & PROVINCE

Its lake is polluted, there is a huge amount of road and rail traffic rushing through on its way in and out of Switzerland, and there are so many factories that there should be an impression of total chaos – yet the city of Varese retains a feeling of peace and green bower tranquillity thanks to its well-kept parks and avenues lined with trees. They make everything in this province, from helicopters to silk, so it is one of the busiest areas in the whole country. Saronno is of course where *amaretto* comes from, and it's also a centre for excellent confectionery.

At the Sacromonte di Varese, about 5 km from the convent of the Romite Ambrosiane, the sisters sell butter, cheese and cream such as I've never tasted. Now I know where the Lombard fame for dairy produce has its roots. While I was there I acquired a couple of bottles of their fiery liqueur, made with many local secret ingredients – it's called *rosolio* and is a digestif *amaro* with belly-burning qualities.

While regarding all the wooded, hilly and extremely green and ferny undergrowth of this province, I knew there had to be a crop of wood-

land berries there somewhere – which had to mean jam. I found the berries and their resulting superb *confetture*, *marmellate* and *distillati di frutta* – jams, preserves and fruit distillations at Bregozzena. This turns out to be the centre for *frutti di bosco* fruits of the woods. At Gavirate, they have wonderful *pasticcerie* where you can buy the local biscuits – *brutti ma buoni* meaning ugly but good.

COMO & PROVINCE

Wandering slowly amongst the well-heeled beauty of the old city of Como, it is nice to know that the sweet smelling, densely wooded hills surrounding the city hide many excellent restaurants, hotels and beautiful villas. *VILLA SIMPLICITAS* is an old family home turned into one of the best hotels I have ever visited, with a marvellous restaurant on the terrace overlooking the lake. With antique furniture, quaint objects and floral murals, the pace is reminiscent of a stay at granny's, though the food is too sublime to be a reminder of sago pudding. The city weekenders from Milan don't even bother to come to their holiday villas once the holiday season is upon them, the traffic is too daunting on the way in and out.

At Brienno, they smoke and sell trout from the lake, and on the opposite shore, at Lecco, I ate some memorably rich ice cream before delving into the intriguing wine shops. They are full of a wide selection of fruit distillations and liqueurs prepared by Trappist and Certosini monks who inhabit the mountain monasteries. At Solzago there is more of the same, with the added bonus of many *grappa* varieties – most of them completely unknown to me, and again produced by the good monks and nuns.

SONDRIO & PROVINCE

This may be the poorest area of the region, up in the Alps, but it is worth visiting just for the cheese. In Sondrio itself, the Tognolina family's shop seemed to be the most helpful and have the best selection of delicious Valtellina cheeses fresh from the mountains, but wherever I looked there were more well-stocked windows filled with delights. In the *PASTICCERIA TAVELLO* I found hand-baked Valtellina *panettone* and took some home as it was nearly Christmas.

BERGAMO & PROVINCE

The city is divided in two – Bergamo Bassa is an ordinary modern city, but to reach Bergamo Alta you have to travel 100 metres up by funicular, to find yourself in a lovely historical and artistic city, surrounded by ancient Venetian walls, now transformed into avenues. Here I bought some amazingly grainy *salame* from the very helpful *SALUMERIA ZANETTI*. They also had another Christmas goodie I had been looking forward to tasting, or at least buying, on its home territory. *Cotechino* is a fat spicy sausage which, after a considerable period of boiling, is sliced up and served on a bed of lentils on New Year's Eve – each lentil representing a golden coin coming your way in the year to follow, ensuring a safe income for the future. Bergamo is also the birthplace of another traditional dish called *Polenta e osei* which is polenta covered with a stew of small birds. In the centre of town there is a very old *pasticceria* guarding the secret of a recipe for a cake of the same name. It's a very realistic representation of the real thing, and should not be offered to vegetarians. . . .

At San Pellegrino Terme, the famous mineral waters full of fabulous properties for clearing up renal and liver problems gush up from the earth and are dutifully bottled for the consumer. At the *RISTORANTE AGNELLO D'ORO* the boss Pino gave me one of his hand-painted plates (he always does this if you order risotto – I suppose it's in return for waiting patiently for twenty minutes while he makes it).

Heading out towards Martinella I found Marco Camponuovo's famous shop with fabulous fruit cakes and tarts. At Gromo there is another wealth of amazing cheese shops.

CREMONA & PROVINCE

Suddenly the shops and markets seemed to be filled with enormous cans, baskets and barrels of the local peculiarity – *mostarda di frutta* – a highly spiced, shiny, sticky candied and pickled fruit concoction which is considered a must with *bollito* (boiled meats and vegetables) and an ingredient for pumpkin *tortelli* to be consumed with melted butter on Christmas Eve. I have never really developed a taste for it myself, although it makes a passable alternative to chutney with cold meat. Much more delicious and equally interesting is Cremona's other speciality, *torrone*, nougat, which comes in all kinds of flavours and textures, and it is ever present throughout the Christmas celebrations.

Here one becomes aware of the proximity of that awesome – at least in gastronomic terms – region next door, Emilia Romagna. Gone is the rice, in comes hand-made pasta in all shapes and stuffed with many fillings. The delicious Soresina butter is widely available, so it does make up for all this pickled fruit.

MANTOVA & PROVINCE

It's hard to believe that these plains are still part of Lombardy, but the Po flows by as a constant reminder, its poplars standing to attention in neat rows. These pasture lands produce most of the veal and beef which is of such fine quality in this region, and the pork – most of which ends up in the *salumeria*.

The glorious city of Mantua was for almost three centuries (1319-1608) one of the most important centres of art and learning in Italy, mainly thanks to the patronage of the Gonzaga family. Mantegna was lured here from Padua; Alberti, responsible for the façade of Santa Maria Novella in Florence, was commissioned to build the church of Sant'Andrea, while Petrarch, Ariosto and many other poets owed much to the financial assistance and interested encouragement of their Gonzaga patrons.

Nowadays it is still a lovely city, with the weight of history heavy in the atmosphere. Nearby, I discovered and was completely charmed by Sabbioneta, little Athens, walled in by its high 16th-century ramparts. The cake shops everywhere were full of marvellous *torta sbrisulona* and *torta di tagliatelle*. At Corte Pasquetta, 3 kms from Mantua, Rosolino Benatti makes the best *grana* you're likely to find anywhere.

SALUMI

Salami, Sausages and Cured Meats

Salumi come into their own in this region. There are those who say that the Lombard love of *salame* and other preserved meats is simply to allow him to get the business of eating over with quickly so he can continue earning his fortune. Certainly, good *salame* tucked inside fresh bread

---

Local Specialities

• *Verzada con i salamini* Cabbage and sausage stew. The delicious sausages used in this time-honoured dish are called *de vers* – for cabbage.

---

with a glass or two of Barbera washing it down is a splendid meal fit for any industrialist – and it can be enjoyed quickly, but I doubt if this is the reason for the love of *salumi* in general in this region.

Much more to the point is the fact that Lombardy raises and butchers excellent pork, and as everywhere else in the country (though less as you travel north), fresh pork bears some kind of stigma and is not madly popular. They say it's hard to keep fresh, you can't eat it in summer months, it will give you worms, it's not good for you, it's *pesante* – heavy on the digestion. So, once slaughtered and carved up, the pig is turned into meat which is preserved and eaten throughout the year.

• *Salame Milano* is one of the most refined of the *salame* family. It has a fine grainy texture, and tiny white spots of fat.

• *Mortadella* is the largest of all the *salumi*, and is fairly fatty. Very popular with children, it tends to be used mainly in *panini* filled rolls, although it is also an essential ingredient in fillings and stuffings. If you come across it, try the superb *Mortadella di fegato*, liver mortadella, which is soft, creamy and delectable – it comes *cotta* or *cruda*, cooked or raw, just like *prosciutto*.

• *Salsicce* are plump, peppery, soft sausages that can be grilled, split and fried, or used to make lovely pasta sauce or risotto.

• *Luganeghe* is the Lombard version of Basilicata's *lucanica* sausage sold in continuous coils, which makes a truly wonderful risotto.

• *Salsiccia mantovana* or *salamella* is a cross between sausage and *salame*, and makes a delicious risotto typical of the province of Mantua.

• *Prosciutto* appears to be preferred in its cooked form, although other types are also widely available – *affumicato* smoked, *di cinghiale* boar, and *capriolo* roebuck; although these other kinds are not necessarily typical of this region – more likely to be neighbouring imports.

• *Bresaola*, on the other hand, is a very typical Lombard way of using beef fillet. The meat is salted, dried, then smoked. Sliced paper thin, it is dressed with olive oil, lemon juice and plenty of freshly ground black pepper. Some like to add a layer of thinly sliced white onion. It is traditionally a dish of the Valtellina province, but in the Grigioni area it takes on a French name, and will appear on your menu as *viande des grisons*.

You may find *soppressata* on offer. This is a nice old-fashioned way of preserving meat, and the local version reminds me slightly of a cross between corned beef and brawn – can be comforting on a cold picnic.

PASTA

This is not really a true pasta region, but there are some stuffed ones such as *agnolini*, *casônsèị* (a sort of twisted *ravioli* and the most difficult pasta in the world to make by hand) or *marrubini*. Then there are *pizzoccheri* which are made with buckwheat. In Mantova they fill *tortelli* with pumpkin, and in Cremona they fill them with crushed *amaretti* and candied fruits *tortelli alla cremasca*.

Maize to Amaze You

In place of pasta, in this region polenta reigns supreme. It started out being the peasant's staple diet. It took the place of bread, and was always cooked at midday. Lunch would be polenta with milk, or cheese, and in the evening, the leftovers would be fried or grilled and served on their own. In less poor households, it would be served with stewed meat, game or fish, with plenty of sauce. In Bassa Padana, hungry children are filled up with polenta mixed with lemon rind, sugar and flour, deep fried and eaten piping hot at tea time.

PESCE E FRUTTI DI MARE

Fish and Seafood

With all these lakes, rivers and canals, provided they can keep the levels of pollution under control, the Lombards have a surprisingly large collection of fish specialities for a land-locked region. They tend to use fish which are elsewhere

Local Specialities

• *Polentauncia* Sliced polenta, layered in a pot, with garlic, butter and cheese, then baked in the oven.
• *Polenta e osei* Polenta covered with a stew of tiny birds cooked in a rich sauce.
• *Risotto alla certosina* Risotto made with vegetables, frogs' legs and fillets of perch or carp, created by the monks of Certosa.

considered inedible or too much trouble to bother with, proof once again that life has not always been so rich.

Tench *tinca* crops up on the menu quite often, but even I, a seasoned fisherwoman, recoiled in disgust when told that this fish, which has the unusual quality of surviving for some time out of

Local Speciality

• *Missoltitt* An unusual fish dish consisting of dried *agoni*, *alosa vulgaris*. The small fish are laid out on trestles in the sun to dry, then fried in butter and sage, or grilled and served with polenta. A marvellously tasty affair, which can be bought in and around the Como area in market towns. They are kept in huge cans, layered in sheets of bay leaves.

the water, is traditionally forced to swallow a large tablespoon of pure wine vinegar, while still alive, in order to cleanse it for the cooking. The alternative, less popular, is to boil it fiercely to death.

Eel *anguilla* appears in stews, with polenta, risotto and in soups. From the lakes, pollution permitting, come pike *luccio*, carp *carpa*, perch *persico*, rainbow trout *trota salmonata*, and a fish I have been unable to identify in English called *lavarello*. You may be offered all these on their own, but quite often they'll end up being combined with polenta, pasta or risotto, or as an ingredient for a finished dish. This appears to be the Lombard rule of thumb in cooking: the combination of different foods so that you end up with something *really* substantial.

CARNE E CACCIA
Meat and Game

Many say that here is the best meat in the country, with plenty of succulent veal, beef, pork, turkey, chickens and other poultry. The quality is consistently good wherever you are – juicy, crumbly slices of tasty meat.

Frogs and snails are also popular. The whole frog is eaten, as opposed to just the legs – look out for *ris e ran*, frogs with rice, to really appreciate them. Snails are treated in a variety of ways – in Milan they will be stewed in a heavy, highly flavoured fashion.

Game is also very popular, but frankly I find eating little birds like larks, finches, thrushes and sparrows is just stretching the point too far. Recent restrictions on shooting have improved the situation, but it is still traditional for the hunters to consume vast quantities of these tiny birds.

The region is so obviously populated by avid meat eaters, I could go on for another mile of paper, but I will cut it short by reporting on a dish I really feel you should be warned about, just in case it turns up on the menu when you're comfortably seated in a restaurant in the Pavese district. *Frittura di sangue di pollo* is a dish of freshly killed chicken's blood, which is allowed to drip on to slices of fresh bread until they are saturated. The bread is then fried in plenty of butter and served on a platter, sprinkled with sugar!

In the Mantua district, the same principle is adapted for the local pudding *torta di sangue*. While the chicken is still alive, the blood from the cut throat is allowed to run into a bowl containing beaten egg yolks and sugar. Butter, flour, lemon rind and a few other ingredients are added, the cake is baked and served tepid.

I did tell you the Longobards were a particularly wild tribe did I not?

Of Nannies and Snails

When I was little, my brothers and I had a Milanese nanny called Angela, who would take us out on snail hunts every morning, during the season, after a night of rain. The brown and yellow-shelled creatures would be whisked into her bucket as quickly as we could spot them. Angela would give each one a name – there were usually about three dozen – and she would keep them in a box without food or water for 7 days and 7 nights, to allow them to purge themselves. Once a day, she'd let them out for an airing in the garden, never losing sight of them. Then one by one, she'd call to them by name and pop them into a clean box. On the 8th day, they'd get about 3 baths in salt water, until they stopped foaming. At this point Angela would extract them from their shells and cook them – the next we knew they'd been eaten. She lived to a ripe old age, did Angela, on red wine for breakfast and stewed snails for tea.

Local Specialities

- *Bollito* A collection of different meat and offal, all cooked together in a big pot. The meats are sliced thinly and served with *mostarda di frutta* or *salsa verde*. A superb meal if cooked properly.
- *Osso Buco* Shin of veal including the marrowbone, cooked with white wine and served with creamy white risotto topped with *gremolata*, a garnish of grated lemon peel, garlic and chopped parsley.
- *Busecca* Tripe cooked with vegetables and highly spiced.
- *Casseula* Originally a Spanish dish introduced by the Gonzagas. A complicated dish of pigs' trotters, *luganega* sausage and lots of vegetables, particularly Savoy cabbage.

FORMAGGIO
Cheese

It's hardly surprising that with all these incredibly well-fed, happy cows, the Lombards have ended up with the country's best dairy produce. As it's rather impossible to carry home a jug of cream or milk (butter *is* easy, because you can buy it in hermetically sealed cans, and it is delicious), cheese is the obvious choice if you want to take home a slice of the best of the region.

- *Grana* will always be sold with a piece of crust on it so as to make grating easier, but if you feel you've been given more than you want to pay for, speak up, and it will be cut off! The older the cheese, the better it is for grating, but a young, moist chunk will be wonderful served at the end of a meal with fruit. Lombard tradition calls for a piece eaten at the end of a meal to cleanse the palate.

• *Robiola* is a pure white creamy cheese, sold in flat rounds. There is a version with chopped smoked salmon in it too, though it seems to me to be rather a waste of both – however, it is perfect for tossing with pasta for a very quick dish.

• *Mascarpone* is hardly cheese at all – more like thick clotted cream. It will cause a great deal of mess in your suitcase unless transferred to a tub. Excellent with pears, and much used in cooking. Neither this nor *Robiola* lasts for long.

• *Stracchino* is a white, slightly sour-tasting cheese, often seen for sale under the name of *certosa* or *certosino*. Lovely melted over polenta, pasta, in omelettes or between chestnut flour fritters. It won't keep out of the fridge.

• *Gorgonzola* is only worth eating when it has *la goccia*, in other words, when it's runny. A fabulous soft, blue and yellow cheese from the town of the same name on the outskirts of Milan, it finds its way on to *tagliatelle*, spaghetti, polenta or as a finishing touch to risotto.

• *Taleggio* is a fairly strong cheese from the northern provinces. It is sold in squares with tiny air bubbles in it. The texture is rather like Camembert and is absolutely delicious.

• *Bel Paese* Anyone who has ever flown Alitalia will have noticed or indeed eaten that circle of creamy processed cheese wrapped in gold foil with a greenish sticker. That is the bastard child of the real thing, a large, mild, generous cheese sold in wedges, and has about as much in common with the little cream cheese as Brie has with Cheddar. Real *bel paese* is well worth eating.

• *Groviera* is the Italian version of gruyère. It's a sweet cheese with huge holes, delicious grated over pasta.

In the Valtellina area, cheese takes on a further dimension, and mountain cheese comes in all kinds of forms and flavours, all worth trying. Many have the added quality of going stringy like *mozzarella* when cooked. They will often be sold without a specific name, simply as *formaggio di montagna*, *formaggio alpino*, or have peculiar regional names in dialect.

FRUTTA E VERDURA
Fruit and Vegetables

All the vegetables thrive and grow healthy on the rich soil. One splendid guide book says that 'it is the elite of the vegetable kingdom, it is nurtured on the limestone by the loving care of man'. Which actually means that you can be sure of growing almost everything successfully, providing it doesn't hate limestone. Two vegetables worth a mention are the pumpkin *zucca* and asparagus *asparagi*. Pumpkin is used a lot in the Mantua area, particularly as a filling for *tortelli di zucca*, the traditional Christmas Eve dish in all Mantuan households. Thin green asparagus – almost sprue – are grown around Milan, and big fat and juicy ones with green and purple heads come from Bassano del Grappa.

Apples, pears, peaches, apricots, persimmons, cherries – all these in many varied forms are grown extensively here. But the prize for fruit goes to the lush crop of woodland berries and

Golden Wedding Gifts

Risotto is the best Lombard cuisine and has almost become an art form. It appears in all versions and flavours – pumpkins, frogs, *salame*, green beans – quite honestly, if cooked with care, anything goes! But the prize must go to that creamy yellow speciality *risotto alla Milanese*. It is surrounded by myth and fable, but the best one is dated 1574, and is connected to the stained glass window of the Duomo, which represents Saint Helen. The artist's apprentice was nick-named Zafferano, meaning saffron, because he used this spice to brighten

up his paints. 'Ah,' his master would cry, 'You'll end up putting saffron even in your risotto, I can see it coming!' Some time later, his daughter married a local merchant. In the middle of the wedding feast, the guests were amazed to see 4 page boys entering the banqueting hall, each carrying a tureen. When the lids were removed, inside was a bright yellow risotto, flavoured and coloured with saffron 'like golden coins'. It was Zafferano's wedding present to the happy couple. Within the week it had become Milan's most fashionable dish.

strawberries. These can all be enjoyed fresh with the lush local cream, or in fabulous local jams and preserves. Delicate *fragoline di bosco* wild strawberries and the black *mirtilli* myrtleberries are especially good.

PASTICCERIA
Cakes, Biscuits and Puddings

Now here I really don't know where to begin. Italians all tend to have a sweet tooth, but in true Lombard fashion, up here everything is bigger and better! Every town, village or province will have a traditional pastry, cake, biscuit, sweet or pudding, so spend a wonderful afternoon in any of the big towns, and go window shopping round the *Pasticcerie*! The triumph of the local bakers, and of Italian Christmas, just has to be *panettone*, that airy synthesis of light fluffy dough, studded with sultanas and candied peel.

• *Sapajean* is the Lombard version of Piedmontese *zabaione*, but made with wine instead of Marsala. To make it you need skill and patience, and a lot of egg yolks – it is supposed to do wonders for your sex life.

• *Busecchina* is the dessert reserved for the feast of Santa Sevina, which falls on the last Thursday in January. It is a delicious pink purée of boiled chestnuts and is always served with cream.

• *Mostaccioli* are made by the nuns of the Sacro Monte convent near Varese. They are fabulous rectangular spicy biscuits which mustn't be confused with the Calabrese version.

• *Pan de Mort* On All Souls' Day the classical custom was for bakers to use up all the bits and pieces they had left over, and turn them into this bread.

• *Pan de Mej* Millet bread made to celebrate the patron saint of dairy farmers, who happens to be St George, on April 23. These used to be washed down with glassfuls of single cream! You can still buy these cakes, and I thoroughly recommend the bright yellow ones made with polenta flour.

• *Chiacchere* and *Tortelli de Carnevale* are prepared at Carnival time, the last final fling before Lent, when everyone dresses up and makes merry. *Chiacchere* are thin strips of dough which are quickly fried, so that they bend and twist in the oil, and are then dusted copiously with icing sugar. *Tortelli* on the other hand are just like stuffed pasta, filled with winey custard and deep

Panettone Toni's Loaf

The legend behind this lovely cake-bread goes like this: There was once a baker called Antonio (Toni in dialect), who was in love with a young lady. But she wouldn't even smile at him. So Toni decided to create a loaf of bread in her honour. He added eggs, candied peel, nuts, sultanas, sugar and butter to a basic bread dough, and baked it in a round tin until it rose up above the edges into a deliciously light and very tall mound. Unfortunately, his love married another anyhow, but Toni became rich instead, because, by the morning, all of Milan's richest society was banging at his door, all asking for *pan de Toni–panettone*.

fried, then covered with sugar. The air is filled with the scent of them frying.

• *Torta Sbrisulona* is found all over the region. With its crisp crust and soft middle it is impossible to cut neatly as it falls into crumbs as soon as it sees the knife.

• *Torta di Tagliatelle* is a very rich, chewy and heavy cake made of *tagliatelle*, chocolate and candied peel.

VINO
Wine

They are fairly serious drinkers in these parts – each tiny corner seems to have its own brand, and claims it surpasses all the others. This spirit of rivalry is growing well on the vine.

SPECIAL REDS
• *Grumello* A delicious Valtellina wine, ruby to garnet in colour. After 5 to 6 years it can be rightfully considered the best of the Valtellina reds. Fairly heady, it is superb with red meat and game.

• *Sassella* As drunk by the Emperor Augustus, and mentioned by Virgil in the *Georgics*. Also from the Valtellina, it is a ruby wine that goes brick red as it ages. Perfect with all roast meat.

RED WINE
• *Valgella* It has many of the characteristics of *Grumello* and *Sassella*, and is supposed to aid

digestion. It's a light coloured red, with a faint rosé flavour and delicate bouquet. Excellent with light roasts and throughout the meal.

• *Franciacorta Rosso* Worth buying just for its amazing colour, red with violet flashes, and its raspberry bouquet with a vaguely almondy flavour. Very good table wine, best drunk young, when 2 to 3 years old. It comes from the lovely Franciacorta vineyards stretching to the south of Lake Iseo.

WHITE WINE

• *Lugana* A wine with very ancient historical traditions. Produced between Peschiera and Desenzana on Lake Garda. It has an extraordinary slightly salty flavour, and a bouquet reminiscent of willow trees. It is sublime with pink trout from Garda, served cold with home-made mayonnaise.

• *Oltrepò Pavese Riesling* Extremely good with *antipasti*, and delicious *Risotto alla Certosina* or fried fish. Tends to be greenish in colour, with a full dry fresh flavour and characteristic bouquet. It comes from the hills of Oltrepò where the most valuable Riesling vineyards grow in ideal habitat. Especially important are the Renano and Italico Riesling grapes.

DESSERT WINE

• *Oltrepò Pavese Moscato* From the Moscato vine, it is best known in its sparkling *spumante* form. It has a straw yellow colour, an intensely aromatic bouquet and a sweet aromatic flavour. Best drunk with fresh fruit, fruit salad or delicate desserts.

• *Lacrima Vitis* A well-known dessert wine produced with *muscato* grapes at Santa Maria La Versa.

BEVANDE
Drinks

There is the popular *Amaretto di Saronno*, a glowing amber-coloured, almond-flavoured liqueur, which in my opinion is especially good poured over ice cream or used in trifle instead of sherry.

Leaving aside this, innumerable *acquaviti*, *distillati di frutta* and *grappa*, which can be savoured all over the region (though most particularly where it is coldest), we are left with a few interesting non-alcoholic drinks. I will tell you that the young, slick, fashion-conscious kids

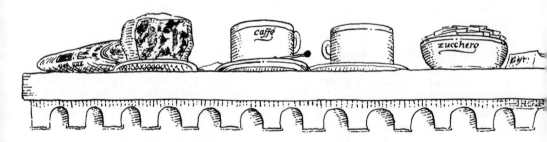

The best label for Oltrepò Pavese wines in general is Frecciarossa.

SPUMANTI

• *Franciacorta Pinot Spumante* Real champagne produced with traditional champenois methods. Enjoy it through the meal like a fine wine or as a superb aperitif. It is produced in very limited quantities, and is therefore valuable and expensive. It is made in *brut*, *rosé* and *pas dosé* versions.

hanging around on the piazzas with their mopeds and scooters drink Coca-Cola, which is perfectly fitting if you're a 15-year-old girl trying to look like James Dean.

• *Rosumada* is, I suspect, another one of those Italian preparations for increasing one's sexual potential – the secret lies in the egg yolk. It consists of sugar with egg yolks beaten to a very light and fluffy texture, with a few good glassfuls of Barbera or other heavy red wine chucked in, though in the summer the wine is replaced with ice-cold water! It will be served as a pick-me-up or refresher – usually mid-afternoon or for breakfast.

• *Caffè Brûlée* is the optional additive for the breakfast *Caffelatte*. It's made with burnt coffee, caramelised sugar and water. It keeps in the fridge for up to a month, and is used to add more depth and waking-up power to the flavour of milk with coffee – into which you dunk your *cornetto*, brioche, biscuits or *panettone* for a complete breakfast.

• *Barbajada* is wonderfully old fashioned and totally delicious. It's a mixture of coffee and hot chocolate, served with peaks of whipped cream in the winter, and ice-cold in the summer. Very much the ladies' drink at elegant cafés at the turn of the century.

• Mineral water features as strongly in this area as anywhere else in the country. The most popular is the famous San Pellegrino, which is also used in soft drinks made by the same company – the *aranciata San Pellegrino* orangeade is very good indeed, and can also be bought as bitter orange – *aranciata amara*.

WORTH TAKING HOME

Take *grana* home with you in huge quantities – don't be afraid of it going bad. If you have to, grate it all and then freeze it. Otherwise, keep it unwrapped, so it doesn't sweat, in the larder, or in an airy drawer. Other cheeses to take, as they're not often available outside Italy, are *robiola*, *stracchino*, *mascarpone*, and *taleggio*.

Torrone from Cremona comes in a convenient shape for tucking down the sides of suitcases. It comes in all sorts of forms – milk or plain chocolate, with hazelnuts, almonds, pistachios, candied fruit or coffee – the permutations go on and on. Best of all are tiny oblong ones to hang on the Christmas tree.

Rather difficult to pack, but you must take at least one *panettone* at Christmas and *colomba* at Easter. In recent years the original version has been bastardised with chocolate coatings and fake *zabaione* fillings. Be wise and buy plain. Almost any other goodies in the *pasticceria* will be worth taking home.

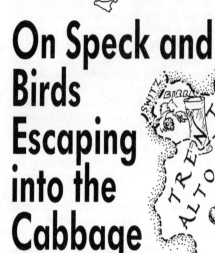

On Speck and Birds Escaping into the Cabbage

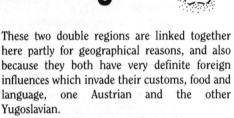

These two double regions are linked together here partly for geographical reasons, and also because they both have very definite foreign influences which invade their customs, food and language, one Austrian and the other Yugoslavian.

At the risk of being accused of making sweeping statements, I will venture the theory that Trentino, Alto Adige and Friuli have definite similarities, all being landlocked and influenced by Austria to a certain degree. Venezia Giulia seems the odd one out, still so obviously part of Veneto, by tradition if nothing else, and very much a sea-loving region. One look at their menus will prove my point. The first three provide hearty, pulse-filled soups with cabbages and sausages, horseradish, beer and polenta galore. In Venezia Giulia, fish and seafood figure strongly alongside risottos and Venetian-style fritters. Once again, the kitchen never lies, and the flavours and ingredients tell it as it really is.

TRENTINO – ALTO ADIGE – Kingdom of the Dolomites

The silent, fantastic, breathtaking mountains lie like a series of 'islands' within the Alps, with little towns and villages, famous for their warmth and hospitality, scattered throughout the lovely green valleys. At the foot of these pinnacles, gigantic steps and blocks of pink and grey are woods and meadows where many tourist centres offer skiers and hikers excellent facilities. Three towns, Trento, Bolzano and Belluno, are the places from which to reach the arcane beauty of the mountains.

Dagger in the heart

This region used to be two separate areas. Trentino in the south is named after the Roman settlement of Tridentum, now Trento, and Alto Adige encompasses the northern branch of the Adige river. Though the Alps form the natural northern frontier for Italy, until 1918 Alto Adige was a dagger-shaped Austrian province called Süd Tirol – still known as that by Austria. At the end of World War I it was finally united with Italy.

This is Italy's most northerly region, touching Austria and Switzerland, with Lombardia and Veneto on either side.

The summers here are generally cool, with plenty of snow in the winter. It is less cold in sheltered valleys, or on lower levels of the mountains, which make up the entire region. There are crystal clear lakes everywhere, surrounded by woods and stunning mountain views – these are solitary beautiful places to visit at any time.

Here there are two distinct populations, with different languages. Over half the people of the province of Bolzano speak German, the official second language. Television, road and shop signs, schools and newspapers all use German, although in Trento everyone speaks Italian. This difference is also apparent in the kitchen. In the province of Trento you'll eat good hearty mountain food, but it will retain its Italianness. Move north into Bolzano and the picture changes; *zweibelröstbraten* beef steak and onions, *gröstl* meat and potato cake, *knödel* dumplings and *erdbeertorte* strawberry cake invade the scene so much you have to continuously remind yourself where you are!

TRENTO & PROVINCE

In a valley of the Adige, surrounded by majestic mountains, lies the city of Trento, the façades of all its old buildings decorated with murals. Rovereto, in the val Lagarina, is a very old city, considered to be the cultural centre of the region, and situated in the middle of a very fertile area, it is also a major agricultural centre.

I was attracted here by tales of a fabulous restaurant on the top floor of a castle which has housed the War Museum since 1921. It turned out to be even better than I'd heard, its owners, passionate cooks, dedicated to unearthing the best of local cuisine. I tasted delicious *carne affumicata di cavallo* smoked horsemeat, *prosciutto affumicato con salsa di mirtilli* a superb smoked prosciutto, served with myrtleberry sauce, *Risotto alle castagne o alle noci* risotto with chestnuts or walnuts, light and fragrant strudel, and all with a marvellous view of the city and surrounding mountains.

BOLZANO & PROVINCE

Known as Bozen in Germany, this city lies on the Isarco river, and its old winding narrow streets are instantly memorable. Merano (Meran) is the other main city in this province, loved for its mild climate – a perfect place for a healthy holiday against a fantastic backdrop of mountains. The prettiest town in this province has to be Bressanone (Brixen), with its old houses and low archways reminding me of Bavarian buildings.

In Bressanone I found *FINK'S* at via Portici Minori 4. Its proprietor had painstakingly researched all the old local recipes and folklore to bring it to the tables of his restaurant. A perfect variety of the very best of Alto Adige cuisine greeted my eyes: *prosciutto di cervo con pane di noci* venison prosciutto with walnut bread, *zuppa di vino* wine soup, *cervo al forno con polenta nera e cavolo rosso* roast venison with wholemeal polenta and red cabbage, *goulasch con torta di grano saraceno* goulash with buckwheat cake. All very Austrian, far removed from *peperoni* and courgettes, but nonetheless delicious, and ideally suited to the blizzard outside.

Smoked Meats and Sour Cabbages

From one end of the region to the other, the most typical dish is a piece of steaming hot, boiled smoked meat, surrounded by a crown of crunchy sauerkraut cooked in lard, washed down with a glassful of local beer or wine.

Yet I was delighted to discover lots of other superb specialities as well, and while the differences between the Germanic and the Italian are obvious, the ways in which the two cultures have intermingled are just as fascinating. If the Süd Tiroler has accepted the *minestrone* made with beans and potatoes as prepared in and around Trento, so the Trento housewife has learned to make the *canederli* and *goulasch* like her sisters in Bolzano.

But if you're beginning to think that this is an unimaginative cuisine, where only heavy, thick warming dishes are served, you'd be wrong. There is, I promise you, a lot more to Alto Adige and Trentino cooking and it's waiting to be explored.

SALUMI
Salami, Sausages and Cured Meats

Wonderful home-made sausages are still being made by the housewives of the more remote villages of the Trentino. Called *probusti di Rovereto*, they are delicious pork and beef sausages, mixed with a little suet. They are usually smoked for three days over a fire of juniper and beech, before being grilled or fried.

Local Specialities

- *Biroldi* Semi-sweet sausages made with freshly killed pig's blood, milk, nuts, raisins and spices. Fried or grilled they can be served as *antipasto* or dessert.
- *Speck* Smoked veal *prosciutto*. Sliced very thinly and served with horseradish sauce, *salsa al cren*, or other piquant sauces.

All over the region, *carne affumicata* smoked meat appears in different guises. Horsemeat, beef and pork are all smoked and served cold in thin slices with bread and butter and pickles as a first course.

PASTA

There are few pasta specialities for this region, as the main standbys are potatoes and bread, but you will find *Ravioli alla Trentina*, a special occasion dish with a filling of chicken, roast meat and *salumi* in equal parts.

In the Alto Adige, dumplings replace pasta altogether, except for *Türteln*, which are *ravioli* made with brown flour, and stuffed with a cumin-flavoured filling, and deep fried.

Local Specialities

- *Canederli* (*knödel*) Bread dumplings, boiled and dressed with melted butter or served with sauerkraut, or as an accompaniment to meat dishes.
- *Polenta smalzada* Buckwheat polenta dressed with anchovies and butter, generally served with roast pork chops.
- *Smacafam* The name means 'kill hunger' – a very substantial and filling preparation of polenta, fried with sausages. There is a sweet version too, served with grappa-soaked raisins.
- *Strangolapreti* Gnocchi made with potatoes or bread and spinach, or chard, boiled then dressed with butter and cheese.

PESCE E FRUTTI DI MARE
Fish and Seafood

The rivers and lakes of this landlocked region yield huge amounts of excellent freshwater fish, such as trout *trota*, perch *persico*, carp *carpa* and pike *luccio*. However, with a few notable exceptions the regional preference is for meat rather than fish.

Local Specialities

- *Brodetto di gamberi d'acqua dolce* Delicious soup made from freshwater shrimps.
- *Trota in salsa di funghi* Trout in a mushroom sauce.

CARNE E CACCIA
Meat and Game

There's a splendid variety of meat from animals accustomed to lush grass in summer and warm stables in winter, accustomed to climbing steep slopes and the taste of open air. It's lean, muscular meat, which lends itself to the smoking and boiling it inevitably gets, whether it's beef, veal,

Local Specialities

- *Cröstl* A popular Alto Adige dish consisting of a little cake made with meat and potatoes or bacon, flavoured with chives.
- *Goulasch* The well-known beef stew made with tomatoes, paprika and various other spices. Of Hungarian origin, it is popular all over the region.
- *Rane embragade* This is a peasant dish of frogs flavoured with herbs, covered in batter and deep fried.
- *Sauersuppe* Soup made with sour tripe, marinated in white wine vinegar flavoured with onions, garlic and celery. Popular on market days.
- *Zuppa di trippa* A really filling winter soup of tripe, cut into strips and boiled with celery, marjoram, carrots and broth. At the last minute square chunks of bread are added.

pork, horse, mutton or chamois *camoscio* – or even roebuck *capriolo*.

Chamois and roebuck are prepared all over the region, in various ways – from marinating the meat in red wine before stewing it, to the dish where the meat is flavoured with wine, and once cooked, served with polenta and sour myrtleberry jam.

Unsmoked meat appears in filling rich stews, or smothered in mushrooms, onions or other sauces – along with hare, chicken and frogs. All kinds of offal are popular, especially brain, spleen, tripe and liver.

FORMAGGIO
Cheese

Cheese generally doesn't feature very much, though *parmigiano* is used to some extent in cooking. In summer months superb *ricotta* is freshly available and is used in *crespelle alla ricotta*, pancakes with ricotta filling. There is a *grana Trentina* which is much like that from Lombardy, though possibly richer, and *cioncada*, a cows' milk, un-fatty cheese, used a lot in cooking. Not a grating cheese, it has a consistency more like Edam.

FRUTTA E VERDURA
Fruit and Vegetables

It is hard to grow very much at all amongst these rocky crags, steep mountain slopes and in the icy winter temperatures. Apples *mele* and pears *pere* grow profusely all over the valleys, indeed the region produces more than anywhere else in the country. Cherries *ciliegie* and plums *susine* also thrive well on the little fertile soil available. Virtually no vegetables grow other than potatoes and rows and rows of cabbages. Potatoes end up everywhere, even in the bread dough, and cab-bage, its flavour enhanced by the stiff frosts, is superquick to prepare, and sauerkraut lasts for months and months in its bath of salted water and vinegar.

In the Trentino a certain amount of wheat is cultivated, whereas barley and rye are the main crops grown in Alto Adige.

PASTICCERIA
Cakes, Biscuits and Puddings

The pastries of this region are a triumph of expertise and refusal to calorie count. A fantastic array of cakes and puddings – rich chocolate cakes smothered in whipped cream, foaming airy omelettes filled with hot jam, fritters made with fruit, jelly and so on. I have divided the lists between Trentino and Alto Adige so you can know the differences for yourself if you come across any difficulty in choosing.

TRENTINO
- *Brazadel* A breakfast cake made with eggs, flour, milk and yeast. Just made for dunking in coffee.
- *Chifelini* Baked envelopes of potato, flour and yeast dough with a jam filling.
- *Crostoli* Crisp deep-fried pastries of odd twisted shapes.
- *Dolcetti all'arancia* Two sheets of pastry enclosing a filling of almonds and oranges cut into cubes.
- *Dolce Trento* A wonderful buttery almond cake.
- *Fiadoni alla Trentina* Purses of pastry with a spicy almond filling, baked in the oven.
- *Fritelle* or *Straboli* Little grappa-flavoured fritters.
- *Fugazza Trentina* Always served to guests with plenty of chilled white wine, a rich cake flavoured with lemon and vanilla.
- *Soffiato alla Trentina* One of my favourite puddings! A layer of sponge cake soaked in rum, covered with custard, then a layer of rum-soaked *amaretti* also covered with custard. The whole dish is then smothered in very light meringue and baked till crisp.
- *Zelten Trentino* A very heavy cake prepared for Christmas. Dried fruit and nuts filling a rich, dark pastry made with grappa and orange peel added to the dough.

Local Speciality

- *Crauti* (*sauerkraut*) Pickled cabbage kept in jars until required, then quickly sautéed in a pan with lard to be served with meat dishes or other specialities.

ALTO ADIGE

• *Cappuccini affogati* (*ersoffene kappuziner*) Odd but delicious dessert of deep-fried bread, drowned in flaming spiced wine.

• *Dolce al vapore* (*dampfnüdeln*) A German teatime treat which has crossed the frontier in no uncertain terms! Little light pastry strips boiled in milk and butter and served with raspberry syrup.

• *Palle di prugna* (*zwetschgenknödel*) Balls of potato and flour dough, each one enclosing a ripe stoned plum, boiled, fried in butter and breadcrumbs and served hot.

• *Schmarrn* Little strips of pancake, the traditional accompaniment to stewed fruit.

• *Strudel* Light, wafer-thin envelope of pastry filled with: apples, nuts and raisins (*apfelstrudel*); a rich custard with sour cream, raisins and spices (*rahmbstrudel*); plum jam, or a traditional ingredient, *mohn*, made with crushed poppy seeds, milk, butter, sugar, lemon juice, honey, cream and currants (*germstrudel*) and this has yeast added to the dough.

The difficult part of making strudel pastry is stretching the dough without it tearing. I can remember having to hang it over the backs of chairs, standing on a table top so as to get gravity to help in the task!

• *Teste di moro* (*mohrenkoepfe*) A dessert made with chestnuts boiled in milk, masked with bitter cocoa, sugar and liqueur. Made into balls, they're topped with cream and cherries and served well chilled.

VINO
Wine

Strangely, the popularity of this excellent wine has only recently spread to Italy – before, most was destined for the overseas market, particularly Germany. However, things are beginning to change (and so they should!). About 50 per cent of the wine produced here receives D.O.C. labelling. Vineyards grow lustily wherever possible, though the quantity of wine is small for the size of the region.

SPECIAL RED

• *Santa Maddalena* Considered the 'prince' of the Alto Adige wines. Made with Schiava grapes, round Bolzano. Ruby red, brilliant wine with an aristocratic bouquet and rounded, velvety flavour. Once aged it rivals the most exclusive French collectors' wines for quality. Excellent with all meat.

• *Teroldego Rotaliano* The 'prince' of the Trentino wines. An intensely coloured ruby red, with a bouquet of violets and raspberries. Very tannic taste, with a bitter almond aftertaste. A wine to drink with special rich meat dishes, it must be aged to be worthwhile.

RED WINE

• *Trentino cabernet* A very well-known wine made in Trento province, with Cabernet Franc and Sauvignon grapes. An intense red wine with orange glints appearing as it ages. Classic with rich meat dishes. It's supposed to have digestive-aiding qualities.

• *Alto Adige merlot* An elegant ruby wine, with a full flavour, and herby bouquet, to drink with sophisticated dishes.

WHITE WINE

• *Trentino Traminer aromatico* A very fine wine, immediately recognisable for its unique and very intense aromatic bouquet. It's got a dry and slightly bitterish flavour which makes it perfect for drinking with seafood, especially lobster.

• *Terlano* A marvellous straw yellow wine, with a characteristic fruity bouquet in contrast to its slightly acid flavour. Traditionally served with the rare and delicious asparagus produced in Terlano, this is an elegant wine.

ROSÉ WINE

• *Alto Adige lagrein rosato* (*Lagrein kretzer*) A superb rosé with a delicate harmonious flavour and bouquet. Perfect for drinking with soups, white meat, vegetable or offal dishes.

SPUMANTI

An excellent variety of *spumanti* is produced in this region, most of it with the real champenois method. They are divided up into categories, *brut*, *riserva*, *secco*, *semi secco* and *extra*. They are made with *pinot bianco*, *pinot grigio* and *pinot nero* grapes and are really quite excellent.

DESSERT WINE

• *Alto Adige moscato rosa* A sweet rosé, with a delicate, aromatic flavour. Delicious as a dessert wine or a drink on its own. Produced in various

parts of the Alto Adige from Adriano to Termeno.
- *Trentino Vin Santo* A wonderful amber to gold sweet dessert wine, which needs to be aged about 4 to 6 years. It's very sweet indeed, made with Nosiola and Pinot grapes on the banks of Lake Garda, in Dro, Lasino and Arco.

BEVANDE
Drinks

Beer and *grappa* are both extremely popular locally – beer is often preferred to wine, especially with the more heavy and peasant-style dishes. *Grappa* is produced in vast quantities and various potencies and is drunk a lot in winter months to warm and cheer.
- *Sciroppi di frutta* Fruit syrups come into their own in this region – sweet golden syrups of grapes or brilliant, ruby-coloured raspberry, strawberry or blackberry syrups diluted with water and drunk cold.

WORTH TAKING HOME

Mountain holidays in this region have given me ample opportunity to shop around and fill every available space with goodies to take home. The jams and preserves made with local mountain berries are a must.

Grappa, though not my tipple, always makes good presents. Here it really is worth taking time in choosing, and if you want to keep your friends, don't go for the cheapest bottles.

Zelten is easy to pack, and it will keep for a long time and go on being nourishing! If you haven't far to go before you're home, I strongly recommend you to take a strudel with you, and when you get home just warm it through in the oven to crisp it up.

I used to bring *biroldi* and *speck* home with me – and in case there are restrictions nowadays, it's best to buy them vacuum-packed.

FRIULI-VENEZIA GIULIA – 'Not really Italy'

Here is another region which is still coming to terms with being an amalgamation. Friuli-Venezia Giulia was formed of two distinct parts, but the two names have a common Latin origin, deriving from the words *gens Iulia*, that is, the family of Julius Caesar. Friuli derives from the words *Forum Julii*, the name given to a major commercial centre founded by the Romans and which is now the city of Cividale.

After World War II much of what had been an enormous region called Venezia Giulia was handed over to Yugoslavia. Italy was left with Trieste and Gorizia and a much smaller amount of land. Combining this with Friuli, the 'powers that be' created the present day single region.

This is the most eastern of Italy's regions, its frontiers touching both Yugoslavia and Austria.

It's a small region with four provinces. The capital city is Trieste, where the Bora wind blows strong, bringing hope of good weather to the area. In general the climate is such that it is never very hot, and there is plenty of rain as well as wind.

In some parts, particularly close to foreign borders, the common language is not Italian but German or Slav. The Government has provided special schools where lessons are in the pupils' mother tongue in places like Trieste's suburbs, or the rural villages of the Carsico.

Unified Cuisine

It is generally thought that there are two distinctive types of cooking, but I don't think this is really the case. Certainly the area round Trieste is influenced by the sea, while the dishes of the inland areas logically won't use seafood. However, as soon as you start talking about freshwater fish, dried fish and other ingredients, the differences between dishes cooked in the two parts of the region vanish into thin air, and there emerges a marvellous unity of flavours and cooking customs.

The fact is that gastronomic habits are linked to the culture and history of the people. So the love of soups, especially those with beans, or the many recipes for cooking rice with vegetables or fish, definitely recall the long domination of the

Serenissima in these parts, in the same way that the flavour of paprika which invades local dishes reminds one of the former presence of the Hungarians. But these influences, here as in other regions, soon lose themselves and become assimilated into the local traditions and way of life, not just changing but adding to the culinary picture. The local roots are those of a people of peasants and shepherds, austere, dour folk, used to long silences, used to dragging out of a rebellious patch of soil all that they need to feed their dear ones.

It is a frugal cuisine with no flights of fancy. There are few vegetables, and what there are are turned into warming hearty soups. Lots of rice and polenta, and on the coast a cuisine that is principally Venetian – fish and seafood with few variations. When you get off the fish theme you suddenly discover yourself eating dishes that are very clearly middle-European – goulash, boiled pork with mustard, Viennese sausages with sauerkraut – all washed down with beer, maraschino or plum *acquavite* to cheer up the coldest windy days.

TRIESTE & PROVINCE

The ancient Roman colony of Tergeste was set up in the most sheltered spot on the Gulf. Today's Trieste boasts the Roman forum and theatre, from the Middle Ages the lovely Basilica of San Giusto, and the fabulous Venetian castle.

For years Trieste was forced into submission by her great rival port – Venice. Every attempt to

develop her sea-going commerce was blacked by Venice, and so the city remained little more than a village until the early 18th century when the Austro-Hungarian Emperor turned it into a prosperous and important port city. All round Trieste in the mountains delightful little villages maintain the charm of the original rural settlements. On the coastline is pretty Guggia, a fishing port situated right in the middle of a heavily cultivated area with fruit trees, olive groves and vineyards. Sistiana is a very small tourist port in a lovely bay surrounded by wooded green hills, well worth seeing. There's a fabulous café here called *COSTA DEI BARBARI*, providing superb pastries and ice creams.

GORIZIA & PROVINCE

Gorizia is a green tranquil city with a marvellous climate. But when I asked my mother about it her reply was a little vague to say the least: '... It isn't an Italian city you know', she said, 'not like Udine or Trieste'. Once in Gorizia I realised what the distinction is – Gorizia is very pretty, with a friendly atmosphere, but it does feel like Yugoslavia. In fact some of the suburbs actually lie over the border.

In the tiny little province is the resort of Grado, which is situated on an islet in the lagoon, and where heavy-set ladies will happily pound you with mud or bury you in sand to cure your aches and pains. It is principally a fishing town, and the local restaurants reflect the ancient culinary traditions based on the best of the sea. *ANTICA TRATTORIA DA NICO* is where I stopped for lunch – I had delicious *tagliatelle* with sole, and a fabulous mixed fish grill. The fish was really fresh, and tasted of the sea, the atmosphere was merry and the wine list crammed with a selection of local Veneto wines.

UDINE & PROVINCE

Founded in the Middle Ages, Udine is the historical capital of the region, and thanks to its ideal geographic situation in a flat plain, it is still one of the most important centres.

The province takes in the whole of the mountainous area, the Carnia and the Tarvisiano, and spreads out on to the plain on the left bank of the Tagliamento. The most charming town to visit is Prato Carnico. Like many nearby towns and villages it is a collection of higgledy-piggledy houses, built to defend the inhabitants against harsh snow, each one painted in its owner's favourite colour with bright balconies and shutters. Admittedly it looks more Austrian than Italian, but it is pretty and in keeping.

If skiing holidays are your thing, then Tarvisio is the local resort for winter sports, while Lignano is the best seaside resort, on a peninsula jutting out into the lagoon. In 1976 four major centres in this province were totally destroyed by earthquakes, including San Daniele, renowned for its wonderful *prosciutto*.

Latisana is a town little known for anything except a marvellous restaurant, the *BELLA VENEZIA*, run with precise and elegant care by the formidable Signora Oneglia. It had been recommended to me by relatives living near here, so I was anxious to see if it deserved the accolades. The menu was bursting – shrimps, prawns, local smoked game, goose prosciutto, bean and barley soup, *bavette* with locally caught crab, sole in white wine, wild boar in a rich sauce with polenta – not to mention strudel with a meringue topping. Definitely worth a long detour.

PORDENONE & PROVINCE

The thriving town of Pordenone sits on the bank of a navigable river, the Noncello, its province stretching out over the plain to the west of the Tagliamento.

If you are near Spilimbergo, you must stop at the restaurant at the top of the 14th-century tower, called *RISTORANTE LA TORRE ORIENTALE*. There is a cellar-level wine bar where you can taste wines with delicious snacks if you can't face a whole meal. If you eat in the restaurant itself, be sure to try the *salumi* (from a local *salumeria* called *LOVISON* which has won lots of prizes) and don't miss the turbot escalopes with Traminer, the duck's breast with citrus fruits, or the wonderful selection of local cheeses. there is plenty to shop for locally too – wonderful *salumi* at *LOVISON* and at a butcher called *PEPPINO DE ROSA*, or cheese from Carlo Tosoni's shop.

Heading away from Spilimbergo a bit, in Gaio you can buy superb peaches and apples (in season) straight off the farm belonging to Alfredo Prevedel, and in Gradisca ask to be shown the way to Silvano Bertuzzi's house – he makes the most incredible honey (or rather his bees do).

SALUMI

Salami, Sausages and Cured Meats

The most famous and exclusive of all Italy's *prosciutto* is the delectable pale pink San Daniele from the little town in the province of Udine. Here atmospheric conditions are particularly conducive to the curing of ham. It is also available smoked. *Museti* is the local name for *cotechini*, the rich stuffed spicy sausages that are boiled for hours and are served with polenta or lentils. Those from San Daniele are especially sought after.

Cooked ham *prosciutto cotto* is very popular in these parts, and is eaten a great deal more than in the south. There is a very special *salame* made locally called *punta di coltello* (knife point) because of its shape.

Also well worth trying is the strongly flavoured *salame di cinghiale* wild boar salame and the superb *prosciutto d'oca* goose prosciutto. *Salame all'aceto balsamico* is another wonderful local speciality flavoured with balsamic vinegar, and *petto di tacchino affumicato* smoked turkey breast. *Speck* appears in these parts too, slightly smoky and rather fattier than the local prosciutto. *Ciar* is served as a *salume*, but is actually slivers of raw beef eaten with lemon juice and cream cheese – very Yugoslavian!

PASTA

Here the pasta may take on new names, but basically they are the same. *Bauletti di carne* are *ravioli* stuffed with meat, and *cialzons* are *agnolotti*, though their stuffing is often quite unusual. It is common in Friuli to have a sweet first course, and you may come across pasta filled

Local Speciality

- *Cialzons* Pasta stuffed with spinach, chocolate, raisins, dry brown bread, candied lime, sugar, cinnamon and parsley, dressed with smoked grated *ricotta*, butter and sugar. Some of the best ones comes from Timau, in Udine, where they are filled with potatoes, butter, parsley, sugar, cinnamon, brandy, mint and onion.

with sugar, spices and dried fruit as well as cheese and vegetables.

Gnocchi are popular, made with potato and cocoa, always cooked in stock or broth.

Offelle are small square *ravioli*, the dough made with potatoes, flour and baking powder, making them very light. They are filled with spinach, sausage meat and minced veal, and dressed with butter and cheese.

☆☆☆☆☆☆☆☆☆☆☆☆☆☆☆☆☆☆☆☆☆☆☆☆☆☆☆☆☆☆

Mellifluous Maize Meal

Polenta is used throughout the region, but always allowed to be quite runny – it doesn't have the sliceable quality of Venetian or Lombard polenta. Yellow polenta is usually the one used for meat, game or vegetable dishes, and white for fish. You can also find sweet polenta dishes, like the one served with prunes cooked inside it.

☆☆☆☆☆☆☆☆☆☆☆☆☆☆☆☆☆☆☆☆☆☆☆☆☆☆☆☆☆☆

PESCE E FRUTTI DI MARE

Fish and Seafood

Freshness is absolutely essential to the Friuli cooks, and if the fish isn't fresh, then you won't be served it. Immense variety is available according to the season, and the conditions at sea. *Cape sante* are also called *capete* or *pellegrine di San Giacomo* and are scallops. There are *ostriche* oysters, in particular the variety locally known as the *piede di cava* horse's foot, and *datteri* sea dates, known in dialect as *cape longhe* are brown shellfish-like mussels, which bury themselves inside the rocks. Fishing them out is hard work, and dangerous, as the fisherman has to bring the rock to the surface or break it up underwater to expose the fish. They are eaten raw with lemon juice or put in soups or risottos. There is *merluzzo* cod, and *gamberi* (*giambars*) shrimps, and in December, January, April and May, the

Local Speciality

• *Brodeto* A mixed fish soup flavoured with garlic, white wine and tomatoes.

local spider crab *granzevola*. This is extremely hard to clean and prepare – if you are self-catering and are tempted to buy them fresh at the market, be sure you are armed with plenty of patience and know-how. *Sardoni* large sardines, *sardelle* sardines, *tonno* tuna, *anguilla* eel, *rombo* turbot, *go* (*ghiozzi*) gudgeon, *scorfani* scorpion fish, *triglia* red mullet, and all kinds of other wonderful fish will be here for your pleasure as long as the fishermen have been lucky!

CARNE E CACCIA

Meat and Game

Plenty of beef and veal, lots of pork and game in season – they like to eat meat up here, and they cook it extremely well. Look out for hare *lepre* and roebuck *capriolo* and venison *cervo*. Beef dishes are stewed thoroughly and made for warming, filling, virile dishes to keep out the cold – for example goulash – another import as made in Trieste.

Meat stews will almost always be served with steaming polenta for substance, and a delicious blending of flavours.

Frogs *croz* are very popular here, in season from September to the end of October.

FORMAGGIO

Cheese

Fresh creamy cheeses are particularly popular here as they are in countries like Bulgaria, Yugoslavia or Hungary. Look out for *carnigo*, *montasio* and the salty cheese called *delicatezza della Val d'Arzino*, *formaggio stravecchio carnico*, a very mature grating cheese, *ricotta affumicata* smoked *ricotta*, also for grating, and *carnico stagionato* a mature mountain cheese. Fresh *ricotta* and *formaggio magro*, a fat-free sliceable cheese, both appear in lots of recipes.

FRUTTA E VERDURA

Fruit and Vegetables

Only the lower plains are cultivated and they are used carefully so as to make up for the rest of the territory being so impossible to farm – either too mountainous or infertile. On the lower plains,

---

Local Speciality

- *Rambasicci* or *Uccelli Scappati nella Verza* – Birds escaped into the cabbage. Cabbage leaves stuffed with minced beef and pork or rice. A Yugoslavian dish which has been carefully reproduced.

---

sugar beet, tobacco, corn, rye and fruit are grown profusely, with apples, peaches and pears coming at the top of the list.

This is not a vegetable-growing area – they simply don't thrive on the soil, though the only vegetables native to the area – potatoes, beetroot, artichokes and beans – are all put to good use. The dwarf radicchio from Gorizia is probably the most interesting, and *fagioli* beans are cooked in such a remarkable way throughout the region as to make them creamier and more delicious than beans anywhere else. They are used especially in the creation of soups with rice, barley, *bobici*, grains of corn, or pasta.

Local Specialities

- *Brovada* Turnips marinated in wine which has turned sour (*vinaccia*), then sliced into thin strips and fried in lard and butter with onions, garlic and parsley. Generally to accompany boiled pork dishes.
- *Paparot* Soup made with nettles, spinach and yellow cornflour. The name means 'crumbling, falling apart' as the soup ends up looking as if it has fallen apart.
- *Risot coi Croz* Local recipe for risotto with herbs, and a garnish of frogs' legs.

PASTICCERIA

Cakes, Biscuits and Puddings

All the sweets and desserts are fairly substantial, filling and heavy, with lots of variations on the strudel theme, stuffed with nuts, dried fruit, honey or jam.

- *Budino alle uova* A creamy custard set in a mould which is wet with Marsala to prevent sticking.
- *Budino di Avena* A milk and barley pudding, reminiscent of Yugoslavian desserts I have eaten.

- *Budino di patate* Deliciously spicy potato pudding of Hungarian origin.
- *Crostata di mandorle* A delicious almond tart, often served for breakfast as well as dessert.
- *Fritole della Venezia Giulia* Carnival time deep-fried pastries strongly flavoured with cinnamon and lemon zest.
- *Fritole Istriane* Similar to the above, these fritters from Istria are very spicy, with cloves.
- *Gubana* Twisted pastry case, filled with walnuts, almonds, pinenuts, candied fruit and eggs, served with plum *grappa*.
- *Kügelhüpf* Traditional Austrian cake with a hole in the middle, made with sultanas, almonds, rum, butter, flour and yeast to make it tall and light.
- *Pistum* This is considered one of the ancestors of medieval *maccheroni* made with similar ingredients. A kind of sweet *gnocchi* flavoured with cinnamon, pinenuts, candied peel etc. They look like boiled rocket-shaped pieces of dough and are cooked in pork broth, preferably one which has boiled *cotechino*. They were served as a sweet course, at the end of a banquet. I have come across other versions where chopped ham and herbs are added to the list of ingredients.
- *Presnitz* A dish from Castagnevizza, a town which was Italian and now is Yugoslavian, this has been adopted by Trieste as its Easter cake. A pastry case filled with nuts and candied fruit, it is twisted into a spiral – very spicy and delicious.
- *Putitza* Another Yugoslavian dish adopted by Trieste, for Christmas and the New Year. Like a strudel, coiled round like a snail's shell, filled with nuts and candied fruit.
- *Pinza* A sweet or savoury plain cake. The savoury one is served with ham and plenty of horseradish sauce.

VINO

Wine

This is a region of really GREAT Italian wines. It is divided into about 6 really valuable areas, the Colli Orientali and the Collio producing exceptional wine.

- *Vini dei Colli Orientali del Friuli* (C.O.F.) The eastern hills of the region are famous for their excellent wines. The climatic conditions and the soil combine to produce superb wines considered amongst the very best the country has to offer.

SPECIAL RED WINE

• *Colli Orientali del Friuli Cabernet* Rivalling some of the most famous French Cabernet wines, this is an excellent ruby red wine, with a herby, slightly violet-scented bouquet and a full, slightly bitter flavour. Perfect with *salumi*, game and all roast meats.

• *Colli Orientali del Friuli Merlot* If aged over two years it is called *riserva* to make it really special. A brilliantly coloured ruby wine which marries perfectly with all the region's best meat specialities.

RED WINE

• *C.O.F. Pinot Nero* Reminiscent of fine Burgundy wines, a clear ruby wine with an intense bouquet and a light dry flavour. Young, it is drunk with stews, and as it ages it goes better with roasts, smoked meat, game and pork.

• *C.O.F. Refosco* This varies a great deal depending on where it's produced, but it is consistently excellent. A slightly austere and tannin-rich flavour, it can also be bought in a sweet version. Perfect for drinking with local mature strong-tasting cheeses.

WHITE WINE

• *C.O.F. Sauvignon* produced successfully in this region for over 50 years, a delightful pale yellow wine with a delicate flavour and dry quality. A very refined wine which also makes a great aperitif.

• *C.O.F. Ribolla* A rounded wine with a good intense flavour – very good with freshwater fish or antipasti.

• *C.O.F. Pinot Grigio* One of my favourite white wines. It's got a fabulous golden colour and smells like wild flowers. A velvety, dry and delectable wine.

• *C.O.F. Pinot Bianco* A sharper flavour than the above, with a scent of almonds. Very good with egg-based dishes, soups and grilled fish.

• *C.O.F. Tocai* Very different from the Hungarian wine called Tokay, which is a sweet dessert wine. This is a dry aperitif wine that can also be drunk with fish.

• *Vini del Collio* The collio is an area which stretches between the Judrio and Isonzo rivers, bordering on the Colli Orientali with Yugoslavia on the other side. The excellent, delicious sought-after wines have only just been introduced into Italy, though they were well appreciated at the Hapsburg court. Most of the above wines appear, with *Collio* in front of them in place of *C.O.F.*, and are arguably better quality. *Collio Traminer* is particularly delicious as an anytime wine.

• *Collio Malvasia* is a fresh vivacious wine to drink with fish.

• *Collio Renano* is a very expensive and fine wine to drink with fish soups and delicate cheeses.

Other wines from this region come under the general headings:

• *Vini delle Grave del Friuli*
• *Vini dell'Isonzo*
• *Vini di Aquileia*
• *Vini di Latisana*

For a very small region they certainly produce a wide variety of wines – and most of them are really amongst the best I've tasted anywhere.

BEVANDE

Drinks

This is one of the main *grappa* regions, and although it isn't really my tipple, I am told you would have a struggle to find better than what's on offer here. These are some of the brands worth tasting or taking home, though home-made ones are often the best: *Giannola Nonino, Romano Levi, Marolo, Pagura di Castions di Zoppola*.

Other strong and warming liqueurs include *acqua vite di genziana* gentian-flavoured acquavite, *nocino* walnut liqueur, *la mentuccia di San Silvestro* mint liqueur and *maraschino di zara* maraschino cherry liqueur.

WORTH TAKING HOME

The region's best speciality is the San Daniele *prosciutto* which you could buy vacuum-packed. Smoked *ricotta* travels well, and if your journey isn't too long, the fresh creamy cheeses *formaggi di malga* would last a while once you got them in the fridge. Plums, cherries and myrtleberries preserved in grappa, sold in jars or wide-necked bottles, would make wonderful presents.

Around Trieste you'll find many *Osmize* – privately owned outlets for home-made wine and home-cured *prosciutto*. They are usually situated inside the courtyards of private houses or in the cellars. Here you can buy whatever you prefer, and it will be authentic with no additives.

VENETO

Spicy Serenissima

Venice dominates this region so much it is easy to forget what lies around the most romantic (and wet) city in the world. I have been bewitched like everyone else by this city, but it is to the region as a whole that I feel I must pay tribute. There is plenty to be seen and enjoyed – historical villages and lush countryside – providing a fascinating contrast to the opulent splendour of Venice.

There is a feeling here that they've got the right idea about things – the ancient beauty of the buildings is being preserved carefully and lovingly. The Venetians love their land, are incredibly proud of it, and it shows. I owe a lot to this region, as my first teacher in the art of food preparation comes from Vicenza, and from him I learned a great deal about this region – and about cooking.

There are two sides to Venetian cooking, the side that reminds you of lace gowns, enticing whispers behind open fans, ships returning from distant shores loaded with spices and strange exotic cargo – and the side that tells you that it gets cold up in these mountains, that man has to fill his belly in order to survive. This second type of cooking, simple, honest and cheap, was what the

man from Vicenza taught me about, and in many ways I have never strayed very far from his basic good sense.

Riches from the Orient

It was during the Crusades in the 11th and 12th centuries that Venice built up its riches by transporting armies to Palestine and eastern Europe, and thus coming into close trading contact with Arab and Byzantine civilisations. The merchants of Venice proved to be more wily and skilful at Eastern trading, and at the shifting of soldiers, than her rivals Pisa and Genoa, and thus developed their systems on a far greater scale, so filling their coffers to bursting point.

At the height of her glory, the Serene Republic of Venice, 'La Serenissima', comprised a strip of Dalmatia, the Ionian islands, other Greek islands, several towns in the Peloponnese, Gallipoli, and had trading stations in Constantinople, Adrianople, Trebizond, Caffa, Tana, Tyre, Sidon, Tripoli, Damascus and Cairo.

The rewards of trade were a whole range of products previously unseen in this part of the world – spices, coffee, fruits, vegetables, precious stones and metals, cloth, as well as foreign customs and traditions.

The Veneto region covers a stretch of land between the Carnic Alps, the Dolomites, and the Gulf of Venice. A brief stretch of its northern frontier touches Austria. There are marshy islands in the lagoons, rocky snow-capped peaks of craggy mountains, tiny unknown villages amongst heavily wooded mountain slopes, built on the edge of rushing torrents, rounded smooth green hills, the shores of Lake Garda (which it shares with Lombardy), a popular Adriatic coast with long beaches *lidi*, and an endlessly monotonous flat plain which has been extensively reclaimed, dotted with towns and villages, each with a bell tower looking like a direct copy of the St Mark's campanile.

The Veneto enjoys a mild climate in the areas influenced by the Adriatic, though Venice itself is prone to winter fogs, while inland they suffer extremely cold and snowy winters with subsequent cool summers.

Though simplicity rules the culinary scene the range of ingredients is enormous – largely thanks to the influx of exotic goods in the past.

The trademark is the creamy smooth risotto, made with thousands of combinations of tastes and textures. Polenta and beans fill in the background, with occasional flirtations with dried fruits and spices, which often give an eastern feel to the dishes.

To complement the homely but stylish dishes, the region produces plenty of bright, cheerful and uncomplicated wines.

VENICE & PROVINCE

In the 5th century AD, the early inhabitants of this area, who were simple fishermen, escaped from the Barbarian invasions on to the islands of the lagoon. From the humble huts erected here, over the course of the centuries, a splendid city was built that was to become one of the richest states of the known world. Even from earliest times these islanders engaged in trading, transporting oil, wine, and corn from Istria and Ravenna and other towns along the coast.

Although Italian in race and speech, they were a cosmopolitan people from the start, since the

city was a natural meeting place for so many nationalities and races. To the merchants and tradesmen, bankers and noblemen living here, can be added the slaves bought in North Africa and the Levant – Africans from Ethiopia and Numibia, pale Circassians, Slavs and Persians, who were sold in the squares of the city.

Venice is 2 kilometres from the open sea, 4 from dry land, built on 117 islands separated by 170 canals joined by 400 bridges. On the islands, the narrow winding streets form an intricate maze, opening out into little squares. At the centre of the city is the lovely Piazza San Marco, with its basilica of St Mark. In or near the square are numerous cafés like *HARRY'S BAR*, and *FLORIAN'S*, where a drink of coffee or a glass of wine can become a real event. In extremely elegant and subdued surroundings, to the sound of orchestras playing, you may pay upwards of L3,000 – but you're here for the atmosphere.

Unquestionably the best and most authentic cuisine is to be tasted at the *ANTICA BESSETTA* in Calle Salvio 1395. Here, with Mum in the kitchen and father and son in the dining room, in an atmosphere of friendly cordiality that is sadly rare to find these days, I enjoyed sublime risottos with fresh vegetables, delicious seafood including soft-shell crabs *moleche*, wholewheat spaghetti *bigoli* and excellent wines. This is the cuisine of the Venetian people, simple yet sophisticated, whispering of times gone by when exotic ingredients and recipes became part of the culinary scene to the extent that they lost every trace of foreignness.

The *ENOTECA AL VOLTO* is another experience not to be missed, especially if you are a wine buff. This splendid old establishment in San Marco San Luca offers delicious *panini* and other snacks filled with local produce, with an extraordinary selection of international, national and regional wines, and 75 kinds of beer. There were 1,320 kinds of wine on offer when I visited – some of them actually 'historical' they were so well aged. There are worse ways to while away the time than to rest your legs and just taste wine. Other places for little snacks, like little pieces of fish, squid or bowls of soup if you're not wanting a complete meal, are the many bars throughout the city, especially round the markets. You may not find any chairs, but it is a good way to taste the everyday fare of the Venetian. Here you can also taste the delicious light *prosecco* wine which the locals gulp as they 'bar-crawl' through the city.

The principal places of interest in the province itself are the Lido, a long island facing the sea on one side, with a long beach and many resorts, the islands of Murano and Burano, and the solitary island of Torcello with its beautiful cathedral and Byzantine mosaics. Chioggia is one of the major agricultural and fish markets in the country.

PADOVA & PROVINCE

Padua is situated on a tributary of the Brenta river on the plains, deservedly proud of its countless important buildings, like the chapel of the Scrovegni and the Palazzo della Ragione. In this historical centre I discovered *DOTTO*, where I had dishes that combined the best of the two sides of Venetian cooking – the fruits of the sea and the fruits of the land.

The province is almost completely flat except for the Euganean hills, and is principally an agricultural area growing rice.

From here you can take a trip down the Brenta Canal to see the many splendid Patrician villas built for the rich nobility as cool summer residences during the 16th, 17th and 18th centuries. Some were designed by great architects like Palladio, and though many of them have been abandoned and allowed to collapse, I recommend you to take this trip between Padua and Venice, especially in springtime when you are less likely to be eaten by mosquitoes.

VERONA & PROVINCE

The second largest city in the region, fabulous Verona lies at the feet of the Lessini mountains on both sides of the Adige river. It has preserved its beautiful Roman arena where theatrical and operatic performances take place in the summer. Like Venice, Verona has not a single jarring visual note to offend the visitor, despite the fact that, situated where it is, between Venice and Milan, it represents an important commercial centre and is on a busy link route.

At Christmas Verona produces *pandoro*, a distant cousin to *panettone*. No Italian Christmas is complete without at least one of each, and it's entirely a matter of which one you prefer. I have long heard discussions round the table about each one's merits, but to my mind they are as good as each other, as long as they're left alone. I have been served *panettone* and *pandoro* with ice cream, whipped cream, hot chocolate or raspberry syrup poured over them, but I can't say I was wildly impressed.

In the province itself Legnano and Villafranca are interesting old market towns, but I fell completely in love with the Garda Riviera, with its peaceful setting, mild climate and delightful little towns.

It would appear that wine-making goes back a long way in these parts – archaeological digs near Verona have proved that the vine was grown here for wine as far back as the Bronze Age. It would seem that the Etruscans introduced it to the Pianura Padana from this area.

VICENZA & PROVINCE

Palladio himself was responsible for the design and construction of most of this city's beautiful monuments. For a really good idea of what Renaissance architecture is all about take a good look at this city.

At Easter, *fugazza vicentina*, a special Easter cake, is made in great quantities by the local bakers. The cakes, varying in size from tiny little ones to enormous two-kilo ones, are given as gifts to the customers, depending on how much they've spent. Sometimes the dough is turned into little dove shapes *colombine*, with hardboiled painted eggs inside. Depending on the colour of your egg, you can expect hope, glad tidings, disappointment or anger, love or sickness in the near future.

Bassano del Grappa is obviously one of the main grappa-producing centres of the country. There are countless varieties produced here, and plenty of experts only too happy to help you to choose.

In Bassano del Grappa there is a very old *pasticceria, L'ANTICA OFFELLERIA*, where the 16th-century recipe for the biscuits called *forti* is still used, but well guarded. This is considered to be the original biscuit recipe from which the wide variety of Venetian biscuits have since descended.

Marostica is at the centre of a rich cherry-producing area, so during the season it is worth visiting. They also hold a human chess game here every other year. Asiago is a winter sports centre, and Recoaro Terme the local spa town, where they make excellent soft drinks, *chinotto, aranciata, limonata,* as well as the lovely mineral water. If you fancy a complete 'cure' you can book in for a weekend of bathing, being pounded and 'taking the waters'.

TREVISO & PROVINCE

Think of Treviso and you think of . . . radicchio of course! There are many varieties, but the best is *trevisana,* which looks different from the others – it has long pointed leaves and a very crunchy central spine.

Radicchio was originally a Venetian endive, which was turned into the now well-known vegetable by a Flemish botanist, Van den Boor. It is used in hundreds of recipes, *risotto,* pasta, pies,

and also excellent in a salad or grilled, or simply fried in olive oil.

I know this area well, and love it dearly. I love its soft gentle hills, its wide fields and foggy light. An extraordinary combination of old and new, simple little *osterie* and delightful family-run shops, but also huge furniture factories and fertiliser plants. I was astonished to see huge plantations of kiwi fruit everywhere. In the city of Treviso itself, the 14th-century walls surround frescoed houses and canals that traverse the city.

Within the province you must visit Asolo, a charming town with steep, narrow streets where they hold fascinating weekend antique fairs. It lies at the feet of Monte Grappa, so it's a good place to acquire this most regional of beverages. But always remember you're in the region whose happy hills produce some of Italy's most refreshing and delicious wines.

It was here, in a little trattoria, that I first tasted *Clinton* – the wine made from the few vines that survived the 19th-century catastrophe, the phylloxera disease which wiped out almost all European vines. Only those which had a really high tannin content survived. Since then all wine produced in Europe comes from vines brought from far-flung parts, that have since nationalised themselves. *Clinton* is served in white china cups, because it stains like berry juice, and has a very strong tannin content. It is delicious, very strong and heady. It's a thick, dark, almost syrupy wine that you don't forget in a hurry.

BELLUNO & PROVINCE

This is an entirely mountainous province with Belluno perched on a craggy peak dominating the landscape. It is a lively, modern city.

Within the province lies Cortina d'Ampezzo, the frightfully chic and upmarket ski resort, surrounded by fantastic views of the Dolomites. Though you'll probably get very international cuisine in such a place, there is a speciality from these parts which is worth seeking out. *Fritole de Pomi* are delicious apple fritters, either served on their own or as part of a *fritto,* with lots of other deep-fried things like meat, chicken, or vegetables, or as an accompaniment to a roast joint of pork. In this last case, they are also served with fresh myrtleberry sauce. They are usually made with Reinette apples, but are wonderful whichever way they're served.

SALUMI
Salami, Sausages and Cured Meats

Soppressata is something you either love or hate, but it's ubiquitous in these parts. It's very similar to black pudding, a dark red, spicy sausage made with pig's blood, beef, pork and fat. It is usually soft and spreadable, and in my opinion makes a wonderful antipasto with bread and butter.

The other glories of Veneto *salumi* are the *salsicce all'aglio* – marvellous pink, soft, garlicky sausages to stew with tomatoes and vegetables, and to eat with polenta or to grill on a glowing fire. A very good *Luganega* sausage is made in Treviso.

PASTA

The most important local pasta are a kind of wholewheat spaghetti called *bigoli*. The classic sauce to accompany them is simply called *salsa*, which consists of oil, anchovies and garlic pounded to a smooth paste.

Other specialities include *Bigoli con rovinazzi* spaghetti with ragù, *Spaghetti con l'anatra*, spaghetti with duck, or sometimes with a duck sauce *in salsa d'anatra*. *Ravioli* here are called *casumzieei* or *cassunziei*. *Fettucine* are called *paparele*.

Local Speciality

- *Pasta e Fasoi* Classic soup changes from household to household, restaurant to restaurant as everyone adds their bit. A thick winter soup of beans and pasta, the beans sometimes puréed, sometimes left whole.

PESCE E FRUTTI DI MARE
Fish and Seafood

The sea brings in a wealth of seafood, like *cape sante* scallops, *cozze* mussels, *seppie* squid, and all kinds of *pesce azzurro* (literally translates as blue fish, and means all kinds of Adriatic fish like mackerel, brill, bass, mullet etc). Inland fishing is carried out in the *valli*, branches of sea lagoons that are fenced off, and where *dorade* mullet and

---

Local Specialities

- *Granseola alla Veneziana* A huge locally caught crab, often served simply boiled with a dressing of lemon juice and oil. The flesh is sometimes used for more elaborate dishes.
- *Saor* is an ancient sauce made with onions, vinegar, pinenuts, sultanas and various spices, in which the little local fish such as sardines and sole are marinated for two days.
- *Spiedino di Scampi* Lovely bright pink scampi, fat and juicy, threaded on to a stick and cooked very simply on a grill with a little oil and some lemon.

---

anguilla eel are allowed to live until they reach the adult stage and go for the open sea – at this point they are caught. Fish is popular throughout the region, and is often combined with rice in risotto, or cooked in a tasty stew and eaten with slabs of polenta.

Baccalà or *stoccafisso*, the delicious, very humble dried salt cod, is prepared in thousands of ways – with milk, onion, and herbs, or with *parmigiano* and parsley or many more – it's extremely popular.

CARNE E CACCIA
Meat and Game

Veneto holds the first place in the poultry production for the whole country. All kinds are eaten: *oca* goose, *tacchina* hen turkey, *pollo* chicken, *gallina* boiling fowl, *faraona* guinea fowl, *anatra* duck, *cappone* capon. All of them crop up cooked in many delicious ways.

Beef, veal and pork are also very much in use; particularly good is the beef that comes from herds that have used the lush pastures on the mountains or hillsides. Offal is also popular – especially liver – the most famous restaurant menu dish in Venice must be *fegato alla Veneziana*. Another popular offal dish uses lung to make the stew called *fongadina*.

Horsemeat is fairly widely used, tending to be rather well hung, which makes it particularly sweet in flavour – you can't miss it. Kid *capretto* is also used to make certain traditional local dishes. In the province of Belluno, it is cooked with lots of butter and herbs. At Gambellara it is roasted on a spit, to make a dish called simply *Capretto di Gambellara*.

As far as game goes, many songbirds end up in dishes like *polenta e osei*, as in Lombardy. Pigeon is considered a traditional local ingredient, and is popular in the Breganze area, where it is cooked on a spit with juniper berries, herbs and olive oil, *toresani allo spiedo*.

Local Specialities

- *Fegato alla Veneziana* One of the most famous local dishes. Finely sliced calves' liver, dressed with soft sweet onions. A wonderfully quick and easy dish.
- *Pastizada de Manzo* A marinade of beef with herbs, oil and vinegar, cooked in the marinade. In Verona, the dish is made with horsemeat.
- *Peverada* Dating from the Middle Ages, this is a strong-flavoured sauce made with stock, chicken livers, anchovies, lemon juice or vinegar, pepper and chilli. Served with roast meats.
- *Sopa Coada* A soup from the Treviso area, made with pigeon, chicken or turkey meat, placed in layers with slices of bread, covered with good broth and cooked very slowly in the oven.
- *Squazzeto a la bechera*. *Becheri* are butchers, and the reason for the name of this is obvious – it is a collection of different bits of offal served in a clear soup.

FORMAGGIO
Cheese

The main Venetian cheese of any note is the delicious *asiago* produced in the mountainous parts of the region. It's a softish cheese with a few holes and a soft outer crust like Brie, a good strong flavour and can also be grated when it's old and dry.

FRUTTA E VERDURA
Fruit and Vegetables

The mountainous areas produce very little, but on the fertile plains there is well-organised production. The Venetians are very fond of using modern farming methods – they like tractors!

Local Speciality

- *Risi e bisi* A very thick soup made with rice and peas, flavoured with onion, ham and celery.

The fields are well irrigated and carefully ploughed and sown. *Granoturco* maize, *orzo* oats, *piselli e fagioli* peas and beans, *mele e pere* apples and pears, *carote* carrots, *barbabietole* beetroot, vineyards and rice are all cultivated here

Rippling Risotto

The risotto is one of the great undiscovered arts of Italian cuisine as far as cooks outside Italy are concerned. It is a delicious way of preparing rice, with endless possibilities. All kinds of vegetables, meat, game, wine and fish can be blended with rice to make a perfect risotto, with little fuss and almost no hard work. This is the basic recipe for a plain risotto – what else you add in is entirely up to you though even on its own, it can be delicious.

Fry an onion in a little butter until soft, add *arborio* rice to the onion and butter, and turn the grains over in the mix to toast them gently.

Meanwhile heat up some water or good stock until boiling. As soon as the rice is coated with butter begin to add one ladleful of the liquid and stir it in. Always wait for the ladleful to be absorbed before you add the next one. Keep stirring at all times. Add salt, pepper, and grated *parmigiano* at the end. It takes exactly 20 minutes to cook a risotto from start to finish. You'll know when it's done as the Venetians like it as there will be rippling waves on the creamy surface – *all'onda* they call it – with a little rice stuck to the bottom of the pot. If you're not sure – taste it!

Masks on the Gondolas

During the great festivities of the Venetian *Carnevale* in February, when the streets are thronged with hundreds of people dressed in the wildest and most opulent costumes, faces painted with coloured greasepaint, the fritter comes into its own. The smell of frying batter, with apples and aniseed, pervades the narrow streets for days on end. Once upon a time the *frittelle* would be prepared in the old shops known as *malvasie*, where along with your boiling hot fritter you'd get a glass of Malvasia wine.

very successfully. As far as vineyards go, the region lies in second place behind Sicily in terms of quantity produced. Bassano is famous for its asparagus, and Marostica for its cherries. Two of Venice's most famous dishes, *risi e bisi* and *pasta e fagioli*, make use of the peas and beans that grow so well in this area.

PASTICCERIA
Cakes, Biscuits and Puddings

Venice, in the forefront when it came to dealing with noble guests over the course of history, has developed many recipes to be eaten over a sociable glass of *vino di cipro* sherry or hot chocolate, often flavoured with spices. Spices like cinnamon and nutmeg, introduced to Venice before the rest of the country, play a big part in Venetian *pasticceria*. There are hundreds of cakes and biscuits representing saints' days and special village festivities, like Verona's *pandoro* or the wonderful Carnival goodies, but sadly, like the Patrician villas, many of them are being forgotten.

● *Baicoli* Crunchy biscuits made very simply from flour, sugar, butter and yeast, the recipe dating from the 17th century.

● *Bussola Vicentina* The traditional gift to godchildren at Confirmation this is a cake with a hole in the middle, made with simple ingredients and flavoured with grappa or Marsala. The proverb goes *chi ga santoli ga busolai* – meaning that those who have protection from high up (or from the *bussola*) will get what they want in the end.

● *Crema fritta alla Veneziana* A great favourite in and around Venice, but I have always failed to make it properly at home. A thick custard, cooled and cut into squares before being deep-fried in egg and breadcrumbs. In some Venetian shops you can buy the custard ready to fry. Not very refined, but delicious and filling.

● *Crostoli* Crisp, golden deep-fried fritters with a delicate grappa flavour in the pastry, covered with sugar and served warm with sweet wine.

● *Focaccia* A plain and simple but very delicious Easter cake covered in chopped almonds.

● *Forti* These biscuits have ancient roots indeed, made with bitter cocoa, molasses and all sorts of eastern ingredients.

● *Fritole alla Veneziana* As sold for centuries by the *fritolari*, at Carnival time, crisp deep-fried puffy cakes made with flour, eggs, sugar, candied peel and nuts.

● *Frittelle di zucca alla Veneziana* Crisp sweet pumpkin fritters with sultanas, dusted with sugar and served piping hot.

● *Pandoro di Verona* A tall pale yellow fluffy cake, lighter than any sponge cake. A Christmas speciality and a relative of *panettone*.

● *Pinza* The local word for pizza – in this case a very simple cake, made with cornflour, sugar, pinenuts, candied peel, dried figs and grappa, that used to be wrapped in thick cabbage leaves and baked in the embers of a hot oven on the night before Epiphany when *la Maratenga* (*befana* everywhere else in the country) comes down the chimney with her sack of toys and sweets for good children, and nasty coal for naughty ones.

● *Rosada Veneta* A smooth lemony cream pudding baked or cooked in a bain-marie.

● *Torta di paparele alla Veronese* Identical to the Turkish *katayif*, therefore one can assume it's a direct result of Venetian wanderlust. The only difference is that this uses butter not oil.

● *Torta Nicolotta* This is one of the oldest of the Venetian cakes, named after the poorest inhabitants of the city – the Nicolotti, who lived as beggars. With the few bits of bread they were given as alms, a little milk and just about any other sweet ingredient they could lay their hands

Paid Back with Interest

Fifty years ago, a gentleman called Harry asked for a loan from a kindhearted barman. Three months later he returned to repay his debt and thank the barman, giving him three times what he'd borrowed. The barman opened up his own place, and naturally named it after Harry. The barman's name was Giuseppe Cipriani, and he has created a legendary café, that you should not miss when in Venice. When Giuseppe died, many were concerned that the sons and daughter following him would betray their father's expertise. But *HARRY'S* – where everybody who is anybody has been, from Hemingway to all the European kings – is just as perfect, subtle and elegant today as when it first opened.

The expertise and sheer talent of Signor Cipriani have also left us with the delightful *HOTEL CIPRIANI*, the ultimate place to go for a honeymoon in luxury, for peace and sublime service and the restaurant on the island of Torcello (open only from March to November).

HARRY'S BAR is famous for the creation of the Bellini cocktail, invented by Signor Cipriani in 1948, by mixing fresh peach juice with excellent Venetian champagne; and for the creation of *carpaccio* – slivers of raw beef fillet smothered in a sauce of olive oil, lemon juice, and eggs – for a certain Contessa Amalia Nani Mocenigo, who was forbidden by her doctor to eat cooked meat. It was named after the artist, because there was an exhibition of his work at the time in Venice, and the colour of the dish was like the red in his pictures.

on, they would prepare this plain and simple, delicious cake. It is popular throughout the region, though sometimes sold under other names.

• *Torta Sabbiosa* The cake everyone loves, simple to make and in the Veneto always on hand to serve with some good cold dry white wine if friends come to call. Its best quality lies in the way it melts in the mouth, crumbly under a crisp crust.

• *Zaleti* Little cakes made with yellow semolina flour with the very unusual ingredient of ammonia in the recipe! (This helps bind the raw semolina.) Very buttery, full of sultanas and pinenuts.

VINO
Wine

The region produces an enormous quantity of wine, which is almost always at the top of the list for excellent and consistent quality. The vineyard has become an integral part of the landscape, pushing its way right up to the edge of the suburbs – sometimes even into the cities themselves, with vines growing in people's gardens and orchards. Valpolicella, Bardolino, Soave and Recioto are produced in the Verona province, Robosco, Prosecco and Cartizze come from the Trevigiano area and Merlot and Cabernet come from the Venetian countryside close to the Adriatic coast. All these names are famous the world over. These mentioned below are all D.O.C. wines.

SPECIAL RED WINE

• *Pinot Nero* Dark ruby-coloured wine with a rich full body to be served with special meals.

• *Cabernet Franc* When young this delicious wine has a ruby colour, and a distinctive herbal flavour, but with ageing it becomes more garnet

Strade del Vino

The value of their wine has been put to good use by the people of this region – it has been turned into a tourist attraction through the introduction of the *strade del vino*, the wine roads. There is the *strada del vino rosso* and the *strada del vino bianco*, both of which start off from Conegliano and snake their way through the most productive wine areas of the region, which also provide the traveller with some of the prettiest scenery around.

This is really an excellent idea, bringing the tourist to see and taste the best the region has to offer, and aiding the economy of some of the more far-flung areas that might otherwise never be visited, lying as they do under the imposing shadow of glorious Venezia.

in colour and the flavour becomes flinty. A harmonious wine that goes well with anything.

RED WINE

• *Merlot* An intensely flavoured ruby red wine, very fine and dry, to be drunk with roasts.

• *Bardolino* One of the most popular wines of the region, this is a light-bodied wine with a very characteristic bouquet and a light colour. Excellent with poultry, or game such as rabbit or pigeon.

WHITE WINE

• *Soave* One of the best-known wines from Italy, it surely needs no introduction. It is always dry and velvety, *brut* to just the right degree – amber yellow and transparent with the lightest of aromas.

• *Tocai* Comes from a similar vine as the Hungarian wine called Tokay, but there the

○○

A Drink in the Shade

A stranger arriving in Venice for the first time could well be asked to stop and drink *un ombra* 'a shade'. You may well enquire as to the origin of this rather odd colloquialism. In days long gone the best wines from Greece and Dalmatia, brought straight off incoming ships, would be sold at a little kiosk situated in the patch of shade at the base of St. Mark's Campanile. As the day went by, so the kiosk would be moved, so as to be always in the shade *ombra* – the passers-by could enjoy a drink here any time, and so the word has become part of the Italian wine culture.

○○

similarity ends. This is a pale, straw-yellow, delicate wine with a slightly sharp flavour. Perfect with soup or fish.

ROSÉ WINE

• *Bardolino rosé* Like the red, this is a consistently good wine with a firm flavour and light, refreshing quality. Also delicious with poultry, and very good as an aperitif.

SPUMANTI

• From the Prosecco wine many spumanti, made with the Charmat method, are derived. Two of the best known are *Prosecco di Conegliano* and *Prosecco di Cartizze*.

DESSERT WINE

• *Moscato di Arqua* A highly aromatic wine, containing lots of sugar. Dark yellow and almost syrupy, it's said to have restorative qualities.

BEVANDE
Drinks

• *Vermouth di Conegliano* This is a very light, white vermouth – the classical Italian aperitif, but this one is made only in this area.

WORTH TAKING HOME

Try buying proper polenta flour to recreate the dish at home – its called *farina di polenta*. Arborio rice is now available widely at home, but that's the one you want for risotto.

If it's near Christmas, don't forget to take a *Pandoro di Verona* with you.

Bottles of Valpolicella and Prosecco wines – and if you're going on the Strada del Vino Bianco at Pedemontana you'll find little local dairies where you can buy delicious home-made cheeses.

SAGRE E FESTE
Festivals

Marostica holds a festival of cherries on one of the first Sundays in June.

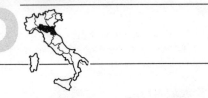

Paradiso dei Buongustai

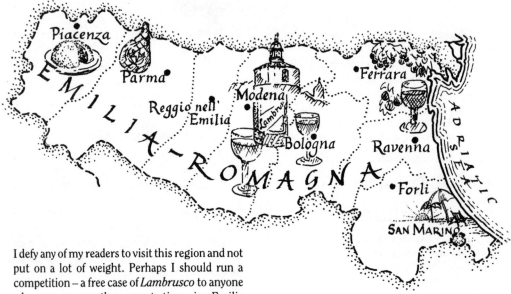

I defy any of my readers to visit this region and not put on a lot of weight. Perhaps I should run a competition – a free case of *Lambrusco* to anyone who can prove they spent time in Emilia Romagna, and did not get any fatter!

The name comes from the via Emilia, the Roman road stretching across it in a straight line for about 250 kilometres from Piacenza to Rimini. It has been a vital communications route for centuries, bringing Attila the Hun (who got lost in the fog), the Longobards, Benedictine monks, the retreating armies of Charles III, the Napoleonic army who planted 'trees of freedom' among the elms and poplars that lined the route, and more recently the escaping Wehrmacht pursued by partisans and the allies. In the 14th century a *provençale* princess travelled the road on her way to Modena, to marry a nobleman of that city. Part of the dowry she carried with her was vines by the name of *Lambruscu*.

This endless number of travellers of every race and creed have left the region with an inheritance of foreign blood, ideas, traditions and languages, all of which have their effect on the cuisine, and have underlined existing contrasts and differences of opinion. These influences, combined with the immense fertility of the soil, which enabled the farming aristocracy to thrive very happily with full larders and bellies, despite internal battles for independence from popes, emperors and cardinals, and the burning feeling of 'we can do better than you', have led to Emilia Romagna being the gastronomic heartland of Italy.

The region lies between the Adriatic, the River Po and the Apennines. It seems split into two, with a mountainous band, and a wide, flat plain, two totally different landscapes. The mountains are rather ugly and bare, their feeling of loneliness in sharp contrast with the pulsating activity of life on the plains, where everything is densely cultivated, and where traffic roars noisily on busy roads. Rows and rows of fruit trees stretch as far as the eye can see.

The plains end at the coast, where once again there are two totally different views – long sandy beaches crowded in summer with holidaymakers, and the tranquil silence of the wild lagoons and salt valleys of the north.

Summers are hot and humid, winters cold with fog and frost, and plenty of snow in the mountains.

The region is divided into 7 provinces, some with more gastronomic claims to fame than the others.

BOLOGNA & PROVINCE

Bologna, once an Etruscan settlement, later inhabited by the Romans, stands at the feet of the

Housewife's Only Choice

In 1891, the very first Italian cookery book, called *La Scienza in Cucina e l'Arte di Mangiar Bene* (*Science in the Kitchen and the Art of Eating Well*) by Pellegrino Artusi, was published here. It is still recognised as being the most complete and authoritative book on Italian cookery. Apart from prayer books, this was the only piece of literature which housewives had access to for many decades. *L'Artusi*, as it is fondly known, is a collection of 760 Italian recipes, although most of the menus he suggests are more than likely to provoke high blood pressure, dangerous cholesterol levels or heart failure. Can you imagine eating *pappardelle* with hare, followed by *crostini* with plenty of Alba truffles, then *budino alla Genovese, salame da sugo di Ferrara*, followed by capon with Roman salad, finishing it all off with a goodly slice of *dolce torino* – on a regular basis? Obviously, these were menus put together for rich epicureans, but I hope that these days one eats less, and more healthily.

Vacuum-packed nostalgia

The Emilians' battle with the problem of retaining the age-old flavour, textures, aromas and spirit of their eating habits, as illustrated by Artusi, and bringing them into the 20th century. When you consider that the region produces 30 per cent of what the rest of the country eats, it is a matter of constantly testing and trying various modern methods of food manufacture, so that the cooking of Emilia Romagna, the emblem of Italian gastronomy at its best, loses none of its acclaim.

In 1985 the annual food fair, held in Parma, was given the name CIBUS – Latin for food – and its object was to show that traditional cooking can be packaged successfully. Emilian cuisine is moving into the 'fast food' world of our time, but with a nostalgic look back at the way things were.

In any case, admired all over the world for centuries, this region represents the heart and soul of the best of Italian cooking. Here they are masters of pasta making, especially fresh egg pasta, they produce excellent *salumi* and they have given the world *Parmigiano Reggiano*, Lambrusco, Parma ham and so-called Bolognese sauce. You can be sure of eating well in this region – good, rich and hearty food prepared with flair and imagination.

Apennine hills on a fertile plain. The medieval and Renaissance buildings still stand intact, though most of the famous towers have collapsed and those that remain are now leaning.

'All that is required for life'

In the early part of the 15th century, Schedel wrote of Bologna 'She is known as the fat one, because she produces such an abundance of grain, wine and all that which is required for life'. The legend of Bologna, still known as *La Grassa*, the Fat, as the gastronomic capital of the region, if not the entire country, has never waned. Every restaurant is guaranteed to be good, every *trattoria* worth a stop, and in every home the lady of the house, the *rzdora*, carries on the tradition of excellence in the kitchen.

But what is it that makes Bologna so enchanting? Is it the wide arcades, opening out under porticoes, that make one so welcome? More likely it's her superb cooking, which fills the air with pungent smells, her restaurants, where it's quite acceptable for the customer to enter the kitchen and explore the pots and pans.

Gifts from God

As everywhere in Bologna is an excellent place to eat, or buy food, I'll give you simply my list of favourite haunts. *RISTORANTE NOTAI*, via dei Pignattari, *RISTORANTE PAPPAGALLO*, Piazza Mercanzia, *RISTORANTE SILVERIO*, via Nosadella, and the *ANTICA OSTERIA ROMAGNOLA*, via Rialto. Buy bread and fresh pasta at the *PANETTERIA E PASTIFICIO ATTI* in via Capraie 7. The windows of *ATTI* are poetry in edible motion. Take your time and really look – the attention to detail, freshness and style are incredible – bet you never knew food could look this good. There are little labels here and there with remarks printed on them referring to the items for sale. For example, next to the *tortellini* is a note reading *'buoni da ingannare i mariti'* 'so good they're enough to fool husbands'.

For *salumi* in general you should go to the fabulous *Salsamentaria TAMBURINI* where there are over thirty types of *prosciutto*, and I don't know how many *salami, mortadelle, cotechini* and so on and so on laid out on the 20-metre-long counter. Cheese must be bought at *FORMAGGI BRINI* in via Ugo Bassi 19 – Antonio Brini is passionate about what he sells – there are over 200 kinds of local cheese here, and every one is a winner. Shopping for food is as much an art as the cooking in Bologna. Just admire the windows, gaze in on all those *'Ben di Dio'* (gifts from God) on offer and you won't be lacking inspiration for long.

More than Lambrusco

For wine, in Bologna itself I would recommend a visit to the cellars of the *TENUTA BISSERA DI NEGRONI*, which are in via Valdossola 16. Outside the city at Zola Predosa, in via Predosa 83, are the excellent cellars belonging to the Vigneto delle Terre Rosse di Vallinia. At Bazzano in via Castelfranco is the Fattoria Montebudello which produces and sells the best local wine. All these cellars will once and for all put to bed the myth that the only wine produced and worth drinking here is Lambrusco – certainly they drink a lot of Lambrusco in Bologna, but the other wines of the region also need to be introduced and savoured to get the full measure of what's been happening since medieval times. If you want to drink a glass of real local wine, amongst real local people, head for *L'OSTERIA DEL SOLE*, the last real *osteria* in the city, where elbow-smoothed old wooden tables are laid out haphazardly, and where you sit and drink the only thing that is available – a really good glass of wine. It opens at 8 o'clock in the morning, and soon after is filled with customers from the nearby local market. All day it buzzes with life, until it closes late at night. It's been here in via dei Ranocchi since 1475, and it doesn't look as if it's changed much.

A family affair

The province of Bologna is the largest and most densely populated in the region. Of all the towns within the province I shall limit myself to Dozza Imolese, 30 kilometres outside Bologna on the way to Rimini. This is one of the oldest and most interesting little towns in Italy. It is famous for 3 reasons: it is the region's wine centre, it has a Rocca – a stately home which used to belong to my ancestors, the Sforza family; and every available piece of wall space in the town has a mural painted on it. Every other year since 1960 over 150 painters have painted the murals, turning the Rocca, its walls adorned with sketches for the works of art, into a modern art gallery in its own right. There is to my knowledge nowhere like this town in the world, ancient buildings tastefully decorated with murals painted by a wealth of talented artists. Come and admire the work and taste the wine, and spare a thought for my long-gone forefathers!

PARMA & PROVINCE

Cheese, ham and violets – there are not many towns whose name is so readily associated with so many wonderful things. Though the origins of Parmesan are disputed between Parma, Reggio and Piacenza (it is correctly called *parmigiano reggiano*), the whole area round Parma is involved in its production. Every morning at dawn and each evening in the provinces of Parma, Reggio Emilia and Modena, about 100,000 people in 35,000 stables milk 350,000 cows to produce 1,300,000,000 litres of milk, out of which 879,000 cwts of Parmesan are produced!

While the pastures round the city of Parma and beyond obviously enhance the milk which produces the cheese, it is said to be the particular quality of the local air, and the exact altitude of the hills which gives the right atmosphere for drying and curing the hams of Parma. These come from pigs which have been fed on the whey of the milk, discarded from the production of *parmigiano*.

In the city of Parma itself the best place to eat is the *ANTICA OSTERIA CON CUCINA PARMA ROTTA*. The wines and olive oil are perfect, and complement everything you eat – from the delicious variety of *salumi* to the marvellous selection of cheese, including a range of Parmesan starting at two years of maturity and working upwards.

Apart from the cheese and the ham, which must be Parma's most famous products, I should also mention the local scent of Parma violets, which is produced by the gallon in local factories. If the wind is blowing the right way, you'll know where it is!

Within this province lies Salsomaggiore Terme, a very pretty and well-organised spa town with hotels and restaurants galore. The healthy water is drawn up from deep wells and is filled with mineral salts and iodine, guaranteed to cure just about anything.

MODENA & PROVINCE

The biggest stock-raising markets in Europe are here. Recently Modena was connected to the International Stock Markets and the prices of day by day sales are dictated through this system worldwide. According to the latest statistics, 17,000 pigs, 250,000 cattle and 25,000 horses pass through the Modenese markets in one year. The cattle market in Modena opens for business at dawn every Monday and Thursday, and for horses it's on Sundays. If you are interested it is possible to arrange visits.

All the world's most important banks are represented here, in the historical centre – Modena has her own 'city' – and it is the very heart of the region's financial well-being. It's a lovely city; like Bologna, it has arcades and porticoes which lead you into ancient streets through to silent piazzas that have the atmosphere of someone's drawing room. But if the 'city' is the financial heart of Modena, then *BIANCA'S* (via Spaccini 24) has got to be the city's gastronomic heart. Opened 30 years ago in one of the less refined areas of the city, it is a meeting place for people who have at least one thing in common – the desire to eat well. This is absolutely my kind of place, a family business, free from all the awful fussiness of so-called chic restaurants, but still retaining attentive, professional service in an intimate and elegant atmosphere. The vegetables are the

freshest, from the family kitchen gardens, and there's *tagliatelle, tagliatelle* and still more *tagliatelle*, dressed with an infinite variety of superb sauces according to seasonal availability. There's wonderful Lambrusco to go with it all, but worlds removed from the screw-top bottles available at home.

The hotel and restaurant *BAIA DEL RE* is blessed by Secondo Vecchi, the owner, who organises marvellous promotional activities to teach everything about the food, wine, and history behind his beloved Modena. From the restaurant you can buy perfect *parmigiano* and bottles of *Nocino* (walnut) and *Laurino* (bay) liqueurs, and Signor Vecchi's extraordinary balsamic vinegar.

The *pasticceria SAN GIORGIO* has mounds of local pastries and cakes, and some beautiful ice cream. The *salumeria GIUSTI* runs a close second to *TAMBURINI* in Bologna, long considered Italy's top *salumeria*. *GIUSTI* is run by a charming husband and wife team and to call it a shop is to do it severe injustice – this is a gourmet's paradise, a real food and wine experience not to be missed. The old ancestral tools are still in use, with a vast variety of preserved meats, and lots more wonderful balsamic vinegar on offer.

Within the province of this green and somewhat sober city, so different in atmosphere from jolly Bologna, are the towns of Carpi, good for wine, cheese – and pullovers, Sassuolo, home of the *Sassolino* liqueur and Vignola, famous for its cherry trees which produce most of the cherries eaten throughout Europe. The trees blossom white and pink throughout the spring, miles and miles of blossom stretching out across the valley, then turning to the brilliant red of the ripening fruits in early summer.

EMILIA ROMAGNA

FERRARA & PROVINCE

Founded in the Middle Ages this city belonged to the d'Este family from the 13th to the 16th century. The Renaissance part of the city was known as the First Modern City when it was built, but the medieval part is no less interesting to visit.

I discovered an extraordinary bar here in via Adelardi. It's named *ENOTECA-WHISKEY AL BRINDISI* and is run by the enterprising author of *In viaggio nelle valli del Whiskey* (Journey in the whisky valleys), and consists of a kind of wine and whisky bar with some food. As far as I could work out, what you ate seemed to depend upon what you ordered to drink, and the price varied accordingly. It used to be the *OSTERIA CHIUCCHIOLINO*, where Ariosto, Cellini, Tasso, Copernicus and Carducci are all supposed to have supped, though not together as far as I know! Now it is the ideal place to stop off for a quick bite to eat and drink of the sublime local wine ... unless of course whisky is your tipple, in which case Signor Moreno Pellegrini claims to have several hundred brands available, including single malts from all the Scottish distilleries.

Mussolini Fails Again

Ferrara is very famous throughout Italy for her bread, though nobody quite knows what it is that makes it so special – it's something to do with its absorption qualities.

Mussolini attempted to hold an Emilian banquet in Rome, inviting several bakers from Ferrara to bake the bread for the occasion. After several attempts they simply gave up – baked in Rome the bread lost all its characteristics.

Within the province lies the delightful, timeless town of Comacchio, a small town built on 13 islands, separated by canals and joined together by bridges. Comacchio is to eels what pasta is to tomato sauce. Fishing is the main industry, particularly eel fishing, with big square nets suspended into the water. Eat the eels as they are eaten here cooked in a delicious rich tomato sauce *anguilla in umido*, or simply grilled, cut into sections *anguilla alla griglia*.

RAVENNA & PROVINCE

Ravenna is of course renowned for the stunning mosaics that are now sadly endangered by the threat of pollution in the air. This was the capital city of the eastern Roman Empire, well-positioned as a stronghold, as surrounded by marshes she was virtually impregnable (although the health of her inhabitants must have been precarious as a result). Nowadays, the marshes reclaimed, malaria is a thing of the past.

The first local industries sprang up on the newly dried ground, sugar factories and mills mostly. In Roman times this was an active port city, and now it is connected to the sea by the Canale Candiano, at the mouth of which lies Porto Corsini, one of the most important ports on the Adriatic.

FORLÌ & PROVINCE

Forlì is a city sitting in the middle of a great ploughed field, with all kinds of fruit and vegetables pouring into her daily markets and shops.

Within the province is the horrible Rimini, which I can only bear to visit in the winter or early spring – before the hordes arrive in their thousands – when I make a point of eating at *RISTORANTE DALLO ZIO*, which is a family-run seaside *trattoria* with plenty of very good fresh fish – I can particularly recommend the *cannelloni* with fish filling and sauce, the stewed sea snails, *lumache di mare*, and the vol-au-vent with fish *pâté*. Skip dessert, because nearby, in the vicolo San Bernardino, is a wonderful traditional *pasticceria*, and the *GELATERIA ROMANA* in Piazza Ferrari makes really fabulous ice cream.

On the via Emilia, between Rimini and Forlì, is Cesena, with its port of Cesenatico, on the canal, dating back to the 14th century. Near Cesena, in a little town called Forlimpopoli, there is a truly magnificent restaurant – *IL MANEGGIO* – run by a young couple called Giorgio and Bruna, who prepare their menu with great care, bringing the excellent traditions of Emilian cuisine right up to date without upsetting anyone. There is a huge selection of local specialities with fresh egg pasta, and beef and veal in the forefront, with a framework of perfect fresh vegetables and fruit to complete the miracle. They have very good olive oil, in particular *Brighisello, (cru Valdeto)* and *Villa Cristina* which can be bought in the restaurant.

SALUMI

Salami, Sausages and Cured Meats

Each province, village and town has its own *salume*. Bologna's *mortadella* is cited in a reference book for visitors, dated 1726, as something to avoid paying too much for in local inns. It is still considered to be among the most refined and delicious *salume* available. It's the largest, about a metre long, and up to a dinner-plate size in diameter, pale pink, with a mild flavour, with dots of pure white fat, black peppercorns, and the odd green pistachio nut.

In the Piacentino area, *coppa*, the peppery and rather greasy mixture of all the odd bits of the pig, pressed together and treated rather like *prosciutto* – delicious in a crusty sandwich – and *pancetta* bacon rule, while *zampone*, stuffed pig's trotter and *Cappelli da Prete*, first created 200 years ago, are from the city of Modena.

Prosciutto, of course, is unlike anything you've ever tasted anywhere outside this region, especially if you chance upon the amazing *prosciutto di Langhirano*.

Local Specialities

- *Rifreddo* is a speciality mainly of the Reggio area and consists of various kinds of *salumi* and very thin slices of veal placed in a loaf tin in layers with cheese and eggs in between each layer. The moulded 'cake' is then gently cooked in a bain-marie and served with aspic jelly in thin cold slices.
- *Salama da Sugo Ferrarese* The delicious, superb and inimitable home-made sausage with its delicious juices and surrounding *sugo*, which oozes out when the sausage is cut.

It is served with mashed potatoes in winter, and melon in summer. If it has been properly cooked by experts this is one of the most exceptional specialities of the region you are likely to eat. It was apparently originally created by Lucrezia Borgia as the dish to be served to men returning exhausted from battle. I don't know how true that is, but nowadays it is the traditional dish served in households when the young men return from doing their military service.

PASTA

This is a paradise for pasta lovers – all kinds of fresh pasta are made throughout the region – you are never allowed to forget for one moment that here you are in pasta land. All shapes and sizes, all kinds of colours and varieties, from *lasagne* to tiny stars for putting into soups. There is masses

Local Specialities

- *Bomba di Riso alla Piacentina* Rice dishes are almost non-existent in this region, but this rich rice mould with a filling of pigeon, butter, cheese and tomato sauce is really well worth trying. It is an ancient traditional speciality of the city of Piacenza, originally created for the Festa della Madonna on 15 August. In some parts of the province, truffles, *prosciutto* and other local ingredients are also added.
- *Cannelloni Ripieni di Tortellini* If you ever doubted that you were in Pasta land, this is the dish to dispel all your doubts. *Cannelloni* with a filling of stuffed *tortellini*, combining ham, *mozzarella*, cream, butter and milk – very rich and filling!
- *Cappellacci con la Zucca* A speciality from Ferrara, a city whose inhabitants are renowned for being great devourers of pumpkin. This traditional liking for that vegetable goes back to the time when *mangiar dolce* eating sweets was in vogue with the court of the Gonzagas in Mantova and the Estensi in Ferrara – this is probably why so many local specialities are the same in both those cities, despite them being in separate regions. In this case, the pumpkin is used to stuff some rather large *ravioli*-shaped pasta called *cappellacci*.
- *Pasticcio alla Ferrarese* A pastry shell, baked golden and crumbling, which hides a dish of short pasta dressed with a white ragù (white truffles and Béchamel), a very popular dish in the 16th century.

of very rich, eggy golden yellow soft pasta. To make the *sfoglia*, the sheet of pasta dough, you need 100g of flour and one egg per person. The egg is the vital ingredient, and the stickler for authenticity will make sure it's a brown-shelled one.

The *sfoglia* is turned into *garganelli* by cutting it into squares, and rolling it into hand-made *maccheroni* over a comb. Other non-stuffed

Strands of Golden Hair

Tagliatelle were created on May 28, 1487 by the great cook Mastro Zafirano as a homage to Lucrezia Borgia's blonde tresses – this does somewhat excuse her from some of her evil deeds – she can't have been all bad to inspire such a delicacy. For centuries the exact width of the *tagliatella* was argued over, until 1972 when a gastronomic law was passed whereby one *tagliatella* has to measure one 12,276th part of the height of the Torre degli Asinelli – i.e. 8mm! Before it enters the pot, it must be no more than 6.5 or 7mm, so as to allow it to swell to its required 8mm in cooking. Or so the jury finally decided! Anything wider or narrower is NOT a *tagliatella*, and will have another name!

shapes are *lasagne, maccheroni, malfatti, pappardelle, paspadelle* – all of which will be accompanied by the so-called Bolognese sauce – in other words *ragù*. Stuffed varieties include *anolini, caplet, cappellacci, cappelletti* to name but a few.

Pasta even finds its way into the cakes – *ravioli* are filled with jam, *taglierini* into a chocolate cake, and *tortelli* are filled with chestnuts and jam to be deep-fried at carnival time.

PESCE E FRUTTI DI MARE
Fish and Seafood

Sea fishing in the Adriatic gives Italy one fifth of the fish eaten, but there are few fish specialities in this cuisine. The fish caught are mainly sardines *sardelle*, anchovies *acciughe*, and the newly-discovered mackerel *sgombro*, previously considered a poor man's fish not worth the trouble, now becoming very popular indeed all over the country. Inland, fishing also takes places in the canals and lagoons in the valleys of Comacchio, where mostly eels are caught, but also grey mullet *muggine* and bass *branzino*.

CARNE E CACCIA
Meat and Game

Meat is certainly big business in this region. Here are bred the country's largest number of pigs destined for the table, most of which are turned into *salumi*, and the lush pastures grow one-fifth of the nation's beef and veal.

Reggio Emilia is the kingdom of the pig and all main European dealers flock in their thousands to the annual Pork Fair.

In recent times the region has attempted to widen its vast meat production by introducing the

Local Specialities

- *Bauletto* or *Portafoglio* A wonderful idea! Two slices of beef, with chopped *mortadella* and ham in between, floured and lightly fried in butter with asparagus spears and plenty of grated *parmigiano*.
- *Fritto Misto all'Emiliana* A very typical regional dish, this is a huge pile of different things fried in batter and all served together. Chicken croquettes, apple fritters, little pork and lamb chops, savoury buns, *ricotta* fritters, *semolino* fritters and naturally *tagliatelle* fritters. It is a marvellous, grandiose dish, only to be tackled if you're feeling really hungry.
- *Osso buco alla Reggiana* From the city of

Reggio comes this delicious recipe for cooking *Osso buco*, shin of veal, in a casserole with butter, spices, Marsala and garlic, served on a bed of yellow saffron rice.
- *Passatelli* A mixture of breadcrumbs, *parmigiano*, eggs, lemon zest and nutmeg that are then pushed through a sieve into boiling hot broth to flavour a soup.
- *Brodo* Broth is a regional speciality and is cooked with great pride and care. Whether it has *tortellini, passatelli* or anything else in it, the *brodo* is always made with several different kinds of meat, and they make sure it harmonises perfectly with what it contains.

country's most important poultry and rabbit breeding farms, situated in and around Forlì. In one year, 314 million eggs, 37 million chickens, and 3 million rabbits, guinea fowl and pigeons were marketed here. Definitely not a region of vegetarians!

Definitely *Not* Spaghetti Bolognese

Here it is! This is what has been misnamed for so long: Bolognese sauce! The real thing, *ragù, is placed on the stove at 6 a.m. to be ready for lunch – it is NOT a quick dish, so for quick pasta sauces try anything else but this. You begin with a gently fried onion, carrot, celery and herbs, and sixteen ingredients later you've more or less got it. (Try prosciutto, oil, butter, garlic, dried porcini,* minced beef, red wine, flour, tomatoes, parsley, marjoram, nutmeg, chicken livers, salt, pepper and broth).

FORMAGGIO

Cheese

Reggio Emilia is considered to be the epicentre for *Parmigiano Reggiano*, and a consortium for the protection and care of the cheese was set up in the city fifty years ago.

The oldest known data on this cheese dates back to the Flavian Emperors, where it is mentioned in a poem by Martial, but the earliest statistical fact goes back to 1870 – in that year 130 cheese-producing plants existed in the region.

Ever since the leading paediatricians and geriatricians of the nation declared this cheese to be the best thing for babies, children and old people, it has been added to the essential diet of everybody under six and over sixty. The fact that *parmigiano* has special properties has been known for a very long time. Petrarch was particularly fond of it, and would spend long holidays in the Enza valley so as never to be too far from a source.

Elizabeth I used to buy it in great quantities in Sassuolo, and it was then shipped to England from Massa. Molière discovered it late in life, and

it is said he managed to finish his last work thanks to this marvellous cheese! He had ruined his stomach lining and intestines by overeating and drinking, but once he began to eat Parmesan, he became strong and ended his days on a diet of nothing else.

Spying on Venus

Tortellini were created in honour of Venus's belly button, which a Bolognese innkeeper happened to spy through her keyhole on a stay there. (She had been banished to wander through Limbo and somehow ended up in Bologna – don't ask me how!) Consumed with passion, the man raced down to the kitchen and instead of having a cold shower, he created the *tortellino* to commemorate what he had seen.

In Bologna they are called *cappelletti*, in Modena *tortellini*, in Parma *anolini*, and though a stranger would certainly not know how to tell the difference between them all, each part of the region claims their version of this little pocket of pasta, stuffed with a selection of carefully minced meats blended with herbs, spices, *prosciutto, mortadella*, Parmesan and other secrets, to be the best. The art of making them is to start with a sheet of pasta which is silky smooth and soft (the *Confraternita del Tortellino Emiliano* says it must be 'as round as the moon and as soft as a caress') on which are laid little lumps of the filling in rows. The sheet is then cut around the filling into neat squares, and each square is folded into a triangle, sealing the filling inside. They can then be cooked in good stock *brodo* – in fact nothing typifies the cuisine of Emilia Romagna better than *tortellini in brodo*, or boiled and dressed with a meat and tomato sauce, or a delicate cream and cheese sauce.

A kilo of *parmigiano* will now cost you around L20,000, depending upon the age and quality. Its value doubles with age, in every sense! Other cheeses of the region include *crescenza* and *stracchino* even though they are made in Lombardy and Tuscany in almost exactly the same way. They are soft cheeses with a rather bitter flavour, and a sourish aftertaste. They are used more in cooking.

Puina is the delicious local ewes' milk *ricotta*. Ordinary cows' milk *ricotta* is also available everywhere, and is of excellent quality.

FRUTTA E VERDURA
Fruit and Vegetables

Not content with providing the country with all that meat, Emilia Romagna produces almost all of Italy's wheat and sugar beet. It also produces barley, rice and wine. Excellent peaches, plums, apricots, cherries and pears for the fruit markets, and onions, peas and tomatoes are the best vegetables.

PASTICCERIA
Cakes, Biscuits and Puddings

• *Bensone* A rich buttery almond cake from Modena, reputed to be made from a centuries-old recipe.

• *Cassatella* A pudding consisting of biscuits soaked in *Alchermes* and *Sassolino* liqueurs, layered with a very rich egg, sugar, chocolate and Amaretto mixture.

• *Castagnaccio con ricotta* A chestnut cake with a layer of creamy *ricotta* cheese. In some parts, especially near Parma, this is traditionally cooked in a bread oven, wrapped in chestnut leaves. It can also be deep-fried in olive oil, *Castagnaccio fritto* – usually for children's tea time.

• *Castagne all'ubriaco* Roasted chestnuts, soaked in a bowlful of good red wine.

• *Cedrino* This goes on sale in grocery shops just before Christmas, made with jam, citron peel, pinenuts, sugar and spices, and is added to boiled chestnuts as a filling for *tortellacci*. I have found it a marvellous addition to good old English fruit-cakes too.

• *Croccante di Piacenza* Hard crunchy caramel, eaten like sweets and made in all parts of the country. In the south they add slivers of orange peel, in the Veneto hazelnuts, and in Rome and Naples it is flavoured with vanilla. Here in Emilia it is made with toasted almonds and sugar with butter and lemon juice.

• *Dolce amore* The 'love pudding' made with layers of biscuits soaked in brandy, aniseed and Marsala with *zabaione*, almonds, jam and more delicious things.

• *Frittelle* Light and fluffy fritters are very popular in the region and can be savoury or sweet. The sweet variety will be made with apples, sultanas, pinenuts or semolina.

• *Pan Speciale* or *Certosino* The monks of the Certosa in Bologna would always prepare this cake for Pope Benedict XIV, who was very fond of it. It's a very rich cake of puréed and candied fruit, chocolate, spices and sugar and honey which keeps for several months.

• *Piade dei morti* A warming, thin, round sweet bread with sultanas, almonds, walnuts and pinenuts flavoured with wine. It has a strange, slightly bitter flavour, but still is always baked in the cold winter months, and a slice kept in your coat pocket will warm your hands and keep out the chill, perfuming your clothes with its inimitable smell.

• *Savor* A paste made with pears, apples, peaches, quinces, pumpkin and *mosto* (wine that has just begun to ferment) and is used as an ingredient in various local dishes, or as an accompaniment to *Bollito*. *Savor alla Modenese* is slightly different, made with apples and quinces, lemon and orange zest.

• *Spongata* A speciality of the town of Brescello, and ancient documents state it was given to my noble ancestor Duca Francesco Sforza in 1454 as a gift. It is a traditional cake for Christmas and New Year, incredibly laborious to make, so it is rare to find it home made. You can buy it factory-made, and it is still good. It is two layers of pastry with a filling of nuts, fruit, wine, a whole grated nutmeg and honey. Less well known is the *spongata di Busseto*, which has a richer pastry and a less involved and complicated filling which includes pickled fruit *mostarda di frutta*. In Reggio Emilia the finished cake is covered with chocolate.

• *Torta degli Addobbi* This is the cake baked to mark the occasion of the Addobbi festival in summer time, when the balconies are decorated and lit up, and processions of revellers walk through the streets. It's made with rice, candied peel, almonds, butter, eggs and milk – it's baked, then soaked through with a generous glass of Amaretto liqueur.

• *Torta di Taglierini alla Modenese* A pasta concoction – a very stodgy cake made with *taglierini* and chocolate. One version leaves out the chocolate but combines freshly made *taglierini* with candied peel, almonds, bitter and sweet, sugar and melted butter baked in a pastry case. Always best eaten the day after it's made. Only have a small slice!

• *Tortellacci di Carnevale* Deep-fried half-moon

shaped *tortelli* filled with chestnuts, jam, *cedrino*, breadcrumbs and cocoa powder among other things. Prepared during carnival time and eaten for breakfast – dipped into huge bowls of milky coffee. The filling varies from one district to another, but remains delicious wherever you are.

● *Savourette* This is a runny jam, made with *sapa* (wine syrup, see *Bevande*), and grated quince flesh – boiled together until reduced to a kind of liquid conserve. It is absolutely delicious spread on bread and butter, and in cakes and desserts and on ice cream.

● *Tortelli di Marmellata* Baked *tortelli* made with a lovely lemony, buttery pastry, filled with firm *amarena* cherry jam, and baked in the oven till golden brown.

● *Tortelli di Natale* At Christmas time the *tortelli* made in this way are deep-fried and filled with a rich and varied stuffing including chocolate, chestnuts, *sapa*, *Sassolino* liqueur, coffee, nuts and jam.

VINO
Wine

Emilia Romagna can boast of a selection of excellent wines that until recently have been completely unknown. The experts say that there are a few wines that definitely deserve the D.O.C. label and have not been awarded this accolade. Pinot Chardonnay and Chardonnay are among the ones that have caused the fuss, and so was the Cabernet Sauvignon dei Colli Bolognesi but this has recently been awarded D.O.C. labelling.

RED WINE

● *Lambrusco* has always been the most famous of Emilian wines (some say this fame is unwarranted – wouldn't you know it, they argue about everything here, they can't even agree about wine!), but my advice to you is to seek out the better quality Lambrusco if you want a measure of what the wine is really about.

● *Lambrusco Salamino di Santa Croce; di Sorbara; Reggiano; Grasparossa di Castelvetro*. These four are all good buys. All good Lambrusco can be drunk in large quantities with few ill effects.

● *Lambrusco Parmigiano* is the one best suited to drink on its own.

WHITE WINE

● *Trebbiano di Romagna* An excellent light table wine.

● *Trebbianino val Trebbia* A wine produced in limited quantities so as to be a delicious rarity. Perfect with fish, it's a delicate golden dry white.

● *Pomposa Bianco* This is a lovely dry wine for drinking all through a meal and especially with fish, produced in the area round Comacchio.

● *Scandiano* Perfect with freshwater fish, in particular trout, this is made with a wide variety of grapes, and pressed in the region round Reggio. Slightly acidy, certainly not a fruity wine.

● *Albana di Romagna* This was apparently the favourite wine of the Empress Galla Placidia, mother of the Emperor Valentinian III, through whom, from Ravenna, she dominated Europe for 25 years. There are two different varieties, a light-coloured dry but fruity wine, and a dark golden sweet version, to be drunk with desserts.

BEVANDE
Drinks

● *sapa* A wine syrup made with *mosto*, the must from new wine, cloudy and sweet, that has just begun to ferment. *Sapa* is the kind of drink you will be offered if you visit a farm. With two litres of *mosto*, five walnuts, and a great deal of patience, stirring over the stove, one bottle of *sapa* is prepared. It keeps for years and years and is useful as

---

Almost an Embrocation

Aceto Balsamico is as typical of the region as fresh egg pasta. Part of the tradition of Modena, its origins lost in time, it tastes like a deep, intense nutty wine vinegar. It consists of vinegar that is aged in special casks, called *vascelli*, and the longer it ages the better and more valuable it becomes. Once upon a time it was so precious as to be part of every girl's dowry. It is distilled drop by drop so that it becomes dark brown, and almost syrupy. Very rarely exported because there isn't much of it. Three drops are enough to dress a huge salad. It must be at least 50 years old before it can be used.

a diluted, refreshing summer drink, or as an added ingredient in cake making.

• *Nocino* A liqueur made with walnuts, produced all over the country, but is traditionally from this region. The old custom dictates that the walnuts be picked at dawn on June 24, St John's day, if they are to be turned into *Nocino*. They have to be damp with dew. Many mystical healing properties are attributed to this drink, but all I can say is that it makes an excellent digestif, and is available in very pretty bottles.

• *Laurino* is a liqueur made with bay leaves. If you like that flavour you'll probably like it!

• *Sassolino* A liqueur from the town of Sassuolo, where they also make fabulous ceramic tiles, which is used a great deal in desserts and rarely drunk out of a glass – you're more likely to eat it in a *zuppa* (pudding).

• *Brandy* Distilled from grapes of course, most Italian brandy is fairly dire (we are definitely NOT talking about Cognac), but is nice when added to a cup of coffee at the end of a big meal. Always extremely dry with quite a fierce flavour. Certainly cheaper than Cognac, or even most Spanish brands.

• *Frutta Spiritata* All kinds of fruit are preserved in jars with a very alcoholic syrup covering them. Wonderful on ice cream, you either love or hate it. I love it! Anything from raspberries to chestnuts are available in this form, and the syrup is like a delicious liqueur. Often on offer as the finishing touch to a meal.

WORTH TAKING HOME

Need I say Parmesan, as much as you can carry? It keeps very well if you don't wrap it up. Let it breathe in the pantry or grate it and freeze it. *Zampone* can be bought in a vacuum-packed sealed box.

You must try to take some *aceto balsamico* because you almost certainly won't be able to buy it anywhere else. A bottle of *frutta spiritata* is always a welcome gift. *Certosino* cake for a different Christmas delicacy, and if you buy some *cedrino* you can add it to your own baking. On your way to the airport, stop and buy some freshly made pasta – if your flight isn't too long, it will be fresh enough to boil and eat the minute you get home, with just Parmesan, butter and a little black pepper. Take a bottle of *Laurino* and *Nocino*, and one of *Sassolino* to try out at the end of your next dinner party. And, finally, pack a couple of bottles of Lambrusco, 'the wine that cheers', to show people back home what the real stuff is like.

SAGRE E FESTE
Festivals

In Acquapartita, in the province of Forlì, on 14–15 August, they celebrate the *Ferragosto Bagnese* with the *sagra* of the *Foccaccia* and *Albana* wine. The grand finale is a vast pyrotechnic spectacular on a very grand scale.

On the coast at Cattolica on 21 August they celebrate the *sagra* of the roasted fish – and that's just what you'll get, along with wine, local dancing and music.

In the province of Parma, around 23 August, Bedonia celebrates the *sagra della trota* the trout festival. They use huge frying pans to cook vast amounts of fresh local trout, which are eaten with polenta. As usual, plenty of wine, dancing and singing.

On or around 1 September, they also hold the *sagra delle torte nostrane*, with all the ladies of the village baking cakes and selling them whole or by the slice to all visitors.

7 TOSCANA

Rustic Renaissance

From a landscape of olive groves, vineyards, rounded mossy mountains and long smooth beaches, there emerges a cuisine that manages to be rustic and elegant at the same time. The Tuscan nature is to be pleasant with ironic overtones. It does not accept compromises and nor does its food nor its wine. The dishes are full-bodied, filling and rich, but without the heaviness that this might imply. The wines are rounded and smooth, firmly based on excellent soil, timeless expertise and knowledge.

In this region, where history pours out at you at every turn, with the glories of Florence at its heart, you will eat all manner of food cooked on the open log fire, for Tuscan cuisine does not lend itself easily to the gas cooker or the electric hob. The people here are much more interested in the excellence of the ingredients than in the presentation or accompaniments; this is country food, even when it's cooked in the city. Tuscans are considered to be the most awkward of all Italians, their palate finely tuned to the perfect preparation of any dish. In the *trattorie* you'll see customers watching with great care their half chicken or steak cooking on the scented fire, and it's they who decide when the meal is ready. Great bowlfuls of rich vegetable and bean soups, served in terracotta bowls even in the most elegant restaurants, and meat grilled or cooked on the spit – these form the essence of Tuscan cooking.

TOSCANA

Casa dolce casa

Tuscany is my second home – all my happiest and most vivid memories are linked to the years I have spent here. The corner of the region I know and love the best is the one that touches the Ligurian border north-west of Florence itself. This is Lunigiana, to my mind one of the loveliest places on earth. When I am asked for advice from friends visiting Tuscany, I urge them first to 'do' Florence, the Chianti valley and Siena, then to leave the tourist scene behind, and head for the motorway exit of Versilia, to travel along the coastal strip of Carrara, Viareggio and Forte dei Marmi, with its exquisite backdrop of the Apuan Alps. Here, according to your mood, you can enjoy smooth, sandy beaches or green, densely wooded mountains. It is one of the holiday areas preferred by Italians from all over the country and retains old-fashioned charm and delights that must be sampled: tiny mountainside *trattorie*, elegant seaside cafés, wonderful ice cream shops, olive groves and wine centres.

In pre-Roman times the Etruscan or Tusci inhabited the territory between the Arno and Tiber valleys. This civilisation reached dizzy heights of social development. Called Etruria or Tuscia (from which the name Toscana was derived), this began a highly civilised culture which continued for centuries. The traditions of art, architecture, trade, and banking which culminated in the Renaissance are well known, and there is still an aristocratic, noble atmosphere here of a people with the enquiring and enterprising spirit of families like the Medici, Sforza, Borgias and others who held the destiny of Tuscany in their hands. You must visit the palaces of Florence for an insight into the fantastic history of the region as a powerful state.

Tuscany is mostly hilly or mountainous with short plains lying by the coastline, forming a harmonious but varied view. Some mountains are bare, others densely wooded. On the hilltops are isolated old villas or villages, in the valleys lie the towns and cities amongst richly cultivated fields, all their famous artistic and cultural treasures guarded within their walls. There are stretches of wild, untamed coastline alongside fashionable beach resorts with countless hotels.

The soil everywhere is richer in minerals than in other parts of the country and all manner of crops grow well. The irregular layout of the land makes the rivers twist and turn and flow fairly fast, often with disastrous results. The coastline is almost all sandy and smooth, with occasional rocky promontories. Seven lovely islands lie in the Tyrrhenian Sea – of these Elba is the largest (though it's the third largest Italian island, it's still 11 times smaller than Sicily).

The region has a fairly mild and pleasant climate, with hot, dry summers and gentle, rainy winters.

Here, as in many parts of Italy, the country folk are turning their backs on the land, and heading for the cities. This is to the advantage of many southern immigrants, who have taken over the farming activity with marked success, and even more so for the English and American families who have bought Tuscan farmhouses and villas as holiday or retirement homes. Hundreds of these properties are available for rent throughout the region.

FIRENZE & PROVINCE

Florence lies in a flat plain surrounded by smooth hills peppered with elegant villas with lovely gardens. The River Arno cuts it neatly into two, on the right bank the city spreads as far as the hills of Fiesole – the ancient Etruscan settlement dominating the plain. The old city centre is stunningly beautiful – two piazzas would be sufficient to give the city its well deserved acclaim – the Piazza del Duomo, containing the church of Santa Maria del Fiore, the Baptistry and Giotto's bell tower; and Piazza della Signoria, with its Palazzo Vecchio, Uffizi Gallery and the Loggia dei Lanzi. Apparently, since the film *A Room with a View*, more tourists than ever have flooded into the city, and many have been overcome by its loveliness and atmosphere – Florentine hospitals have been filled with swooning tourists!

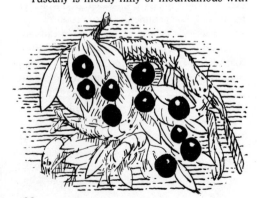

To sample Tuscany's beautiful meat dishes try *IL LATINI* in via Palchetti. At *COCO LEZZANE* in via del Parioncino, I had *cavolo nero* black cabbage, another Tuscan speciality, with my *bistecca di maiale*.

SIENA & PROVINCE

Siena is built on 3 hills at the centre of which the shell-shaped Piazza del Campo annually holds the famous Palio. This is an historical race on horseback, with the various *contrade* or family teams competing at fierce speed in traditional costume with their flags and banners.

Siena is one of the most characteristic of Tuscan towns, its palazzi and churches reminders of its great standing as a medieval power. Much of its commercial success comes from making sweetmeats: *panforte di Siena, ricciarelli* and other biscuits and pastries and dairy products. The surrounding hills favour the cultivation of vines, so that here in this province are all the major wine centres of the region: Montepulciano, Montalcino, San Gimignano, with its amazing collection of towers ('medieval skyscrapers' as a friend called them), Chiusi, and all the villages and hamlets of the Chianti hills.

AREZZO & PROVINCE

In a fertile little plain where the Arno valley joins the Chiana, Etruscan Arezzo is a thriving agricultural market town and craftwork centre, known for its small succulent hams.

The province contains the towns of Camaldoli and La Verna, set in lovely woody scenery. I found a wonderful restaurant at Anghiari with a marvellous name – it's the *LOCANDA CASTELLO DEI SORCI* (*sorci* is a dialect word for rats). The castle here dates back to the 13th century. It was inhabited in the 16th century by a gang of friars who enjoyed rather unecclesiastical habits, including robbery. The restaurant is surrounded by fabulous views of the upper Tiber valley, and the menu is fixed – but what a menu! It changes according to the day of the week. On Wednesdays you'll find *quadrucci e ceci*, a soup of tiny pasta squares cooked in a thick soup with chickpeas. *Ribollita*, a superb minestrone with a covering of onions, will be on the menu on Fridays. Here, too, you'll find roast duck, sausages and all kinds of simple and delicious dishes, their ingredients

from the adjacent farm, and everything on sale should you wish to take some away: cheese, *salumi*, wine, *prosciutto* and so on.

MASSA E CARRARA & PROVINCE

At the estuary of the Magra river lies the little province of Massa e Carrara, which includes part of Lunigiana. It takes its name from the 2 cities standing a few kilometres apart at the feet of the Apuan Alps. Massa is the area's administrative centre, and Carrara the major European centre for marble. It was to these mountains that sculptors from Michelangelo to Henry Moore would come to choose the marble for their masterpieces. Even if you're not looking for marble, these mountains are worth visiting for the tiny little restaurants like *IL MURAGLIONE* in Avenga or *LA LOCANDA DELL'ANGELO* in Ameglia, perched up among the trees with lovely views of the coastline.

LUCCA & PROVINCE

Originally founded by the Ligurian tribe, Lucca became an Etruscan and then Roman settlement. It is a really charming town on the left bank of the River Serchio. It has a marvellous old centre through which one can slowly meander, taking in the beautiful Duomo and the churches of San Michele and San Frediano. This is the major olive oil centre, so if that's what you came for you're in the right place.

Within the province is the marvellous and elegant seaside resort of Forte dei Marmi with boutiques and superb ice cream shops like *CERVINO* and *PRINCIPE* – which is also a café, and has tables set under plane trees where you can idle away the hours watching the best-dressed Italians on holiday pass you by. Forte, as it is affectionately called by those who, like me, have been coming here for several generations, also has some of the best restaurants, night clubs and discotheques in the country, like *CANNICCI*, and *LA CAPPANINA*, and the most interesting food shop you are likely to encounter along this bit of coast. Called *I PARMIGIANI*, it is run by a passionate family of gourmets from Parma, who have gathered together the very best of everything under one shop roof, and whose incredibly lovely window displays of vegetables preserved in olive oil, *salame* and other luscious wares practically drag you in off the street. Near Forte dei Marmi is Viareggio – another seaside resort, much busier and more crowded, but nonetheless privileged to have some of the country's best fish restaurants like *DA BOMBETTA, DA ROMANO* and *FOSCOLO*.

Well worth a visit in the province are the marble centre of Pietrasanta, the oil and wine town of Caponnori and the thermal spa town of Bagni di Lucca.

PISA & PROVINCE

During the Roman era and the Middle Ages, Pisa sat on a lagoon at the estuary of the Arno and was one of the most important ports of the country. In the 16th century the wealthy Marine Republic of Pisa fell, and the port slowly disappeared, buried by mud and gravel and transported downstream by the river. Nowadays, Pisa stands a few kilometres away from the coast, with the fantastic Piazza dei Miracoli at the heart. The name *miracoli* refers to the miracles of art, and there is no doubt that the Duomo, Baptistry and leaning tower are all miracles indeed, drawing in thousands of tourists.

Volterra is worth a visit, especially if you have lunch at the fabulous *RISTORANTE ETRURIA* in Piazza dei Priori, where you'll get the very best of Tuscan cooking, with dishes like *Pappardelle sulla Lepre* thick strips of pasta served with a sauce of hare, and lots of other wonderful local game. Another specially memorable dish was *cinghiale in agrodolce*, boar in sweet and sour sauce, and the *dolce di riso*, a delicious concoction of rice, eggs and milk.

LIVORNO & PROVINCE

This is a relatively recent port town, whose development came about in the 15th century when the Medici decided to convert the village which stood on this site into a vast, impregnable city with a well-equipped port and a huge arsenal. Cosimo I declared it to be a *porto franco*, free port, and as such it was a safe refuge for all kinds of adventurers and refugees. From all over Europe and the world Jews, Muslims, merchants and pirates, political refugees and runaways flowed into the city and its commercial success developed accordingly. By the 18th century

Tuscany had renounced her position of power as a maritime force – agriculture had taken over as being the most important form of commerce, but the ships and fishermen kept Livorno going with boats arriving from the Atlantic, the Orient, and other parts of the world and shipping companies set up under the Dutch, Armenian, Greek, Levantine and English flags. All this has given the local cuisine a huge variety of exotic and un-Italian specialities, of which *il cuscussu*, couscous, is the clearest example. The local fishing trade produces enough fish to satisfy the local needs, but from Livorno big motor launches with sophisticated fishing gear on board head out for the deeper and richer waters of the Atlantic to bring home enough fish to qualify for international export.

The traditional Livornese beauty, with her olive skin, very black hair, and sultry elegance, is an obvious result of the mixture of races that has taken place here, and she knows well how to make the superb dishes from the wealth of seafood available. The most famous of these is the delicious *Cacciucco Livornese*, a fish soup, which local tradition demands contains as many different fish as there are Cs in its name.

From Livorno ferries leave for Corsica and the archipelago of islands that come under its provincial umbrella. These include Elba, where Napoleon spent his exile. Perhaps it is this Napoleonic adventure which has made the customs of Elba somewhat different from those elsewhere in Tuscany. There is still a distinctive French flavour in the air here. Fish and game abound on the island – *seppie coi carciofi*, squid with artichokes, was supposed to be Napoleon's favourite dish of all, and there are many rabbit, chicken and vegetable dishes, one of the best of which is the superb tiny tender *zucchini ripieni* stuffed courgettes.

GROSSETO & PROVINCE

This is a very ancient city that has known desperate times during malaria epidemics which have swept through it time and time again from the marshy ground of the Maremma plain (nowadays the Maremma is almost completely reclaimed and cultivated). Grosseto depends largely upon the agricultural development of this plain for its success. Orbetello is a fishing centre on the coast and one of the prettiest little towns in the area, very popular with holiday makers, especially as you can catch ferries for day trips to the lovely island of Giglio, known as the place *'dove si mangia bene'* – where one eats well.

SALUMI
Salami, Sausages and Cured Meats

The *salami* of the Casentino valley are famous for being better than those from Siena – less salty and much drier. *La finocchiona* is a huge Tuscan *salame*, with large white spots of fat, and a rich, strong texture, flavoured with fennel *finocchio* seeds, and is best made in Florence or Siena. *Salame Toscano* is also more full-bodied and tasty than those from Lombardy or Emilia Romagna – no subtlety here! *Biroldi*, the blood pudding, flavoured with pinenuts, currants and spices, is also called *buristo* or *mallegato*, depending on where you are.

The local *prosciutto* has a darker meat, and a stronger, more robust taste than the one from neighbouring Emilia, and *prosciutto di cinghiale* wild boar is quite strong too.

Bacon is called *carne secca* in Tuscany, and is used to flavour many sauces.

☆☆☆☆☆☆☆☆☆☆☆☆☆☆☆☆☆☆☆☆☆☆☆☆☆☆☆☆☆☆☆☆☆☆☆☆

Abundant Advances

The endless selection of *antipasti* of various kinds is a recent innovation into Tuscan cuisine, but has become one which typifies the meal almost everywhere. What you are likely to be served is a selection of *crostini*, pieces of toasted bread, spread with a kind of pâté, made with liver and spleen, and a selection of *salumi* – *prosciutto, finocchiona, salame Toscano* – and if you are near the sea, you will also get a few stuffed mussels, some baby squid in their ink and lots of other tiny portions of seafood.

☆☆☆☆☆☆☆☆☆☆☆☆☆☆☆☆☆☆☆☆☆☆☆☆☆☆☆☆☆☆☆☆☆☆☆☆

PASTA

In this region of plenty, where somehow even the hearty rustic dishes manage to be sophisticated, there are not very many pasta shapes. However, you will find *bavette*, a kind of flat spaghetti, and *pappardelle*, very wide *tagliatelle*. Polenta is sometimes made into *gnocchi* and served with mutton stew.

Local Specialities

- *Pappardelle sulla Lepre Pappardelle* are hand-made pasta strips, thicker and wider than *tagliatelle*, and in this recipe are prepared with a simple sauce of chunks of stewed hare with tomato, celery, onion and bacon.

PESCE E FRUTTI DI MARE
Fish and Seafood

Eels, *anguille*, are cooked extensively, in many different ways, including *anguilla alla Fiorentina*, a casserole of eel with white wine and sage, *anguilla alla Fiorentina con piselli*, another casserole with peas and tomatoes, and *anguilla*

Local Specialities

- *Cacciucco* Fish soup made with a huge variety of fish, both in size and texture, cooked with *peperoncino*, garlic, wine and herbs, and served over slices of garlic bread.
- *Cieche alla Pisana* Newborn eels fried in oil and baked, covered with a mixture of breadcrumbs, eggs, *parmigiano*, and lemon juice, until golden.
- *Triglie alla Livornese* Delicious red mullet caught off the rocks and cooked simply with tomato, garlic and parsley.
- *Polpo alla Piombinese* Chopped reef octopus cooked in its own juices and plenty of *peperoncino* – eaten with no accompaniment. Usually bought from street-sellers in Piombino, where you catch the ferry to Elba.
- *Spigola all'Imperiale* Bass is marinated for several hours in wine vinegar, then boiled briefly with onion, garlic and bay leaves. Served tepid with mayonnaise.

marinata, which is eel, floured then fried and covered in spicy vinegar and left to marinate until required. *Cieche* are new-born eels, fished from the Arno in springtime. The name means 'blind', since at such a tender age they cannot yet see. *Baccalà* and *stoccafisso*, salt cod and stockfish, are both extremely popular in the inland provinces – this method of preserving good fish easily and cheaply obviously appeals to Tuscan ideals of

Waifs in the Storm

There is a lovely legend surrounding the origins of *cacciucco* about a fisherman who died at sea in a storm, leaving his widow and children in darkest despair. When hunger became unbearable, the children went out begging for food among their father's fishermen colleagues. As they were not rich either, each one gave the children a piece of fish or a handful of shrimps or shellfish to take home to mother. The woman put the ingredients together, adding all she had growing in the garden – a few herbs, garlic, and some spices from her larder.

The smell of her delicious soup pervaded all her neighbours' houses so that soon a crowd gathered to peep into the poor widow's kitchen, and so *cacciucco* was born.

This dish of such poor origins (who knows if this story is true – the soup has always been made with the cheapest and most commonly available kinds of fish) was soon to cross over into Provence, where the locals became experts in its preparation calling it *Bouillabaisse*, but it wasn't till the end of the 16th century that two of the most vital of Mediterranean ingredients (tomato and chilli) entered the scene and it was from then on that *cacciucco* finally looked like we know it today. It's best accompanied with dry red, if possible, slightly sparkling new wine.

no waste and carefully cooking good food with the least possible fuss. It is usually cooked as a casserole, with tomatoes, herbs and vegetables, *in Zimino*.

The most important fish dish of them all has to be the inimitable *cacciucco alla Livornese*. There is a huge variety of fish soups all over the country, but to my mind there is none that tastes quite like this one.

Clams *vongole* are also cooked in soups with *peperoncino*, tomatoes, wine, garlic and parsley. Red mullet *triglie* are the basis of Livorno's other speciality, *Triglie alla Livornese* in which the fish are first fried, then covered with a rich tomato sauce.

Caught in the Arno, trout are popular in the Arezzo area – *trota affogata* is the city's fish speciality. Here the trout are coated in flour and fried in oil with garlic and parsley. They are then covered in white wine and cooked through.

CARNE E CACCIA

Meat and Game

Pride of place just has to go to the *bistecca alla Fiorentina*, that enormous, thick, T-bone steak that flops over the side of your plate and should be cooked over an open fire with scented pine or juniper wood to give it that special something. A *fiorentina* can weigh up to one kilo (2 lb)! They are never cooked with oil, and are always salted at the end of cooking.

La Fiorentina

To cook this properly you need three things:
● An old fireplace or outdoor fire with a grill placed over red hot coals.
● A huge steak on the bone, tender and full of flavour as only Tuscan beef can be.
● A drop of the finest olive oil with which to caress the meat when it's cooked.

It sounds so simple, but you need art and expertise to do the dish justice.

Pork, beef, and poultry are the most popular meats, preferably cooked with the least possible fuss – no sauces, just a few herbs. Veal is used less, and lamb and mutton are practically non-existent. Especially traditional is the *arista alla Fiorentina*, a piece of pork loin with deep holes pierced into the meat, which are then stuffed with chopped rosemary, pepper and salt. The meat is either roasted or cooked on a spit. It is best cold, but can also be served hot with potatoes or vegetables cooked in the juices from the meat. Its origins go right back to when it was cooked for the Ecumenical Council of 1430 in Florence when the Greek bishops pronounced it *aristos*, which means excellent, and so it got its name.

Wild food

Rabbit *coniglio*, hare *lepre*, pheasant *fagiano*, guinea fowl *faraone*, frogs *rane* and thrush *tordo* are all popular and will be served to you all over the inland areas. *Scottiglia* is a kind of meat version of *cacciucco* – a rich stew of all kinds of meat cooked with tomatoes, wine, garlic, herbs and onion, which is served, just like *cacciucco*, on slices of toasted garlic bread. It's a traditional dish from Arezzo, and will include pork, pigeon, chicken, rabbit, veal, guinea fowl or other meats. It dates from times when friendly neighbours would all come to one house, each bringing their share of the meal to put in the pot.

Local Specialities

- *Arista* Roast loin of pork with rosemary, salt and pepper.
- *Beccaccini allo Spiedo* The spit is the kingpin of Tuscan cuisine, and in this case little snipe are roasted, accompanied by *crostini* covered with their giblets.
- *Lepre in Agrodolce* Not a common dish, but it dates back to the 16th century when Tuscan cuisine had a leaning towards the sweet/sour flavours mixed together. The hare here is cooked with pinenuts, candied peel, sugar, chocolate and vinegar.

FORMAGGIO
Cheese

With Emilia Romagna and all that *parmigiano* so close by, I don't suppose the wily Toscani ever thought they need really bother about creating cheeses of their own. However, look out for *marzolino*, a very strong-tasting *pecorino* which is made in the Chianti valley. The best one is made in Panzano. In Massa Carrara seek out the little *formagette di Zeri*, made with a mixture of cows' and ewes' milk with a distinctive milky smell.

Mucchino is a cheese made in and around Lucca, with cows' milk, using the same procedure as for *pecorino* – it's sweeter, less fatty and less flavoursome than *pecorino*. An excellent cheese from the town of Brancoli is the soft, fatty and very tasty *brancolino*. Mountain *cacciotta* as made by shepherds is made to individual recipes and is always superb. Very good local *ricotta* is also available.

FRUTTA E VERDURA
Fruit and Vegetables

Half a century ago oil and wine represented the major commerce of the region. It's inevitable but nonetheless sad that industry has taken over, and the abandoned houses, uncultivated fields and empty farms dispersed amongst the greenery of the countryside bear witness to that fact. But that's not to say that oil and wine have lost all their importance. Lucca is one of the main oil-producing centres in the country, and the Chianti hills produce wines that are world famous. The region is also rich in chestnut forests, although unfortunately there is not much demand for these today. Mushrooms are wonderful here, both in quality and quantity. The province of Pisa grows lots of vegetables, especially the traditionally Tuscan ones like all the beans and pulses (don't miss *fagiolini di Sant'Anna* – thin, knobbly and deliciously sweet runner beans which can grow to enormous lengths) and *cavolo nero* black cabbage with which a superb soup is made.

Local Specialities

- *Fagioli al Fiasco* A dish of typical Tuscan invention, in which *cannellini* beans are cooked slowly in a straw-covered wine bottle over embers. They therefore lose none of the flavour or texture, and once cooked are poured out and dressed with oil and salt and pepper.
- *Fagioli all'Uccelletto* A common accompaniment for roast meats, these are beans cooked with tomato, garlic and sage.
- *Insalata Mista* A lovely selection of the most tender, fresh, tiny-leaved lettuces.
- *Pappa al Pomodoro* Soup, eaten hot or cold, of tomatoes, bread, garlic, and good stock, cooked till smooth. It was famous in the 60s throughout Italy, thanks to a pop song that became Italy's biggest hit since *Volare*!
- *Ribollita* Arguably the most famous Tuscan soup, with countless variations. The most classic calls for green and black cabbage, cannellini beans, and bread arranged in layers. Whatever version you come across, it will always be delicious, simple but filling and tasty. The name means 'reboiled', coming from the original method of reheating the soup from the day before.

Olive groves on the doorstep

In Lunigiana, my family has always had olive groves. Just like all country family homes, those that had vineyards would also grow olives, if the terrain permitted. When my mother lived in the old family house on the hills with her parents, uncles and various other members of the family, her favourite uncle, Cesare, would take her and her brother to taste the oil at the press. For this treat, Zio Cesare would have two loaves of bread specially baked for the two children each with their initials on them – an F for my mother and an S for my uncle. Proudly carrying their bread from the family bread oven the children would follow their uncle and his two dogs, Topetto and Tommi up to the olive press where pieces of bread would be torn off the loaves and used to soak up the dribble of oil coming out of the special little hole and be tasted. Together they would spend a morning deciding which oil was worth bottling, which was the best, and so on. These simple family traditions are still going on in certain parts of the country, although sadly to a much lesser extent.

My old school was situated in an ex-olive press, and in the playground were the old grinding stones, upturned and set out in a pattern for us to play and sit on like a ready-made climbing frame. As a child I never realised what the huge wheels of stone actually were, but I had great fun on them.

Onions grow here too, and bitter turnip tops *rape amare* are popular, and so are artichokes *carciofi*, cardoons *cardi*, peas *piselli*, broad beans *fave*, celery *sedano* and there are plenty of different kinds of tomatoes.

Fruit trees grow very well so apples *mele*, pears *pere*, peaches *pesche*, plums *susine*, apricots *albicocche* and nectarines *pesche noci* are all available. In June and September black and green figs *fichi* are harvested, and at the end of the summer persimmons *kaki* grow huge and squashily juicy. The climate and fertile soil are ideal for all kinds of soft fruit: raspberries *lamponi*, myrtleberries *mirtilli*, strawberries *fragole*, blackberries *more*, medlars *nespole* – just about everything in fact.

The Mangiafagioli of Tuscany

The Tuscans are known as *Mangiafagioli* – bean-eaters. They love beans of all kinds, and cook them in every way imaginable, even in a straw-covered wine bottle. Haricot beans were introduced into Europe in the 16th century, and the fashion for eating them started in Florence with Duke of Florence, Alessandro de' Medici.

PASTICCERIA
Cakes, Biscuits and Puddings

● *Biscottini di Prato/Cantucci* These are the most more-ish biscuit ever invented. They are hard and knobbly, studded with almonds, and are dipped into glasses of sweet *vin santo* at the end of a meal. The end of a meal can last a very long time indeed!

● *Bomboloni* All over Tuscany you can sniff the scent of these wonderful doughnuts which are fried until crisp on the outside, but still soft on the inside. Sometimes thick chocolate sauce or custard is injected into the fluffy hollow centre. One is never enough! You'll find them on sale on the beach, in market squares or in special shops. Do not miss out.

● *Brighidini* Simple little cakes made with special irons that are cooked over a hot fire. Made with aniseed, flour, butter and sugar they are crisp and golden and are on sale from kiosks at village feast days or on market days.

● *Buccellato di Lucca* A very old, traditional cake from Lucca, made with bread dough to which sugar, milk, lemon, Marsala and butter are added.

Buccellato competitions are held in the surrounding countryside – sometimes they are as big as a cartwheel. At confirmations, the Godmother makes this cake and offers it to her Godchild in a public ceremony.

- *Castagnaccio* A poor man's cake this one, but nonetheless delicious. It's a fairly thick *focaccia* of chestnut flour mixed with rosemary, pinenuts, sultanas and water baked in the over and dredged with a little olive oil.
- *Cavallucci* Delectable crunchy biscuits from Siena made with walnuts, orange candied peel, aniseed and other spices.
- *Cenci* Traditionally prepared to celebrate the Berlingaccio, the last day of Carnival. They are ragged squares of light pastry fried in fat and coated with sugar.
- *Corona di San Bartolomeo* From Pistoia comes this 'crown', prepared on August 24, the saint's special day.

Traditionally children of the town would be led up to the altar wearing the crown round their necks, for a special blessing. Nowadays this has fallen into disuse, probably for reasons of hygiene. It's made with little lumps of pastry, threaded on to a piece of string with a wider medallion at the end of the chain, with a B inscribed on it.

- *Frittelle di Riso* Prepared to celebrate San Giuseppe on March 19, these delicious rice fritters are a typical example of the simple frugality of Tuscan cuisine – a frugality not born out of poverty but from a profound dislike of waste or fussy cooking.
- *Ricciarelli di Siena* Another speciality from Siena, soft, chewy, diamond-shaped almond cakes with a rice paper coating.
- *Sticciata alla Fiorentina* Yeasty buns flavoured with Marsala, orange blossom water and aniseed. Perfect for breakfast or teatime.
- *Torta di Riso* From Siena again comes this thick rich eggy rice cake with pistachios, candied fruit, walnuts and vanilla.
- *Zuccotto* A delicious dessert of a sponge cake casing with a creamy chocolate flavoured filling with candied fruit, almonds and hazelnuts. The modern version has a filling of ice cream and is just as wonderful.

VINO
Wine

So much of such excellent quality is produced in this region that it's hard to know just where to begin. Wherever you are, look out for the signs reading *Enoteca* or *Cantina* – here you will be able to buy a wide selection of locally-produced wines and if you're lucky, you may be able to taste some of them.

SPECIAL RED
- *Brunello di Montalcino* produced exclusively from Brunello di Montalcino vineyards in the area around the lovely historic town of Montalcino in the province of Siena. The experts say the longer it is aged the better – even up to a hundred years. It is intensely dark and ruby red but tends towards garnet as it ages. It has a dry, austere, velvety flavour, and an intense, instantly recognisable bouquet. The *normale* is aged for two years, the *riserva* for three, and the *riserva speciale* for four. Perfect with roast meat, and high quality game dishes.
- *Vino nobile di Montepulciano* Produced with Mammolo grapes in the Siena province round Montepulciano, it was described by poet Francesco Redi in the 17th century as being the 'king of all wines'. It is the wine that marries best of all with *Bistecca alla Fiorentina* but is also good

Panforte di Siena

This is a marvellous cake of candied fruit, nuts and spices which keeps for months. It's very rich and filling, and has become a traditional Christmas speciality. Its origins are ancient indeed – some say it was first prepared as far back as the 12th century, according to the interpretation of a verse from Dante's *Divina Commedia* in which, in Inferno, a certain 'Niccolò' mentions something about rich clove cakes – it is thought that Dante was referring to the Sienese traveller Niccolò Salimbeni who, from one of his many voyages to the Orient, brought back bread loaves that were 'honeyed and peppered', scented with cloves – from which you can easily recognise the ancestors of the modern-day *Panforte di Siena*. There is another version, called *Panforte Margherita*, created in honour of Queen Margherita of Savoy, during a visit to Siena. it was made by Galgano Parenti, owner of the oldest *Panforte* factory in the city. You will still see the name *Parenti* inscribed on the box of the *Panforte* you buy today. The box is worth the expense on its own – colourful and octagonal, it is easily packed, and makes a terrific present.

with other red or white meats, particularly roasts. It's a robust, full-bodied ruby red wine, with a bouquet of sweet violets.

RED WINE

I will list the eight most important Chianti wines that you will doubtless encounter. All of them are an excellent buy:

- *Chianti Carmignano* - *Chianti Classico*
- *Chianti Colli Aretine* - *Chianti Colli Florentini* - *Chianti Colli Senesi* - *Chianti Colline Pisane* - *Chianti Montalbano* - *Chianti Rufina*

The differences between all these are subtle and fine, and I wish you much pleasure in discovering them for yourself. They are all excellent table wines, with the Chianti Classico being perhaps the most full in body and flavour.

WHITE WINE

- *Vernaccia di San Gimignano* A very ancient wine, drunk by Dante and Boccaccio. The original Vernaccia wines are reputed to have been brought to the little town in the Siena province in the 13th century. It has a delicate golden yellow colour, an amazing bouquet of flowers, and a light harmonious and slightly bitter flavour. Undoubtedly

one of the country's major white wines, it is perfect as an aperitif, or as a table wine with fish. Also can be drunk with antipasti, soups and white meat dishes.

- *Pitigliano* A straw-coloured wine with a delicious dry flavour. After 2 or 3 years it improves considerably, making it an excellent table wine, with fish dishes or antipasti.
- *Elba Bianco* This fabulous slightly fruity white wine is produced on the iron-rich wine terraces of the lovely island of Elba, some of which are high above sea level.

NB: From the island, you can also find *Elba Rosso* which is an excellent coral red table wine. On the island itself, look out for *Aleatico di Portoferraio*, a delicious sweet wine for dessert, and the unusual *Elba Spumante*, a sparkling white champagne-type wine.

BEVANDE
Drinks

I discovered a list of extraordinary cordials and liqueurs which my mother tells me were in frequent household use when she was growing up in Tuscany, so some of them must still be around.

- *Ratafia* These long-life syrups came originally from France, but became very popular throughout the region. They are alcoholic and keep very well – they can be made with coffee, *Ratafia di Caffè*, cherries, *Ratafia di Visciole*, or Muscatel grapes, *Ratafia d'Uva Moscatella*.
- *Liquore Perfetto Amore* Made with ripe *cedri*, the Italian version of limes with a very thick knobbly skin, this is a purple liqueur of mostly lime peel, acquavite and cochineal. It is left to mature for a week before being mixed with sugar and water, then it is left to macerate again before being strained and bottled.
- *Rosolio Bianco di Cannella* A liqueur made with cinnamon, sugar and alcohol. It is also made with vanilla instead of cinnamon to make *Rosolio Bianco di Vaniglia*.
- *Certosino* this is the oldest herb liqueur known. The first to make it were the friars of the Certosa of Florence, and it can still be bought in various convents and monasteries. It contains lemon balm, juniper berries, hyssop, angelica seeds and roots, coriander, spearmint, fresh lemon rind, cinnamon, mace, nutmeg and cloves, mixed with pure alcohol and left to mature for

---

Bosoms
for a
Poorly Prince

Latte di Vecchia The story behind this weird drink is one of my very favourites. The son of the Granduca Ferdinando III was delicate and frail. At the age of 17, after a severe illness, it was suggested by the court doctor that he should undergo a cure of 'women's milk'. All the most beautiful wet nurses of Florence came to court to offer him their full breasts from which he suckled like a baby. The story got out, despite all the understandable secrecy, and although poor Leopoldo was mercilessly teased, he was also much envied for having all those 'gifts from God' at his disposal. For those who were not able to get hold of real 'mothers' milk', they invented a substitute called *Latte di Vecchia* – old woman's milk. It consisted of alcohol, mixed with orange blossom water, sugar, benzoine tincture and vanilla.

Just a
Pink Liqueur

Alchermes is a cordial, with deep, mysterious and extremely old origins. Alcohol was first distilled in the 13th century, and thought to be the answer to eternal youth. In the 15th century it was first made palatable and many believe that this was the original *Alchermes*. I unearthed a recipe for *Alchermes* as my mother used to drink it, and which was kept in the house to revive swooning ladies or poorly children, though nowadays is used mainly in cake-making. It called for: live silk worms with their cocoons, rose water, apple juice from red apples, cochineal, sugar, aloe wood, cinnamon, ground lapis lazuli and ground pearls, mixed together and left to mature, then strained and bottled! Alternative additions include ground amber, musk, syrup and sandalwood. Fragments of emeralds, sapphires, topaz, rubies and a stone called hyacinth, along with red roses, earth, ground deer horn, red and white coral, ivory, lime syrup and various seeds went into *Alchermes Confezione Jacintina*, a more elaborate preparation. *Alchermes Liquido* was common in the 18th century, and consisted of several secret ingredients mixed with acquavite, coriander, cloves, cinnamon, mace, cochineal and yellow lime peel and apple juice left to mature for several days, then strained. It was used to cure 'weak stomach troubles', and was sold by Florentine chemists at vast expense – hence the secret ingredients. There are many other recipes for *Alchermes* which only vary slightly, but basically it's a sweet, spicy, syrupy pink liqueur.

one month, after which sugar is added to make it syrupy.

• *Sciroppo d'Agreste* Once used all over the Chianti area this is a syrup made with unripe grapes which is excellent for quenching the thirst on hot summer days. It is made very simply by fermenting the juice of unripe grapes with sugar. A vinegar, *Aceto d'Agreste*, is also made by using the juice of unripe grapes.

WORTH TAKING HOME

I go home to Tuscany each and every year, and the selection of things I bring back to England hasn't varied in thirty years. It used to be possible to bring *prosciutto* and *salame* and sausages back, but these days there are certain rules that make it illegal in some cases – please do check first. However, chestnut flour *farina di castagne*, always goes into my suitcase, as does a plait of local little garlic bulbs, a couple of strings of red onions, a few bags of dried pulses for reproducing at home delicious Tuscan soups, olive oil, *parmigiano* and plenty of wine.

If we take a trip to Siena we load up with *Panforte*, *Ricciarelli* and a selection of other pastries and sweetmeats. If we go to San Gimignano we stock up with a few bottles of Vernaccia, and some of the delightful pottery made in the town.

Every year we take a boat trip into neighbouring Liguria for lunch at the Cinqueterre, so we take home at least a bottle of the Vino delle Cinqueterre.

Bags of *Brighidini* make light presents to bring home, but as they are totally crumbly, they must be packed with care. A *caciotta Toscana* is always a good buy, because being quite mild, everyone will probably like it. Don't forget some *vin santo*, and a big bag of *Cantucci* biscuits to dip into it – the easiest dessert there is!

For self-caterers I urge you to follow the traditions of real Tuscan cuisine, and cook out of doors as much as possible – grill and barbeque all the succulent meat, sausages and fish of this remarkably rich region, so as to get the full measure of the flavours and superb textures. Do make sure you taste the lovely local vegetables – the extraordinary *fagiolini di Sant'Anna*, the unique *cavolo nero* and the wonderful selection of salads.

8

Sober and Joyful

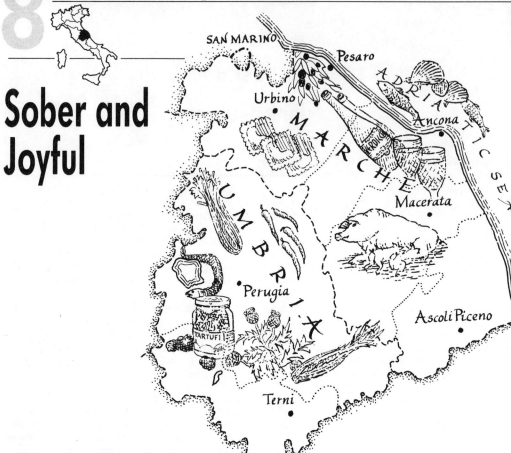

SAN MARINO

Pesaro

Urbino

MARCHE

ADRIATIC SEA

Ancona

Macerata

UMBRIA

Perugia

Ascoli Piceno

Terni

These two adjoining areas are little known at least to foreign tourists, and both of them remain peaceful, unfashionable and relaxing. But while landlocked Umbria stays tucked into the very heart of Italy, Le Marche has the sea, throwing herself outwards from the ports of Ancona, Porto Recanati and Pesaro.

In both regions you will discover gentle, rolling hills and smooth mountains, plenty of greenery and miracles of medieval architecture in towns like Urbino, Perugia, Iesi and many others. In both regions you'll find delicious food and generous hearty portions, full-bodied red wines and light refreshing whites. Here you'll be able to walk and admire the scenery without the fuss and thunder of crowds – and you will want to treasure the memories and return.

Umbria Verde

Cypresses, endless rows of cypresses that stand like sentinels in the magical light of this soft landscape. Though little known, Umbria is much loved, and the clever visitor will make time to come here and linger in the tranquillity of its beautiful places. The first thing that strikes you is just how green everything is – *Umbria Verde* they call it, because wherever you turn there are woods, vineyards, fields, meadows and orchards. There is plenty of water, not least the Tiber, which flows south straight through the region towards Rome, fed by many tributaries. With Lake Trasimeno too, the largest lake in this part of the country, there is no lack of fresh water, and fish abound.

The climate here is unaffected by the sea, so there is a tendency towards cold sharp winters, and extremely hot, still and humid summers.

Pigs and truffles

In gastronomic terms Umbria has 2 important contributions to make to the world of Italian food.

The first is the unique and delicious flavour of the tough black truffle that grows profusely here and is chopped into substantial chunks to be added to just about everything from scrambled eggs to pizza. In Umbria *il tartufo nero* is not treated with any real regard for its value or rarity – the Umbrians use it almost like other people use parsley or potatoes.

Umbria's other culinary claim to fame is its traditional ability in the pork butchering trade, which centres mainly round the city of Norcia. In Italian the words *norcino* and *norcineria* have since come to mean butcher and butcher's shop when referring to pork, sausages or other pork *salumi*.

Pork and truffles then, are at the basis of this region's cuisine, and both are used with great expertise and nonchalance. It's a simple cuisine with no secrets, and no pretence to be anything other than very good, basic, honest cooking, using the best of the locally grown and produced ingredients. And I have discovered another Umbrian speciality: its olive oil is green and smooth and sublime like few others I have tasted. These olive groves that cling on to the rocky mountains are more silvery than olive trees I've seen anywhere, and the oil they produce is well worth finding and keeping locked away for special occasions.

Heart of the Country

It would be easy to dismiss this little region – it hasn't got so many of the attractions which the visitor often seeks in a Mediterranean country, but you'd be hard pushed to find a summer theatre more exciting than the one held in Spoleto in June and July, and lucky to find a more beautiful university than Perugia, which offers so many courses to foreign students. There are many religious sanctuaries dotted amid the rolling greenery, and castles speaking of times of rivalry and battles now long past. Umbria is in many ways the heart of the country, and not just geographically.

PERUGIA & PROVINCE

The fascinating university city of Perugia rises up on a hilltop which dominates the Tiber valley. There are 3 very distinct faces to the city – Etruscan, medieval and modern. It was a flourishing commercial centre in the Middle Ages, and

you can feel that atmosphere as you wander round the winding backstreets. In contrast to the beautiful medieval and Renaissance buildings the new factories producing mainly sweets (especially chocolate) seem naked and cold.

You can buy superb *pecorino*, *grana* and *ricotta* from Bruno Cappellini's shop in the via dei Priori. The best *salumeria* in town, for *salumi di Norcia* is *CORRADI* in the most characteristic street in the whole town, Le Scalette di Sant'Ercolano.

In Scheggino, near Perugia, at the *TRATTORIA DEL PONTE*, you can taste *gamberetti del nera*, freshwater shrimps caught in the Nera River, and served *al verde* in a green sauce. Try to go there, you'll thank me for the tip. Gourmets and lorry drivers flock there in droves, to have the marvellous fresh trout from the river flowing so close.

For another fishy experience in this area, go to Isola Maggiore, in Lake Trasimeno. There's a restaurant called *SAURO* where every day the man of the house goes fishing for his customers' lunch. When he can't catch anything, his wife Lina gets dreadfully upset and forces herself, tearfully, to serve you land food instead. If Sauro has been lucky, you'll get carp *carpa*, eel *anguilla*, perch *persica*, or the mysterious lake fish, *pesce di lago*, which remains anonymous – served either on their own or in sauces on pasta or on vegetables. This island is a fabulous place to go for the day – the only people living here are a few fishermen and women who embroider what I can only call miracles – especially since I can't sew to save my life.

To the east of Perugia you'll find Assisi, the *città santuario*, holy city, which will give you an eerie feeling on first seeing it. It's completely intact and unspoiled, just as it would have been in the year it was consecrated – 1253.

On the plain below Assisi is Bastia, an active market town with flourishing produce tumbling out at you from shop windows and market stalls. At the far end of the Valle Umbra, under *la montagna santa* the holy mountain, once inhabited by hermits and anchorites, is the beautiful city of Spoleto. Here the food is characterised by the use of fresh herbs, especially marjoram, which are only very lightly cooked to retain their strong flavour.

Near the border with Le Marche along the via Flaminia is Norcia, famous for both its black truffles and the pigs who freely roam the fields.

Also black, they are turned into sausages and *salami* better than you've ever tasted elsewhere in Italy.

TERNI & PROVINCE

Terni is one of the very few Umbrian towns that has not sought a hilltop on which to exist. It lies in a dell crossed by the Nera River, surrounded by one of the most important industrial areas in central Italy. All the electricity required for this hive of activity is provided by the waterfall *La Cascata delle Marmore* created by the Romans.

To the north of Terni are the two mineral water spas called Acquasparta and Sangemini, the latter producing the most expensive and special of all the mineral waters you can buy. It's the one given to new-born babies, mums-to-be and invalids. The list of chemical ingredients and specifications is longer on this than on any other label. Both these spas are very well-equipped for 'taking the waters' and thus, in theory, making yourself feel really healthy.

The other main town of this province is Orvieto, which couldn't be a bigger contrast to Terni. Built on top of a steep, flat-topped hill, Orvieto is easy to find, overlooking the main Rome-Florence *autostrada*.

As modern and industrial as Terni is, that's how medieval Orvieto is. It's absolutely delightful, with narrow streets, beautiful churches and lots of excellent *trattorie*. Don't be put off by the very unartistic doorway of *MORINO'S* in via Garibaldi – it doesn't mean that the food will also be irreverent in this *città d'arte*. Once inside you'll be guaranteed the best of local cuisine, cooked with love and care, and served with classic politeness and charm. The specialities of the house naturally include black truffles, but also memorable is the *Sella di vitello con funghi porcini* saddle of veal with *porcini* sauce.

Larder in the well

In Orvieto is the incredible St Patrick's Well, dug right into the hill – actually the remains of a dead volcano – and built with shallow steps so that mules and donkeys could carry panniers down to the storage space at the bottom. Apart from being a clever way of keeping food fresh, it was built in the 16th century to provide water and protection and sufficient food for the population should they come under siege.

Orvieto sits right in the middle of a wine-producing area and has its own delicious dry and refreshing white wine that carries the town's name – just what you want when you've climbed the 248 steps up from the well.

Two towns worth visiting if you have shopping in mind are Amelia, rightfully famous for its figs, wonderful both fresh and in fig jam, *marmellata di fichi*, and Narni, a stunning medieval town set right in the middle of an olive grove. Both have excellent daily markets and good food and wine shops.

SALUMI

Salami, Sausages and Cured Meats

The *salumi* of Norcia of course are the very best you can buy in this part of Italy. *Salsicce* sausages come in various kinds, and are soft, moist and very tasty. You can even buy them preserved in olive oil so that they don't dry out.

The very best *prosciutto* comes from the mountains, *prosciutto di montagna*. There is also an uncured version baked in the oven and served hot called *prosciutto cotto al forno*.

Local Specialities

• *Torta sul Testo* The perfect companion to local *prosciutto*, this *torta*, rather like a pizza, is made with flour and water, and cooked on red-hot stones.

Lots and lots of different kinds of *salame* – mostly home-made to individual recipes, with only slight variations on the theme. However, the ancient *salame mazzafegato*, made with pork liver, pinenuts, candied orange peel, raisins and sugar, bypasses all the rules and stands out on its own like an Umbrian medieval town on a hilltop.

With all the pigs being used for *salame*, *lardo* lard is used a great deal as the basis for sauces. It is chopped with garlic and herbs to form a *battuto* to which other ingredients are added.

PASTA

Spaghetti in general are very popular throughout the region, their sauces using the best of local ingredients, homely, delicious, no-fuss dishes that satisfy and are not full of things that are 'bad for you'. The delicious dish of spaghetti with truffles is repeated over and over again in local *trattorie*, but personally I'll never tire of it. It is a simple dish, but actually very difficult to prepare properly – it only takes an extra bit of garlic, a slightly rancid bit of truffle, or a minute's too much cooking time for the entire thing to be spoiled.

Spaghetti are also served with asparagus *asparagi*, or a simple bacon sauce *col rancetto* which is very similar to *spaghetti all'amatriciana* as eaten in the Abruzzi and very popular round Rome.

Stringozzi are hand-made hollow spaghetti made with a very thick, coarse dough, using hand-milled grain so as to retain that particular flavour of fresh wheat.

PESCE E FRUTTI DI MARE
Fish and Seafood

As this is a landlocked region all the local fish is provided by the many rivers and lakes. All over Umbria you'll find trout *trota* served in a thousand and one different ways, including with truffles and wine.

CARNE E CACCIA
Meat and Game

Lamb *agnello* crops up a lot on restaurant menus, and at home too. Veal *vitello* is excellent here, and widely eaten. But pork rules the meat menus in Umbria.

If you've ever been to the Castelli Romani area, you'd imagine *porchetta* suckling pig to be originally from Lazio. Actually it is native to this region, where the black pigs seen running wild in the fields, eating acorns and mushrooms, are so exceptionally good to eat. After all, it is the

Umbrians who have the reputation for knowing just what to do with pork meat. You'll also find guinea fowl *faraona*, duck *anatra* and chicken *pollo* taking their place in the local specialities.

Game provides some interesting dishes too, and in autumn pheasant *fagiano*, pigeons *piccioni* and thrush *tordi* will be found in casseroles or roasted.

All other types of meat, steaks, chops and so on, whether they're beef, kid, lamb, or pork, are often simply grilled *alla griglia* with salt and pepper and a squeeze of lemon juice.

FORMAGGIO
Cheese

Locally prepared ewes' milk *pecorino* comes in various forms – very piquant, sweet, fresh, matured, for grating or for slicing. Otherwise cheese doesn't seem to figure very much traditionally, and is hardly used in cooking. Who needs cheese when you've got black truffles instead?

FRUTTA E VERDURA
Fruit and Vegetables

In general terms, not very much of it, but what there is will be very good. That's the way it is in Umbria. Land here is divided up into small sectors, mostly worked by tenant farmers, so the farming methods tend to be rather old-fashioned,

Local Speciality

- *Minestra di farro* One of the most common of the local peasant dishes, it's a soup of semolina, which is made tastier than usual thanks to the addition of a meaty ham bone.

and produce only enough to feed small numbers. This in itself is a very good thing, as it means agriculture has not been turned into a major industry. Fruit and vegetables are still mostly grown organically, not because of some cranky idea, but because that's just the way they've always done it.

Grain grows everywhere and is the most common crop. The lush green valleys produce beans *fagioli*, peas *piselli*, onions *cipolle*, and the celery *sedano* from Trevi is well known. Olive groves and vineyards produce small quantities of oil and wine, but they are much sought after for their excellence. The most important vegetable is of course the spectacular black truffle *tartufo nero*, whose season lasts from Christmas until the end of March, with a peak at Carnival time.

White truffles can also be found, especially near Gubbio but in smaller numbers. Cardoons *cardi*, *gobbi* which, incidentally are my favourite vegetable (like delicious artichokes) are grown and cooked a great deal here – best of all in dishes where they are layered in lieu of pasta, and cooked in the oven, *cardi al forno*, *pasticcio di cardi*. The figs *fichi* of Amelia are absolutely delicious.

Buying Black Magic

When you buy truffles you must smell each one carefully, and choose slowly. The most famous local truffles come from Norcia or Spoleto, and are offered for sale between Christmas and March. If the season is a good one, the very best time to buy them is during Carnival time, when the truffle reaches its peak, and is at its most tasty and heavily perfumed. In other months truffles are really not worth having, and you'd be better off buying them in tins.

PASTICCERIA
Cakes, Biscuits and Puddings

Umbria has few specialities. On the whole they are simple country-style cakes and pastries made with few ingredients, and not a tuft of whipped cream in sight.

- *Birbanti* Light, fluffy, golden buns with pine nuts and orange rind for flavour – traditionally baked in a bread oven.
- *Ciaramicola* A wonderful meringue-coated *focaccia*, flavoured with the liqueur *Alchermes*, and decorated with coloured almond sweets.
- *Cicerchiata* A round cake with a hole in the middle, made to celebrate carnival. Deep-fried dough, pine nuts, candied fruit and almonds are rolled in honey and moulded into a shape.
- *Pan nociato* A speciality from Todi, which consists of a kind of bread, containing *pecorino* and raisins, which is baked wrapped in vineleaves, walnuts, cloves and red wine.
- *Pan pepato* A traditional 'cake' prepared at harvest time in the provinces of Spoleto and Foligno. It's very hard, like a really crusty rock cake, with bits of chocolate, candied fruit, nuts and honey mixed into the dough.
- *Pinoccate* A speciality of Perugia, prepared for Christmas and sold wrapped in coloured paper. Only three ingredients plus water: sugar, pine nuts and rice paper hosts.
- *Pizza dolce* A country cake in which you can really taste the flavour of the olive oil, the freshly laid eggs and all the love and tradition that has gone into the making of it. Served at country festivities.
- *Serpentone delle monache cappuccine* As the name suggests, a speciality of the nuns of the capucine convent in Perugia. Shaped like a snake, it is an envelope of plain pastry, richly filled with dried fruit.

VINO
Wine

It is generally thought that Umbria's wine explosion is yet to begin – they are very good at making wine here, and enjoy experimenting. Few other regions can boast of having such ideal conditions for growing so many kinds of wine grapes, from Cabernet to Traminer to Nebbiolo to Pinot and

Chardonnay – they all thrive beautifully in Umbria's climate. Only 3 wines of any real note so far, but they can be exceptionally good.

• *Colli del Trasimeno* Can be red or white. The red version is garnet-coloured with a bouquet of violets and a smooth, harmonious flavour. Very good table wine, especially with light roasts or egg and vegetable dishes. The white version is straw-coloured, with a delicate bouquet and flavour. Perfect with all freshwater fish or *antipasti*.

• *Orvieto* There used to be a slightly sweet version of this lovely wine which was perfect for drinking with the local pastries, but it seems to be disappearing nowadays. Some of the private vineyards where wine is made just for family drinking do still produce it in very small quantities. The dry, pale, clear version is very well known, and is refreshing and delicious with fish or salads.

• *Torgiano* This wine used to be very well known in medieval Umbria, and has come back into vogue in recent times. It is produced in the province of Perugia. The red version is a brilliant red ruby wine, one sip and you know you're drinking a really exceptional wine of excellent breeding. To be drunk with rare game, or roast meat dishes – including pork. The white version is another pale golden wine with a slightly fruity flavour – perfect with various local specialities like *porchetta in bianco* roast pork or *antipasti* with fish or vegetables.

I tasted a delicious and relatively new red wine called *San Giorgio di Torgiano*, which was a marriage between Rubesco and a tiny proportion of Cabernet Sauvignon – the effect was stunning. This sort of wine marriage-service is carried out all over the region with great success – I predict great things to come in the next few years.

BEVANDE
Drinks

In a region where religion figures so strongly you would naturally expect to find *vin santo*. This is a delicious end-of-a-meal amber-coloured nectar into which you can dip biscuits and let the conversation linger on. It comes in two versions, *amabile* fruity, and *dolce* sweet. *Solleone* is amber and dry, and makes an amazing aperitif.

WORTH TAKING HOME

Though fresh truffles should be eaten as soon as possible, you can prolong the pleasure with tinned ones, or even truffle purée in a tube. The marvellous olive oil, especially that flavoured with garlic, sage, or basil, home-made in the area around Assisi and Corciano is on sale at the *OSTERIA DELL'OLMO* just outside Perugia.

Chocolates from Perugia, either the well-known *Baci* or *torrone di cioccolato*, *nocciolato*, *cremini*, or *pralinati*.

A bottle of *Orvieto*, *vin santo*, or *Solleone*, the very dry, amber-coloured aperitif wine.

SAGRE E FESTE
Festivals

Spello, in Perugia province, holds the *Sagra della Bruschetta*, a garlic toast festival, on the last Sunday in March.

LE MARCHE – Huge portions and merry-making

The Umbrian is a steady, sensible fellow, not prone to flights of fancy, or sudden decisions. Umbrian cuisine so well illustrates the personality of the people – good hearty dishes, perfectly in tune with the passing seasons and perfectly balanced according to requirements. Le Marche is a place where laughter and music flow – they like to dance, sing, eat and drink and are merry – so their dishes are always stuffed and drowned in wine. Everything is stuffed – chicken stuffed with olives, olives stuffed with minced chicken, and the whole thing merrily swamped in a good dousing of wine.

Le Marche is a lovely region, tucked away between Emilia Romagna, Tuscany, Umbria, Lazio and the Abruzzi, with a fabulous stretch of the Adriatic coast. In a little pocket of land between the border with Emilia Romagna lies the tiny republic of San Marino.

The reason for the plural name derives from its Roman Empire days when the three Marquisates of Fano, Camerino and Ancona were ruled by independent administrators under the general rule of the Emperor. They now form a single region under the collective name.

The *Marchigiani* have a reputation for being big eaters, and for being the kind of house guest who takes root in your spare room and refuses to budge, eating you out of the house in the process.

The landscape here is partly mountainous, with a long rolling slope leading right down to the shoreline. It's as though a gigantic rake had been pulled from the mountain tops to the sea. Gorges turn to valleys with tiny farming communities, ancient military fortresses, abbeys and medieval or modern towns scattered about the hilltops. The landscape is green and lush with cultivated fields, open green countryside, orchards and olive groves, vineyards and mulberry bushes. The hills come almost right down to the water's edge, leaving just a thin strip of real plain.

The coastline is perfection, straight and smooth, sandy beaches alternating with pebbles, and one single promontory, *il Conero*, where the port of Ancona (Greek for elbow) is situated. This 'elbow' has a direct influence on the climate, which is affected by winds. North of the Conero, they suffer from cold winters, south of it the climate is much milder. The whole region is affected by the Bora Nera, the cold dry wind which here becomes damp and cold after crossing the Adriatic, and pounds this region with the worst it's got.

Head for the Hills

The coast is busy and flourishing, drawing people from the enchanting mountain villages and towns, leaving them practically deserted. For me the real beauty lies in the forgotten hills and mountains. At the most you'll meet an old charabanc of tourists on a day trip to San Marino, and otherwise you will discover complete peace and quiet, stunning views and lots of lovely little villages to explore – with a marvellous *trattoria* on nearly every main square. They are extremely keen on eating well in these parts, so whatever else may happen to you, you won't go hungry!

There is a noticeable division between seashore and mountains – particularly when it comes to cooking. I noticed the difference between the two types of cuisine much more obviously here than other places with a similar layout. There is still an underlying influence of the 18th-century Austrian occupation, and of the specialities brought home by ships that sailed from Ancona to Yugoslavia, Greece and beyond since the port was first founded by Trajan. There is *strudel* at Christmas time, and sweet milk dumplings, *gnocchi dolci di latte*, flavoured with cinnamon and Parmesan, and, like in much Greek cooking, olives are often served with the ubiquitous lamb.

Above all in Le Marche the enormous portions are what characterize the cuisine, along with plenty of good cheer and fun. Be sure you're hungry when you sit down to eat in these parts!

ANCONA & PROVINCE

Ancona was an important city during the Holy Roman Empire, and later was a flourishing maritime republic. Today it is one of the most active Adriatic ports, and represents the commercial and industrial centre of the entire region. Sadly, much of the city's cultural heritage was destroyed during earthquakes in 1972.

Inland, smack in the centre of the greenest, most fertile, and picturesque area of the region, stands Iesi – home of the delightful Verdicchio wine. It is a charming medieval town of yellow stone which rises up proudly on its hills, surrounded by the strong battlements of the 14th-century city wall that binds it.

PESARO & URBINO & PROVINCE

I approached the province of Pesaro and Urbino from the hills, down the via Flaminia Vecchia which winds its way to Fano. I found a tiny little rather scruffy village, completely off the beaten track, called Calcinelli where I was amazed to discover as wonderful a restaurant as *LA POSTA VECCHIA*. The *salumi* we began our meal with were mostly home-cured, delicious *salame* sliced thickly, and greasy but tasty *prosciutto* served in chunks. These were followed by delicious truffle soufflé and roast pigeon with plenty of the ever-present olives. To end the meal the inevitable fresh sweet *pecorino* cheese, and sweet hard almond biscuits *cantucci* to dip in the delicious sweet wine. In all the little towns in this province – Fiorenzuola di Focara, Gabicce Monte and others, the main and best restaurants are in the central village square, and all have the same

things in common – friendly family-run service, local produce and a well-chosen wine selection. Huge portions add to making them definitely the kind of places where you like to linger on well into the afternoon.

The city of Pesaro is situated on the short area of plain formed by the estuary of the Foglia river. To the north of the city the coastal strip of Romagna stops by the first hills of the Marche, the imposing rock of Gradara and the slightly smaller Gabicce Monte. I decided to climb the latter, to look at the view, and found a lovely restaurant called *IL GROTTINO*, where all the best locally caught fish is cooked simply and carefully by Irzio and his charming wife. The amazing view from their windows simply makes everything taste even better.

The little city of Urbino is isolated in the centre of the region, lying on the slopes of two hills with a view sweeping from the Apennines right down to the sea. It is rare to find such a wealth of cultural heritage and beauty concentrated into such a small space. This is a fairy-tale town – a mass of turrets and archways, balconies and tiny piazzas, sloping alleys, domed churches and tall medieval buildings that are as beautiful as they are imposing. It ought to be put in a glass case and tucked away somewhere. Yet within its walls life carries on normally. Will the children of Urbino ever really know how fortunate they are to grow up with this visual feast before their eyes?

MACERATA & PROVINCE

On a spine between the valleys of Chienti and Potenza, Macerata spills out beyond its 14th-century walls, its new suburbs are green and pretty with lush gardens, Civitanova Marche and Porto Recanati are situated on the coastline – they are both fishing ports and seaside resorts of some importance, while their inland counterparts sit up in the hills – Recanati and Civitanova Alta.

I'd heard about the *Circolo Enogastronomico* (wine and gastronomy club) that had its centre somewhere near here, and eventually tracked it down to Montanello – a small town not far from Macerata, in the restaurant called *FLORIANI*. Apart from being a centre where members can taste and experiment with antique recipes discovered in mouldy old textbooks, or out of family albums and scrapbooks, it turned out to be an innovative and original establishment, set in an idyllic situation between olive groves and vineyards, where the pursuit of 'real' Marchigian cooking is carried out with smiling passion. I tasted the local *grappa* for the first time – it is flavoured with aniseed and wild fennel and was absolutely delicious, and the house wine (*Villa Magna Montanello*) was really superb. The olive oil also bore the *Villa Magna* label – so telling me it was home-made. It was a marvellous experience, particularly exciting to find that people care to this extent about their traditional dishes.

ASCOLI PICENO & PROVINCE

Ascoli, the ancient capital of the Piceni tribe, stands on a peak where the Tronto and Castellano rivers cross – at the feet of the Sibillini mountains. The whole city is built with Travertino stone, similar to marble, which makes this place particularly beautiful. You get a true impression of the mountainous aspect of the region from here. Ascoli is particularly renowned for the wonderful dish of stoned and stuffed huge green olives.

San Benedetto del Tronto seems to have cast its ancient traditions to the winds – it is a chaotic modern seaside town with a wonderful climate, proved by the fabulous lines of swaying palms that continue along the seafront all the way to the other resort of Porto d'Ascoli. It is an important fishing town, but the fishing is not limited to the local coastal waters – boats that leave here are equipped with electronic equipment enabling them to go after shoals of sardines, mackerel and other fish which live further out to sea, and they have packaging and freezing facilities on board. Some boats go as far as the Atlantic from here.

Travelling along the via Salaria you will discover Acquasanta Terme. This spa was used by the Romans as a place to come and restore their health. The springs yield delicious mineral water designed to improve your skin and rid the body of most common ailments from arthritis to varicose veins, heart problems to kidney stones.

SALUMI

Salami, Sausages and Cured Meats

According to the locals they are the best in the entire country. I wouldn't go quite so far, but they really are very good. The locally cured ham is not cut into slices as elsewhere, but chopped into nice hearty chunks for lengthy chewing. *Salame* is also very good, and generally speaking all the *salumi* have a good hearty home-made feel about them. All will be served as *antipasti* along with handfuls of olives and good crusty bread. The further inland you go, the tastier and more appetising the *salumi* become.

PASTA

In Le Marche everything gets stuffed. The most special of all the local pasta dishes is the amazing *Vincisgrassi*. It is the most triumphant of all the dishes the region calls its own, and you must not

---

Local Specialities

- *Lasagne Incassettate* First cousin of the Bolognese version, which is called *lasagne pasticciate*, it's a dish of layers of green *lasagne* with a filling of minced beef, chicken, plenty of grated Parmesan, shaved truffles and a lot of butter.

---

miss it. Indeed, cook this for your next dinner party and I personally guarantee your guests will still be talking about it in a year's time.

It was named after the Austrian general Windisch-Gratz, who was even more fond of it than I am. An 18th-century recipe book says you 'prepare a very thick bechamel sauce and add to it diced ham and black truffles, add plenty of cream and boil the whole thing. Alternate layers of lasagne, cut into small squares, with this sauce, adding a good deal of butter and *parmigiano* as you go. Then bake in the oven.' My recipe was given to me by a full-blooded Marchigiana, and it is rather different from the above, but you get the general picture don't you? It is very delicious if not exactly light!

In the area round Urbino, they make a large version of *tortellini* called *tortelli*, which are filled with a mixture of vegetables and meat, and the dressing is always a wonderful meat sauce.

PESCE E FRUTTI DI MARE

Fish and Seafood

The region steadily holds third place after Sicily and Emilia Romagna in the national stakes for the amount of fish caught in its waters.

All manner of delicious fresh fish is caught and cooked along this delightful coastline with its perfect fishing waters. Everything from mussels *cozze* to sole *sogliola* to prawns *gamberetti* to squid *seppie* and cod *merluzzo*. *Garagoli* are delicious shellfish whose shell resembles an ice cream cone. They are extremely tasty, and in season only in May and June – wonderful in a soup or stew. In Italy fish change name according to local dialect, and *nocchie* follow that rule, and although they appear all along the Adriatic coast, they are called *pannocchie*, *ranocchie* and so on. They are long grey-pink shrimp-shaped shellfish.

They are served very simply with oil and lemon juice.

The great variety has naturally produced a fine local fish soup – the delicious *Brodetto* – with apparently two very specific methods of preparation. From Pesaro to Numana they use thirteen different types of fish, cooked with garlic, tomato, onion, parsley and a splash of vinegar. From Porto Recanati to San Benedetto del Tronto they adopt a recipe that is much more southern and uses only nine varieties. Whichever one you use, the perfection depends on the quality and freshness of the fish.

Good restaurants will tell you what fish is fresh and what is frozen *surgelato* and will advise you on the freshest (therefore the one most worth eating) fish of the day *pesce del giorno* accordingly.

Local Specialities

- *Brodetto* Fish soup made with a variety of fish, cooked with garlic, tomato, onion, parsley and vinegar. In the south of the region a large pinch of saffron makes the dish a brilliant golden colour.
- *Garagoli in porchetta* Traditionally served along the coast from Pesaro to Ancona, shellfish cooked with wild fennel, garlic, oil and a great deal of freshly ground black pepper.
- *Stoccafisso all'Anconetana* Dried cod requires a lengthy preparation before it can actually be cooked. In Ancona it is often prepared with tomatoes, herbs and potatoes, then covered in milk and baked in the oven.

CARNE E CACCIA
Meat and Game

Good pastureland means good beef and here it is supplemented by pork, a great deal of which is used for *salumeria*. It is surprising then that few veal or beef specialities crop up on the menu. Certainly they make an excellent variety of roast meats *arrosti* in which beef *manzo* and veal *vitello* do figure, but the most famous of all the meat dishes of the region is the perfect suckling pig *porchetta*, which is cooked out in the open air on a slowly turned spit, its skin gradually turning from golden to dark burnt orange like the colour of terracotta.

Local Specialities

- *Ciaramboli* are pieces of pig's gut, dried in the open air, and fried with cabbage, oil, garlic and rosemary. The smell and smoke will be quite alarming, but as soon as they're cooked the smell becomes a delicious perfume as the dense smoke dies away.
- *Coniglio in porchetta* Stuffed roast rabbit basted with the water in which wild fennel has been boiled to give it a particular flavour.
- *Lumache alle nove erbe* A dish of snails cooked with nine wild herbs.
- *Petti di pollo trifolati* Superb chicken breasts cooked with *prosciutto* and truffles, flavoured with brandy and a little *parmigiano*.
- *Piccioni in casseruola* Pigeons cooked in a casserole with plenty of juicy black olives.

- *Pollo in potacchio* Light chicken fricassee in which the chicken pieces are cooked in olive oil with herbs, garlic, tomato, *peperoncino* and white wine.
- *Pollo con i pinoli* Fricassee of chicken with pine nuts and olives.
- *Quaglie al risotto* Quails cooked with a creamy risotto.
- *Trippa di mongana alla canepina* Extraordinary rather heavy winter dish, enough to keep anyone going for a week. Tripe stew containing ham bone, garlic, tomato and cheese, though there are often variations to the basic recipe.
- *Trippa di vitello casareccio* Veal tripe served with great slabs of bread toasted in the oven and dressed with a sprinkling of olive oil.

The cuisine of the hills gives us delicious game in season – quails *quaglie*, pigeon *piccione* and partridge *starne*, kid *capretto* and delicious chicken, snails and offal dishes too. If you have the misfortune to be hit by heavy rain, one consolation is that snails *lumache* are always at their best after rain, and these local ones seem particularly delectable. Tripe *trippa* is popular too, and there are some delicious dishes, but for the squeamish, steer clear of *testina di agnello al forno* as it's the head of a lamb cut in half and roasted, with the eyes and tongue left in place, not to mention the brain.

FORMAGGIO
Cheese

The most important cheese is superbly sweet, fragrant *pecorino*, which is always served at the end of a meal in lieu of a dessert (or as well as in some cases – they are BIG eaters in this region). It's much sweeter and milder than the same sort of cheese eaten in other parts of the country. Delicious puddings are made with the incredibly creamy local *mascarpone* cheese too.

FRUTTA E VERDURA
Fruit and Vegetables

Agriculture here is mostly run as smallholdings, though it is hoped that eventually all these tiny properties will manage to join under a co-operative of some description and eventually begin to produce the quality and quantity of crops of which the region is capable. At the moment, it seems to produce a little bit of everything.

Absolutely top of the list come olives – big ones, small ones, and medium-sized ones, they get stuffed, fried, baked, but very few of them actually get turned into olive oil. This is the region of table olives – mostly green ones – although the small quantities of privately produced oil are really superb. Barley and wheat are two main crops, along with sugar beet.

PASTICCERIA
Cakes, Biscuits and Puddings

The *pasticceria* I was able to uncover as being genuinely regional was very simple and plain, with no real high points. A typical meal here centres round the main course or pasta course, rather than paying too much heed to the finale.

● *Beccute* Speciality of Ancona, little biscuits with raisins, almonds dried figs and nuts worked into a plain maize flour and olive oil dough.
● *Calcioni* Oven-baked *ravioli* filled with sweet *pecorino*, and shaped like a crescent.

Local Specialities

● *Pizza di Pasqua* Traditional Easter cake that changes name and flavour depending where you are. Bread dough to which you add eggs, fresh and mature *pecorino*, *ricotta* and spices. In Pesaro it's called *crescia di Pasqua*, in Urbino and Macerata *crescia di cascio*, and in Ancona *pizza al formaggio*.

● *Ciambelline di Pasqua* Round cakes with a hole in the middle flavoured with cinnamon and pine nuts, traditionally served at Easter time or at the time of the wine harvest when *sapa* cooked wine must is added to the dough.
● *Frustenga* From Ancona, a sweet polenta baked rather than boiled. Pine nuts, walnuts, sultanas, dried figs and *sapa* are added to maize flour.
● *Frustingolo Marchigiano* The Christmas

Risotto alla Rossini

Quite apart from being a great and vivacious composer, Rossini was also a keen cook and gourmet. He has left us with many memories of the time he spent at the kitchen table, among them the most famous being Tournedos Rossini as served in old-fashioned British hotels and the world over. Rossini came from Pesaro and it is apparently here that he learned to make a dish of rice cooked with boletus mushrooms *porcini*, eggs, Parmesan and cheese, cooked slowly in a good broth. It is a good deal simpler, but to my mind much nicer than the Tournedos.

speciality of the city of Ascoli Piceno. A delicious cake made with honey, bran, dried figs, almonds, walnuts, candied fruit and baked in the oven.

• *Piconi* Shortcrust pastry *ravioli* filled with *ricotta*, eggs, cinnamon, rum, sugar and lemon.

• *Scroccafusi* Little cakes for Carnival. Deep-fried or baked, they emerge round and light with a fluffy middle.

VINO
Wine

The most famous of the local wines is the unmistakable *Verdicchio*, which is specially popular in the States. However, the ones most acclaimed by those who consider themselves to be experts, are the *Rosso Piceno* and another D.O.C. red, the equally delicious *Conero*.

SPECIAL RED WINE

• *Rosso Piceno Superiore* A ruby red wine with a strong winey perfume and a harmonious dry flavour. Made with Sangiovese and Montepulciano grapes in almost equal proportions. Must be aged for at least one year to qualify as the superior variety. Perfect with roasts or red meats.

• *Rosso Conero* A white meat, roast and game drinking wine if aged over two years. A distinguished wine with an aristocratic flavour, it is made with almost all Montepulciano grapes and produced on the slopes of the mountain from which it takes its name.

RED WINE

• *Sangiovese dei Colli Pesaresi* A garnet-coloured light wine with a slightly bitter aftertaste. Considered a good table wine.

WHITE WINE

• *Bianchello del Metauro* Produced in a vast area in the province of Pesare using Bianchello grapes with a tiny addition of Malvasia. Very fresh, crisp and delicate. A table wine if under a year old, thereafter it becomes an excellent fish wine.

• *Verdicchio di Matelica* Extremely rare version of the above but produced in a competitor's vineyard in the province of Macerata. Very much sought after, it's a very special wine indeed.

SPUMANTI

• *Verdicchio dei Castelli di Iesi Spumante* is made as dry *secco* or sweet *amabile* sparkling wine. The dry is drunk with very refined and complicated fish dishes, or as an aperitif. The sweet version is a sweet champagne, which is served extremely well chilled with desserts.

• *Verdicchio di Matelica Spumante* is also served cold with desserts. Very rare, it tends to be rather more elegant than the two above.

• *Vernaccia di Serrapetrona* This is unquestionably the oddest but certainly one of the nicest wines I've ever drunk. It's a red champagne, produced by the proper champagne method in very limited quantity round the province of Macerata. It can be *amabile* fruity or *dolce* sweet.

BEVANDE
Drinks

• *Grappa Marchigiana* For once I really liked the local *grappa*! It's flavoured with aniseed and fennel which seems to be what everybody likes to drink in these parts.

• *Mistrà* a local aniseed drink, like *anisette* or *sambuca*. I noticed that every time a local ordered *espresso* it was *corretto* (added to) with a generous measure of *grappa* or *Mistrà*.

WORTH TAKING HOME

Olives, all shapes and sizes, are better and more varied here then you'll find anywhere else. If you can find it, olive oil is special. Fresh *pecorino*, particularly if you can buy it in Carpegna.

A bottle of the heady, aniseedy *grappa*, and of course any of the delectable Verdicchio wines in their characteristic green amphora-like bottles.

SAGRE E FESTE
Festivals

Ancona has a fish fair at the end of June and beginning of July.

In the Shadow of Rome

Lazio isn't so much a region as a piece of land around Rome, a mosaic of steep arid mountains like those in the Abruzzi, and others which are green and fertile, covered with woodland and olive groves like those of Umbria. There are islands, mountains and lakes, some of volcanic origin. There are areas which are almost completely barren, and abandoned by the population, and others which are rich and fertile and overcrowded. There are the ruins of ancient cities and civilisations, then modern, apartment-block towns, only a few decades old. Two-thirds of the region is crossed by the snaking form of the Tiber, but the real point is that once you start thinking about Rome you forget all about Lazio. In the northern part of this region, the mountains are formed by old volcanoes, but coming south across

the Tiber, the inclines become softer and smoother to form the Alban Hills, *I Colli Albani*, with vineyards everywhere amid rich greenery. In total contrast are the harsh dry mountains of the south, crumbling and stony, yielding nothing.

The countryside immediately around Rome is known as *La Campagna Romana*. It's peaceful farmland, a huge vegetable garden for Rome. This area, together with the Maremma Laziale and the

Agro Ponentino, was in part rescued by the passion of Mussolini, who whipped up a frenzy of activity as only he was capable of, and very quickly the area was drained and turned into rich fields, pastures and vineyards.

The coastline stretches from the ancient Etruscan settlement of Tarquinia right down south to the port of Gaeta. The beaches near Rome are enormous, overcrowded, organised with rows and rows of umbrellas and deck chairs. Further south the sea is cleaner and crowds less frantic. Right in the south, in the Gulf of Gaeta, lie the Isole Ponziane, 6 little islands formed by submerged volcanoes, unspoilt so far, but very popular.

Inland, the volcanic lakes of Vico, Bolsena, Bracciano, Albano and Nemi are all surrounded by pretty countryside. Then there's Canterno, near the thermal station of Fiuggi with its marvellous mineral water, a lake of different geological origin, which empties itself into the ground of its own accord every two or three years.

The sea breezes have a substantial influence on the weather along the coast, and across the plains, freshening the summer temperatures and making for mild winters, and most importantly, making the suffocating summer heat in the cities more bearable. Inland the summers tend to be hot and dry, and the winters cold – especially in the mountains. Rain is scarce on the coastline and along the plains, but in the mountains it's very wet in winter and spring.

Not for vegetarians

Lazio's food is not for the fainthearted or the squeamish, typified as it is by offal dishes and plenty of oil and garlic. It's strong, vigorous, manly food, not designed for those with small appetites – it's the food of people who work hard for a living.

The people of Lazio are generous, warmhearted and lusty – and all of this is reflected at full volume in the taste, smell and texture of all their favourite dishes.

VITERBO & PROVINCE

This province is the home of two important drinks – Sambuca, that sweet, clear liqueur, and Est! Est! Est!, a wine with an extraordinary history. It's a mountainous area, except for its short coastal strip. Viterbo itself is an agricultural town on the slopes of the Cimini Mountains. Just outside the town at Bagnaia is the Villa Lante, country home of many popes. Almost next door to this I found the cool and welcoming *TRATTORIA CHECHARELLO*, where I tasted pasta with plenty of local *pecorino* and tender veal cooked with artichokes and lemon juice.

RIETI & PROVINCE

Rieti is a little country town in the green valley of the River Velino, surrounded by fields of grain and vineyards. Its main claim to fame is that it was the capital of the Sabines, whose women were subject of the infamous rape at the hands of the early Romans. This is a dairying area, and many of the local cheeses are wonderful. The town of Amatrice is in this province, and has given its name to a spaghetti sauce of bacon, tomatoes and onion *all'Amatriciana*, prepared all over the country.

FROSINONE & LATINA

The provinces of Frosinone and Latina are mostly agricultural too. Frosinone is a province full of tiny old villages and towns nestling in valleys or perched on hilltops, almost all treasuring Roman or medieval ruins, while Latina, with a good coastline, counts among her specialities excellent lobster and a large scampi called *mazzancolle*.

THE PROVINCE OF ROME

Although the city of Rome takes all the credit, a few towns and holiday centres dotted about her province should be mentioned. The main town is Civitavecchia, which is Lazio's most important port, and where ferries leave for Corsica and Sardinia. Also along the coastline are the exceedingly ugly seaside resorts of Ostia, Anzio and Santa Marinella. Fregene and Ladispoli are less disturbing. Tivoli is a wonderful place to visit at any time of the year – it's absolutely bursting with medieval and Roman monuments, but my personal favourite will always be the lovely Villa d'Este with its fabulous gardens full of fountains.

After all the sightseeing, head out of town a little, and find yourself one of the many *trattorie* up in the hills with views over the waterfalls cascading into the greenery. For the health-conscious, you can also visit the nearby sulphur baths for a smelly but very good-for-you wash.

Castelli Romani

If you're short of time but want to escape from Rome's chaos for an afternoon, head out for the *Castelli Romani* in the Alban Hills. Here is the tiniest of Lazio's volcanic lakes, Nemi, called Diana's mirror by the ancient Romans. Here they would hunt deer and carry out ritualistic water battles. In the hills surrounding this lake and the larger Lake Albano are the *Castelli Romani*, or Roman Castles: Frascati, Genzano, Velletri, Castel Gandolfo – where the Pope has his summer residence – and several others. Since the very beginnings of Rome, this has been the area where the rich have built their holiday homes, and kept cool in the heat of the summer. Palaces, ornamental gardens, churches and villas are scattered across the hillsides. Many of the smaller villages have no roads for cars, and you have to park in the first piazza before beginning the ascent. Of these villages, Monte Compatri is probably one of the most complete and intact. Here, in the cool breezes, you can sit and rest and enjoy *porchetta*, a huge, whole roast pig, thickly sliced and eaten as sandwiches with fresh crisp rolls and plenty of cold white wine, *vino di Frascati*.

Share the shade

Unfortunately, during the warmer months you will find there will be several hundred people sharing the pig and the shade with you. But in the really hot months, like July and August, everyone who can will have escaped for the coast, so you'll be surrounded by a few working Italians having a day out rather than Japanese tourists.

At Cerveteri you can explore the Etruscan tombs, then head on a little way to see where the living passed their days in the pretty town of Ceri, perched on top of a hill with marvellous views over the green valleys. There are three restaurants here, but after waiting two and a half hours for lunch one Sunday, I would strongly recommend that you either book at *LA TERRAZZA, LA LANTERNA* or *SORA LELLA* – or, take a picnic. If you do get a table, in early spring you might find yourself eating *broccoletti all'agro* greens from the hillside, *polenta al sugo* polenta with a sauce, or *fettucine fatte in casa con sugo di capretto*, home-made fettucine with kid sauce. It will all be authentic regional food, with some

of the dishes served on wooden platters.

Other alternatives for outings from Rome are a trip to the ancient city of Veli, now called Isola Farmese, which has a fortified Etruscan settlement, or to Subiaco, which is famed for the many Benedictine monasteries built there, many of which sell herbal preparations, liqueurs and honey *miele* to passing visitors.

ROMA – LA CITTÀ

With thousands of people coming to visit the treasures of Rome all year round, she has no real need to be anything other than a tourist attraction. A visit to Rome means filling your head with culture, your suitcase with new clothes, and your stomach with good food! More than enough has been written about the history and monuments of Rome, and this is not the place to write about fashion, so I'll limit myself to describing Rome in the context of the latter.

Roman food hard to find

On the whole, I was fairly disappointed with investigating the restaurants and *trattorie* of Rome itself. In the areas where the tourists are most likely to be – the area round the Vatican, or downtown, there are hundreds of restaurants with the same boring old *menu turistico* in the window. I'm sure I would have eaten well, and satisfied my hunger pangs, but that isn't the point. I wasn't out to 'play safe' with the dishes I could eat any old where – I wanted proper local cuisine. It took some finding! I could get excellent Japanese, Ethiopian or even dishes from other regions of Italy throughout the city (which of course is a good way to savour the varieties of the whole country if you haven't time for a Grand Tour), but for really good Roman food, I discovered I either had to pay through the nose, scour the back streets, or go further out of town. The little towns of Lazio are less prone to crowds of hungry tourists, so the food is more genuinely local, and in the suburbs and less salubrious areas of Rome, you will find a very good cheap and cheerful meal from a menu filled with local specialities.

Perhaps this has something to do with the fact that quite a few of the local specialities are a bit 'too much' for the average visitor, but, in my opinion, you ought to be given the chance to try – after all, when in Rome . . .

GASTRONOMIC WALKABOUT IN ROME

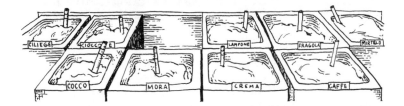

Il Centro Storico

To get the real feel of Rome and her relationships with food, you need first to get into the old historical centre, *Il Centro Storico*. This area, takes in Piazza Campo de' Fiori with its wonderfully colourful daily market and marvellous collection of various food shops and cafés all around it, including a *salumeria* called *VIOLA* and a proper *Norcineria* (a butcher's shop with Norcia traditions and methods – Norcia being considered to be the Italian pork butchery capital above all others). Once you've walked around the market and explored the square at your leisure, I would strongly recommend a saunter down via de'Giubbolari where you will discover a terrific food shop called *PANTAGRUEL* and a bit further along a really superb gelateria called *CHIATTI-MINETTI*. Soon you'll come into Largo de' Librai (so called because several open air bookstalls and their sellers gather here sporadically). Largo de' Librai is worth finding for 2 things apart from the second hand books. On the right there is an *Osteria* called *I FILETTI DI BACCALÀ*. This is all that they cook: fillets of salt cod deep-fried in batter and served with squares of paper with which to hold them – no knives or forks. When you sit down to eat the waiter asks you how many you want, not what you want. Washed down with rivers of ice cold dry white wine, it makes a delicious supper. It is an unusual restaurant for sophisticated Rome, but the *filetti* are really delicious and the place is permanently packed with local residents, workmen and the occasional vagabond, and mink-coated ladies of aristocratic lineage.

You can be sure there will always be something going on to watch, sometimes live music – certainly plenty of local colour and atmosphere. When you've had your fill (get here early or join the queue – frying begins about 6 p.m.), wander across the Largo to the enchanting little Baroque church of Santa Barbara on the other side.

Lungotevere Del Centro

Crossing the pedestrian bridge from Castel Sant'Angelo you will be on one of the oldest stretches of the riverside buildings – *Lungotevere*. If you turn left and make your way along as far as Piazza Umberto I and drop down to the lower level via the steps you will be standing outside one of the old Roman *Osterie* called *OSTERIA DELL'ORSO*, which has been turned into an up-market and exclusive restaurant with items on the menu such as chicken Kiev and beef Stroganoff. Whatever you eat here will be very good but not terribly Roman, although the restaurant is very beautiful to be in.

The road ahead of you is via di Monte Brianzo and if you follow it up it will lead you straight into Piazza di Spagna, the Spanish Steps, so stunning in the spring with the terracotta pots of azaleas creating a floral extravaganza. In autumn and winter the scent of roasting chestnuts fills the air as the street seller toasts them in an old tin pan – delicious, fat, soft and cooked perfectly. On the way there you will pass via della Campana. In this street is one of Rome's oldest established *trattorie*, *LA CAMPANA* – it's been here for over four centuries. All the buildings along this stretch of riverside road used to be where the craftsmen such as cartwrights, joiners and blacksmiths used to work on the ground floor with tenement-type apartments above. Nowadays this is one of the most sought-after places to own or rent a flat, and the old workshops on

Under Cover, but Uncharacteristic

Most Romans do their shopping in one of the wonderful street markets scattered throughout the city, filled to overflowing with the astonishing array of produce from *La Campagna Romana*.

Unfortunately I understand that there are plans to remove all the lovely outdoor markets and replace them with larger covered markets, for reasons of hygiene. Many have already gone,

the traders glad to be under cover, warmer in winter and cooler in the summer, but the atmosphere will never be quite the same.

The best street markets are in Piazza Campo dei Fiori, Piazza Vittorio Emanuele and via Andrea Doria. They are all open daily except Sundays.

On Tuesdays the public can go to the marvellous covered flower market in via Trionfali.

---

the ground floor are fast being replaced with boutiques and art galleries.

In via della Campana, *LA CAMPANA* will offer you a selection of old-fashioned working-class dishes which the erstwhile inhabitants of this area have been ordering for several generations. This is real authentic Roman cuisine, *coda alla vaccinara, pagliata, spaghetti ajo e ojo* and many more. The clientele here is faithful, made up of people who come here because they know they'll get what their grandfather and greatgrandfathers and mothers were served before them.

Via Veneto

For a much more refined gastronomic experience and some really great people watching à la Mrs Stone, have a coffee, ice cream or aperitif at any one of the cafés strewn along via Veneto. If it happens to be raining choose one of the ones with a glass canopy over the tables. The best time to go is around midday – 'l'ora dell'aperitivo' when everyone joins in the fun, or alternatively about 6–7 p.m. Savour canapés or tartine, washed down with cocktails, vermouth or a glass of wine. When you've had your fill of the fashion show and the extraordinary behaviour of the season's gigolos, walk down the hill past the Hotel Excelsior, turn left into via Boncompagni then right into via Lucullo. Turn left into via Sallustiana and then right for via Aureliana. At the bottom of the road, on the T-junction with via Flavia is the excellent *TAVERNA FLAVIA*, which has never let us down in the 60 or so years that our family has been frequenting it.

It's a very pleasant place to lunch or dine, filled by those who care more about what they

are eating than about being seen in fashionable establishments. If it happens to be full try *LA LAMPADA* or any one of the other similar establishments set in this quiet backwater.

Il Centro

The shopping centre of the city, known as *il centro*, lies roughly along either side of the via del Corso (or il Corso) from Piazza del Popolo to Piazza Venezia taking in via della Vite, via del Gambero, via Frattina, via della Croce, via Borgognona and Piazza San Silvestro, Piazza di Spagna and many others.

The best thing is to start at one end. If you begin with Piazza del Popolo you should at least have a drink and a perfect sandwich, such as a *tramezzino ai funghi*, at the *CAFÉ ROSATI*, where all the smart intellectuals hang out, and then head off down via del Corso. Turn left into via della Croce, then right into via Mario de' Fiori and look out for a fantastic fresh pasta, bread and cheese shop, which also lures you over to the window display with the perfume of freshly cooked doughnuts, pastries and cakes. This is *FIOR FIORE* and it really is worth a browse.

Il Centro is basically boutiqueville – virtually every single shop down or up every single little narrow street or even on busier street corners is a clothes shop, shoe shop or handbag shop, with interesting alternatives like specialist sock/tights/stockings shops or 'ideas in marble' – anything from a full-scale obelisk to a fireplace or bath, or door handle shops, china and glassware shops or marvellous bookshops – *in centro* you will find what the rest of Rome does not stock.

There are countless little *trattorie* without a

name outside, or at least not a madly distinguishable name, tucked in between the big names like Mila Schon, Ferragamo and Versace – all serving good honest food at honest prices. There are a few smarter restaurants that have been done up – 'interior designer' restaurants tucked away here and there, but these are the ones that always seem to be empty. It is just the fact that these slightly grubby, understated *trattorie* look so out of place which makes them guaranteed to be good. All these streets and their side streets here are very much alike with more and more boutiques and various kinds of shops interspersed with the odd *gelateria*, *salumeria* or *trattoria*.

Via Condotti has to be the most elegant street in the world, with the inimitable elegance of the *CAFFÈ GRECO* opposite the wonders of Gucci. Go into either and see who you can recognise. The Caffè is of national public interest – its been here for so long and has seen so many of the great literary figures sort out the world's problems at its tiny tables in the original 19th-century heavy red-satin wallpaper atmosphere. Further down via Condotti the street is crossed by via Bocca di Leone. The right-hand section of this street is where the *mercatino* is – lots of fresh fruit and vegetables of the very best quality and bunches of red chillis – roots and all hanging down the sides of the stalls. The market traders offer a sharp contrast to the smart people buying here.

Turning left down via Bocca di Leone you eventually reach via Frattina – and more boutiques. Walking down towards the Corso, on the corner with via Belsiana you'll find *VANNI* – one of the city's most famous, elegant and expensive cafés *gelaterie* with just a few tables scattered outside on via Frattina itself. At the bottom of via Frattina, cross the Corso and turn right to find Piazza San Lorenzo in Lucina with its fabulous Basilica. In the far right-hand corner of this piazza is a narrow turning – via del Leoncino, which leads into via della Fontanella Borghese, where if you turn left and walk up the street you will find a really exceptional bookshop called *Libreria Fontanella Borghese* which sells a good selection of English language books, maps and guide books. Crossing over and entering via delle Medaglie d'Oro, you will be on your way to an amazingly cheap and delicious lunch in a little *trattoria* about halfway down with no name on the outside. Much frequented by local residents and shopkeepers, this is always a safe bet when shopping in the area. Almost all the food is laid out for you to see so you can really whet your appetite before ordering. Three of us had lunch with two courses, wine, mineral water and coffee for a very reasonable 33.000 Lire including the tip. The dishes are good, wholesome standbys like *Minestrone con le Lenticchie* minestrone soup with lentils, *Spezzatino* stew, and such like. After lunch, you are within easy walking distance of Castel Sant'Angelo.

Around The Vatican

The very old buildings and streets and *piazzette* grouped around the Vatican walls are called *I Borghi*. The atmosphere here convinced me I would find some really typical Roman *osterie* offering proper authentic Roman cuisine. Instead of which the *osterie* and *trattorie* were there, but a glance at the menu pinned up in the window revealed once again the predictable

---

Roman Foodie Update

In spite of a few oddities, the Roman recipes and eating habits were not all that different from today. True, dormice aren't bred for stuffing and eating with hens and rabbits, and ostriches aren't boiled and covered in a sauce. Italians on the whole don't eat in a prone position, and the ancient Roman habit of eating an enormous breakfast of all the previous night's leftovers has disappeared.

Coffee, tomatoes and pasta as we know it may not have been around, but the general range of ingredients and the way in which they are cooked are not that different today from what they were almost 2,000 years ago.

According to Martial, who is responsible for much of the information available regarding ancient Roman cuisine, the Mediterranean was much richer in seafood that it is today, and fruit and vegetables grew in abundance. The basic ingredients were poultry, pork, lamb, kid, fish, cheese, fruit, vegetables, herbs and cereals. Sauces were very popular and so were *antipasti*.

menu turistico in 6 languages with its boring repertoire of safe dishes like steak, escalope of veal in breadcrumbs, spaghetti bolognese etc. However, this is one of the most 'Roman' parts of Rome, so a walk down these streets is still worthwhile, even if you'll probably end up eating tourist food.

I started at the end of Borgo Pio and headed in the direction of the Vatican. About halfway down I stopped for lunch at the *TAVERNA 3 PUPAZZI* on the corner of via 3 Pupazzi. I chose the most Roman items on the menu and had *scamorza ai ferri* grilled *scamorza* cheese and *insalata di puntarelle con le alici* puntarelle salad with anchovies. I wandered on a bit and was struck by a very pretty fountain with what

the availability seems to change rather erratically from one season to the next.

San Giovanni In Laterano

For authentic cuisine without offal, there is the excellent restaurant called *CANNAVOTA* (hollow cane) in the piazza of the imposing Basilica of San Giovanni in Laterano. The name of the restaurant is the nick-name of the incredibly skinny owner, Dante Funari. This is a typical *osteria*, noisy, crowded and jolly, with fast, efficient service and huge portions of dishes like *carciofi alla Romana*, artichokes cooked in the Roman style, *linguine agli scampi* linguine with scampi and *pasta all'amatriciana*.

Bene Cenate!

Breakfast was important – it consisted of eating the leftovers from the main meal of the night before, and it was considered best to eat it standing up so as to aid digestion. The average Roman (men only of course) would then spend all day out, and the habit was to grab a quick bite at an *Osteria* (then called *Popinae* or *Thermopolia*), where ready-to-eat simple dishes like chickpea cake (*Cecina*, as still eaten today), *focaccine* or bread and cheese were on sale, with cold wine in summer and mulled wine in winter

The main meal of the day was at sundown, after a cleansing visit to the spa. The meal was always made up of 3 courses: GUSTUM (antipasto) MENSA PRIMA and MENSA SECUNDA. In the case of an everyday meal each course would only have one dish with accompaniments, whereas for a more important occasion there would be two or three dishes per course. On the whole it was just like Italian cuisine as we know it today – and since those times peaches have come from Persia, tomatoes from Peru, maize from America, rice from the orient, and oranges from Arabia. But the

Romans had beer, mustard, vinegar, oil and wine. It is obvious that the ancient Roman was as keen to take care of his table as the modern Italian!

GUSTUM
 Crostini alla Polpoliva
 (toast with olive paste)
 Souffle di Asparagi con Quaglie
 (asparagus soufflé with quails)

MENSA PRIMA
 Dentice Arrosto con salsa alle Erbe
 (roast fish with herb sauce).
 Various vegetables and salads
 Favaone Arresto in salsa Agrodolce
 (roast guineafowl in sweet and sour sauce)

MENSA SECUNDA
 Pasticcio di pesche (peach pie)
 Crema Fritta (fried custard)
 Melograni (pomegranates)

Sounds good to me!

looked like cool pure water spouting out from its marble mouth – but over it there was a plaque reading *Acqua Marcia* – rotten water.

All over this area there are various monasteries, convents and other religious organisations who take in guests as in a hotel but at very low cost and with really rather good food. To get information your best bet seems to be to inquire at any of the local shops or bars as

The Ungrand Central Station – Stazione Termini

In via Marghera, right close by the main railway station, amongst all the multilingual chaos of bars, cafés, bedsits, traffic and hotels, there is a diamond of a restaurant called *GEMMA E*

MAURIZIO. Here you'll get things like *baccalà con pinoli e uvetta*, salt cod stewed with pinenuts and sultanas, *abbacchio* suckling lamb, *porchetta al forno* roast pig etc. Very honest prices and excellent service, plenty to see and watch, but ladies please don't be around this part of town on your own after dark – take somebody bigger and braver than yourself along to cope with the hustlers, beggars and crazy people who hang around here.

Testaccio & La Piramide

To get more authentic Roman cuisine at its most characteristic you have to head out past the Colosseum and Terme di Caracalla, past the Pyramid and get to Testaccio. The Testaccio itself is a hillock formed by the broken pieces of the amphorae that were dumped here over many centuries. Opposite the hillock is the now abandoned central abattoir. The tradition of the very best meat being available 'on site' continues despite the abattoir being abandoned. And all the most authentic Roman specialities are without a doubt meat based.

There are two restaurants in this area that are famous everywhere in Rome for being the ones that serve the best and most traditional Roman dishes. These are *PERILLI*, which is nearer the Pyramid, and *CECCHINO DAL 1887*, which is situated exactly opposite the abandoned abattoir. This is the most elegant of the two, with as much emphasis being placed on the largely French wine list as on the food. For my taste the rather snooty atmosphere and small, elegant portions were not in keeping with the kind of dishes we were eating. Perilli has a much more relaxed family atmosphere, huge portions, shorter bill and excellent house wine. At both restaurants expect to find *pagliata, coda alla vaccinara, nervetti in insalata*, sliced calf's head and pickles, *trippa* and all the other offal-based, strong-tasting and full-bodied Roman dishes, along with artichoke dishes, delicious jam tarts and many more.

Cafés, Gelaterie, Pasticcerie, Paninoteche

If a quick snack and a drink is your style or desire, there is absolutely no need for you to miss out on the very best Rome has to offer you. There are lots and lots of famous cafés, snackbars and similar places that are serving the very best in pastries, sandwiches *tramezzini* filled rolls and baps *panini* and ice creams.

HUNGARIA is in Piazza Ungheria near the Parioli residential area – excellent cakes, especially the *Dolce Hungaria* with an H inscribed on the top.

EUCLIDE has branches dotted about the outskirts of central Rome, but the main one is in Piazza Euclide itself. Their main speciality has to be the sandwiches *tramezzini* which are softer, fresher and with more original and flavoursome fillings than you're likely to taste anywhere else.

BARBERINI is near the Testaccio in via Marmorata and they make the very best *millefoglie (millefeuilles)* cake I have ever tasted.

ANTONINI is not far from the Vatican in an elegant residential area in via Sabotino. They make incredibly light and delicious pastries as well as *tartine* – little open sandwiches with toppings like caviar, oysters, mushrooms, lobster, shrimps, *prosciutto* etc.

VANNI is nearby and is frequented by all the TV personalities working at the RAI studios just around the corner. Here they do ice cream, *tramezzini, panini*, cakes and pastries and other snacks and they even have a tearoom upstairs.

RUSCHENA is more old fashioned and sober, frequented by an older and more sedate clientele. It's on the lungotevere Mellini and offers a fantastic selection of perfectly cooked pastries and delicious ice creams.

These cafés, *gelaterie*, snack bars etc, represent the contrast between the rough and ready Roman *trattoria* and the sophisticated modern Rome, yet both are as much a part of the city as each other. They are always frequented by a massive cross-section of people, which has to mean interesting atmosphere. The oddest of them all is *BABBINGTONS* tea rooms at the bottom of the Spanish Steps which is a perfectly reproduced English tea shop with muffins, scones and chintz galore.

Almost all the cafés and bars mentioned do an outside catering service for parties and functions and have a very well-managed take-away service.

SALUMI
Salami, Sausages and Cured Meats

The Romans and Laziali seem to be inordinately fond of offal in all its forms. Hence *coppa*, the only real Roman *salume*, which is not a sausage, and not *salame*, but consists of all the bits which couldn't be used for anything else. They get shoved into a *coppa* bowl, squashed together, and then turned into a sort of *salame* with a rind, which is hung up and sliced like any other *salame*. It's frankly a bit nondescript, and definitely not for the squeamish – you just don't know which bit of the pig you might be eating! Sometimes it is marinated in oil and herbs for extra flavour.

Guanciale, *pancetta* and *lardo* are all extremely fatty pork *salumi* which are used for cooking, rather like bacon. *Guanciale* is perhaps the meatiest of the three, while *lardo* is just a very highly flavoured version of lard, with herbs, salt and a great deal of pepper added to make it more interesting. All three make extremely useful bases for all local cooking, or any kind of pasta sauce.

PASTA

Spaghetti come to the fore in Lazio, served with very simple rather coarse dressings, quick to cook and ideally suited to the Roman temperament, such as *ajo e ojo*, garlic and olive oil; *cacio e pepe*, grated *pecorino* and pepper; *alla carbonara*, a

---

Local Speciality

• *Bucatini all'Amatriciana* The famous dish from the town of Amatrice, made with a sauce of tomato and bacon. Must not be missed.

---

sauce made with beaten eggs, pepper and *parmigiano* poured over the boiling hot, drained spaghetti, along with a generous panful of fried cubes of *pancetta* bacon; *al tonno* with tuna; *con le acciughe* with anchovies; *con vongole* with clams, and so on.

Then there is *maccheroni alla ciociara*, served with a sauce of *guanciale*, another sort of bacon, slices of sausage, ham and tomato, and named after the imposing dark-haired women, covered

in gold jewellery, from the green valley known as La Ciociaria in the south of Lazio, who used to be employed as wet nurses by wealthy families.

Gnocchi, small potato dumplings, are cooked and dressed just like pasta – best to eat on Thursdays, as tradition dictates.

In Rome there are lots of thick soups containing pasta along with vegetables, pulses and so on.

PESCE E FRUTTI DI MARE
Fish and Seafood

The most popular and available fish in Rome is *baccalà*. This is filleted and dried cod, which hangs in shops and on market stalls looking just like dishcloths. It is then soaked for a night or so in cold water, and returns to its fleshy self. It can be stewed or deep-fried.

From the rivers come eels *anguille*, the very big ones called *capitone*, and in May the tiny little ones called *ciriole*, which are stewed with peas.

The long coastline produces seafood like

Local Speciality

• *Filetti di baccalà* A recipe from the Ghetto – strips of dried salt cod, deep-fried in batter.

---

arselle, little semi-oval shellfish that hide under the sand, and are scraped up in nets, clams *vongole*, and mussels *cozze*. To make a traditional *zuppa di pesce* in Rome, you would need the following fish, all of which are delicious, but the nature of the seas and the season dictate their availability. They can all be bought frozen. *Pesce San Pietro* John Dory, *ombrina* umber, *orata* gilthead, *grongo* conger eel, *occhiata* ray, *martino*, *scorfano* scorpion fish, *cefalo* mullet, *seppia* squid, *merluzzo* cod and *palombo* dogfish.

CARNE E CACCIA
Meat and Game

The overriding passion for offal results in the popularity of tripe *trippa* which is stewed with mint, kidney *rognone*, spleen *milza*, sweetbreads *animelle*, tongue *lingua*, head *testarella*, oxtail *coda di bue*, and the most popular of all is *pagliata*, the innards of a calf, removed from the cow's womb, gutted and then the innards, still

Local Specialities

- *Abbacchio* Unweaned lamb, roasted with a very rich dressing of oil, vinegar, sage, rosemary and garlic. Delicious, but very heavy on the digestion!
- *Brodettato* A sort of stew made with little pieces of lamb, cooked in an egg sauce and flavoured with lemon zest.
- *Coda alla vaccinara* Thick pieces of oxtail, stewed in a very thick rich tomato sauce, flavoured with a great deal of celery.
- *Coratella* Lamb's heart, lung, liver and spleen cooked in olive oil with lots of pepper and onions. A very old traditional dish with working class origins.
- *Cotiche* Trimmings of pork skin which are cooked until tender and jellyfied, very popular with beans.

- *Saltimbocca alla Romana* The name means 'jump in mouth', because it's so delicious. Slices of veal cooked with a slice of prosciutto, mozzarella and plenty of sage and a sauce made with Marsala.
- *Scottadito* Literally means 'burnfingers'. Lamb chops grilled or turned quickly in a heavy pan and eaten with the fingers.
- *Testarelle d'abbacchio* Lambs' heads seasoned with herbs and dressed with lots of oil, then baked in the oven.
- *Trippa alla Romana* Thin strips of tripe, first boiled then stewed for hours with a tomato sauce flavoured with plenty of mint, to hide the rather nasty smell of the tripe.

filled with the mother's milk, are cooked gently and eaten.

Abbacchio is young lamb, not yet weaned, and *castrato* mutton which has been castrated virtually at birth, so that it grows fat and juicy. Lazio produces a lot of poultry – chicken *pollo*, guinea fowl *faraona*, capon *cappone* and turkey *tacchino* are all very popular and plentiful.

Local Specialities

- *Crostini con la milza* Spleen, cooked and made into a sort of pâté, spread on toasted bread.
- *Crostini con la provatura* Slices of bread dipped in egg, then baked in the oven with slices of *provatura* cheese on top, which melts right into the bread.

The countryside round Rome is fairly rich in game – hare *lepre*, pigeon *piccione*, quail *quaglia*, rabbit *coniglio* and pheasant *fagiano*, though these tend to be more popular in the country towns than in the city.

FORMAGGIO
Cheese

The most important cheese of this area is *pecorino Romano*, which is similar to *parmigiano* but made with sheep's milk. It has a pungent, stinging smell, and is very peppery with

Local Specialities

- *Supplì al Ragù* Rissoles made of rice with meat sauce, dipped in breadcrumbs and fried in olive oil.
- *Supplì al telefono* These are the same as *supplì al ragù* with the addition of pieces of *mozzarella* cheese inside, which melts in the frying and so produces the characteristic 'telephone wires'.

a black rind. Essential accompaniment to all the strong tasting pasta dishes.

Provatura, a Roman cheese which is becoming scarce, is often used to make *spiedini*, kind of cheese kebabs. It has a firm texture which softens when cooked and doesn't fall apart.

There is also a local big round *mozzarella* made from white buffalo milk, and soft, sweet *ricotta* made with sheep's milk.

Then there are many local *cacciotte*, which, like in many other parts of Italy, are made to individual local recipes.

FRUTTA E VERDURA
Fruit and Vegetables

The countryside round Rome produces just about everything that grows, filling the Roman markets

Local Specialities

- *Carciofi alla Giudia* Artichokes are immensely popular. In the Ghetto in Rome you'll find them cooked in the Jewish fashion, fried in plenty of olive oil and flattened so as to look like great big roses.
- *Carciofi alla Romana* Artichokes stuffed with garlic and mint, and cooked with oil over a slow heat.
- *Fagioli con le cotiche* Beans stewed with pieces of pork skin, for a long long time, so that the pork turns to soft jelly.
- *Fave al Guanciale* Broad beans cooked with bacon.
- *Fave col pecorino* Raw fresh broad beans eaten with a good wedge of *pecorino* at the end of a meal.

to bursting point with brilliant colours, pungent smells and extremely keen stallholders. At the big markets you can buy meat, fish and cheese as well, whereas the smaller ones will stick to vegetables – but what a choice! Artichokes, cardoons, spinach, chard, sprouting broccoli, broccoli, chicory, all kinds of lettuce, green and white cauliflower, Savoy cabbage, tomatoes, courgettes, peppers, aubergines, onions, garlic, leeks, carrots, runner beans, French beans, and *corallo* beans, pale green, bent and knobbly, borlotti, cannellini beans, lentils, chickpeas, cucumbers, celery, potatoes and all the herbs. There's a very odd salad plant called *puntarelle*, which is mostly white with green points, and when trimmed curls up like seaweed.

Not every greengrocer or market stallholder will sell all these at once – they are quite selective, choosing what they want according to the quality or their mood.

In the fruit department, the same thing applies and anything and everything grows in *La Campagna Romana*, even if some of it's under plastic.

Strawberries are available almost all year round, growing in the sheltered area round Lake Nemi in the volcanic valley. They do grow elsewhere too, and their season seems to begin towards the end of April – by the time it was Wimbledon week, our yearly visit to London, we were all sick of the sight of them! In the summer months plums are available in all colours, shapes and sizes.

Peaches, both yellow and white, including that variety called *spaccarelle*, which used to split right through to the kernel from the top when ripe. Earwigs loved these peaches, hiding quietly inside until you decided to eat them, then tearing round the plate and tablecloth, to the great amusement of us children and the absolute horror of us aged aunt. Each peach used to hide about six of the things, but modern insecticides have put paid to that innocent party piece.

Nectarines *pesche noci* are the most spectacularly coloured fruits, ranging from deepest red through all shades of yellow and orange to pistachio green.

Apricots, also often inhabited, by white worms, need careful inspection before being eaten.

Grapes, in particular *pizzutello*, that odd-shaped one which looks as if somebody squeezed each individual grape to see if they were ripe, and left them looking peculiar. It's white or black, and very sweet and sharp-tasting at the same time. *Uva Italia* is the huge white variety, with each grape filling your mouth with crisp, juicy flavour. You can only eat one at a time! *Uva Fragolina* is supposed to taste like strawberries. Very dark, small grapes with a loose skin which you're not meant to eat. If you squeeze each grape lightly between your finger and thumb, the fruit pops out into your mouth. I can't say I've ever really noticed the similarity with strawberries – perhaps it's the smell rather than the flavour.

Raspberries grow all over the area in vast numbers. Melons, watermelons, *anguria*, and figs, black and green, are also plentiful in two seasonal bursts, June and September. As soon as the strawberries have stopped being exciting, cherries come into season – all different kinds, from the black ones to the sharp *amarene*, perfect for jam, followed immediately by medlars *nespole*, with their bright orange flesh and skin and four black, shiny central stones. After this come all the other soft summer fruits, and at the end of the summer the pomegranates *melograno* and the persimmons *kaki*. *Kaki* are brown and soft and squidgy and very sensual, but be careful that you only eat ripe ones as the unripe ones coat your mouth and throat with a horrid numbing film which can ruin the whole meal. They are impossible to export, because they are so soft – the ones that do arrive in England are hard and revolting.

In the autumn and winter the markets are flooded with all kinds of apples and pears. The most interesting local apples are *anurche* and *limoncelle*. Pears – buy Kaiser.

PASTICCERIA

Cakes, Biscuits and Puddings

To balance the huge list of vegetables and fruit there are relatively few specialities in this category. Bread is important, with lots of different kinds, including *pizza bianca*, pizza dough baked with no topping other than a good smearing of olive oil. Most of the cakes, tarts, puddings and pastries for sale are not originally from Rome or Lazio.

• *Bignè* Big puffs of choux pastry filled with cream or coffee custard, plain custard, chocolate or *zabaione*.

• *Crostata* This is usually a jam tart, often made with cherry jam, *marmellata d'amarene*, or *marmellata di visciole*.

• *Maritozzi* Light oval buns with sultanas, often split open and filled with sweet whipped cream.

• *Quaresimali* Dry Lent biscuits of flour, eggs and toasted almonds.

VINO

Wine

Mostly white wines are produced in this region, all of them pleasant, and right for everyday drinking with no real 'greats' emerging. The wines of the *Castelli* are just right for cooling down on summer days.

RED WINE

• *Cecubo* Made in the area round Gaeta and Sperlonga. To drink with roast meat.

• *Falerno* A good dry red.

• *Velletri* Fairly strong, good with roasts.

WHITE WINE

• *Est! Est! Est!* Perhaps the most famous, surrounded by legend. It exists in both dry and demi-sec versions.

• *Cannellino di Frascati* Typical of the light and breezy afternoon drinking white wines of the *Castelli*.

• *Grottaferrata* A deliciously sharp-tasting wine, with a very distinctive bouquet.

It Is! It Is! It Is!

There was once a German man, some say he was a Cardinal, called Defuck, who was travelling through Lazio. He was very keen on wine, and would send his faithful servant, Martino, on ahead to seek out the best wine cellars as they approached a village. Martino would dutifully taste the wines, and when he found a household where good wine was kept in the cellar, he would write *EST!* on the door, so that Defuck would know where to stop. (*Est* – Latin for 'it is' – *vinum est bonum* – the wine is good).

At Montefiascone he came across a wine that was so excellent, he wrote *EST! EST! EST!* on the door. When Defuck turned up, he obviously agreed in full with Martino's opinion, because he died here from overdrinking, and his body was buried in the local graveyard, where his tombstone reminds all visitors of his sad end. Do go and look for it if you don't believe that this was really his name.

- *Zagarolo* Slightly flinty tasting, very dry.
- *Malvasia di Grottaferrata* Made with specially selected wines from local wineries, it's a demi-sec wine with a pleasantly sharp aftertaste. Dark golden yellow.

DESSERT WINE
- *Moscato di Terracina* Delicious, with the unmistakable flavour and bouquet of Muscatel.
- *Canzanese* A wine from the resort of San Felice Circeo. Unusually it's a sweet red wine.

BEVANDE
Drinks

- *Sambuca* This is a syrupy drink made with aniseed. In Italy it is either drunk straight as it is, with ice or in coffee. I can assure you that setting fire to it with coffee beans is just a tourist invention and you can enjoy it perfectly well without all that performance.

WORTH TAKING HOME

A wedge of *pecorino romano* is a must. Then a couple of bottles of Frascati wine, a string of good Roman garlic and one of onions, dried chickpeas, beans and lentils. Anything else you may want to buy, whether local of from any other region, will be available to you here, and will usually be of excellent quality – the secret lies in shopping around, which in Rome is never a hardship.

The best food shop in Rome is *CASTRONI*, in via Cola di Rienzo, across the Tiber, north of the Vatican. It's *molto snob*, and upmarket, but full of all regional and international specialities from regional cheeses from all parts of the country to Christmas puddings from England.

SAGRE E FESTE
Festivals

At Sutri, on 17 January, St Anthony's Day, they still carry out a ceremony called *Il Rinfresco del Deputato*. During the *Cavalleria*, a jousting contest, held on that day, raffle tickets are sold amongst the people. The winning ticket holder has to buy dinner for all the competitors – in exchange he carries the banner of St Anthony through the streets during the procession which marks the end of the festivities.

In Tuscania on the same day they celebrate the *Sagra della Fritella al Cavolfiore* – a village fête where they fry great panfuls of cauliflower fritters, drink the local wine and sing and dance the day away.

In Rome itself there are festivities throughout the year.

On March 19, St Joseph's Day, stalls sell *fritelle* fritters in the area called Trionfale, near the Vatican.

Easter Monday is the traditional day to have the first picnic of the year, and many people head out for the Colli Albani.

For the *Festa di San Giovanni* (St John) on June 23 and 24 there are feasts of snails and *porchetta* in Piazza di Porta di San Giovanni.

In July the banks of the Tiber are covered with stalls displaying regional food and wine, arts and crafts from all over Italy. On 4 July the American community has stalls, fireworks and hamburger feasts. In the last 2 weeks of July *La Festa de Noiantri* demonstrates Rome's best traditional feasting in Trastevere, when mountains of *maccheroni*, lamb, chicken and *pecorino* are tucked into, and wine flows happily.

Superstitious Peperoncino

because of the terrain, and the traditions and gastronomic specialities of sheep-farming links the two areas. Food is similar in both regions, though the famous *chitarra*, which makes the thick square spaghetti, is absolutely Abruzzese.

ABRUZZI – Cooks of Success

The entire region is mountainous and hilly, cut by green deep basins. The highest Apennine peaks

These 2 regions started off together in Roman times – they were the Fourth Roman Region. After the fall of Rome, Molise had a monstrously tormented history – passed from hand to hand by the Longobards, Saracens and Byzantines, ending up as a Norman possession under Frederick II, followed by years of misery and deprivation until it finally rejoined the Abruzzi in 1860. In 1963 the 2 regions were divided again for good, although in most people's minds they still remain linked.

They share a similar landscape, though the Abruzzi is more mountainous and densely wooded than Molise. Agriculture is difficult here

of the Gran Sasso massif soar up amongst vast plains covered with lean pastures and scraggy woods. It's a grandiose and awe-inspiring view which is both desolate and sour at the same time. The view of the valleys is green, gentle and rich, sweetened by rivers and streams. Then there's yet another sharp contrast – the jump from mountains to seashore. As the crow flies, only about 50 kilometres (approx. 30 miles) separate the highest peaks from the long sandy beaches lapped by the Adriatic. For about 120 kilometres (approx. 75 miles) the coastline stretches in an almost perfect straight line broken only by one high promontory, Punta della Penna. The land behind

117

the narrow sandy or pebbly beaches is fertile and cultivated.

These coastal areas enjoy a very mild climate, and thus good garden produce is found here. Inland, however, snow and rain fall in vast quantities during the winter months while the summers are extremely hot and dry. Since the year dot the region has been plagued by earthquakes – often with tragic consequences.

Magic and mystery

This is a region where magic is still very much part of the culture. The numbers 3, 7 and 13 are considered especially lucky. Take for example the legend surrounding *vitrù*, the classic Abruzzese *minestrone*, which says that it was originally prepared by 7 virgins, each of whom put in a special secret ingredient, creating a soup which is mysterious and virtuous at the same time. Or the fact that 7 soups are traditionally eaten on Christmas Eve, and that 7 meals are prepared and eaten on Harvest day. Spells, incantations, witchcraft, all are part of life in this region, and you can feel it in the air – it even surfaces in the cooking!

I'm unsure of what to make of such an odd combination of magic and food, of a region which boasts the world's most precise and careful chefs – it is generally considered that if a large household or a restaurant has an Abruzzese cook, then they need not worry about what they put in their mouths.

The common denominator which links all the dishes of this region is the strong *peperoncino* chilli pepper which livens up every mouthful. Being a sheep-farming and relatively poor region, pasta and mutton, lamb and kid form the basis of the cuisine, and *peperoncino* is used with careless abandon in all these dishes. Considered to be the most healthy spice available, guaranteed to prevent or cure all kinds of problems from neuralgia to arthritis, it is known locally as *pepedinie*, and none of the superb local stews, sauces or casseroles is complete without it. Many is the time I've tucked into what looked like an innocuous tomato sauce on pasta or meat to find myself gasping for the water jug. But the locals told me that the way to put out the fire was with a glassful of iced *Centerbe*, a liqueur made from herbs. This put out the fire but replaced it with a tingling glow from my toes upwards!

So the symbol of the cooking of these simple

La Pandarda

In this region they still carry out the rites of the ancient banquet which used to form part of long-gone pagan rituals. It's called *La Pandarda* and begins at midday with up to 30 or more courses. The idea is to go on eating until all is finished. It is NOT a good idea to turn down dishes if you are invited to one of these functions as you would mortally offend your hosts, and it is best not to get too involved in the ancient meaning behind the occasion.

cheery meals has to be *pepedinie* which manages to find its way in everywhere, and best complements the strong flavours of the local produce – even the fish get their fair share – *brodetto di pesce alla marinara* calls for 15 whole chillies for six people!

L'AQUILA & PROVINCE

According to legend, at some point in deepest history 99 castles were built on this site, high above sea level, surrounded by a crown of glorious mountains. The castles formed the beginnings of medieval Aquila. I really like the historical centre of this little place; simple and unprepossessing, it respects its past. I spent a week in a villa just outside the town, my bedroom window looking out over the red roofs and cedar trees.

I went to Coppito, a tiny town nearby, and had dinner at the *SALETTE AQUILANE*. The place felt as though the owner had moved in the previous day and hadn't yet organised the decor, but my friends assured me that it always looked like that, and indeed it seemed part of the charm. The service gave me an immediate insight into the warmth and friendliness for which the Abruzzesi are famous. And I ate one of their most famous dishes – wonderful *spaghetti alla chitarra*. These are made by rolling out the pasta dough over a specially made 'guitar' *la chitarra* of steel strings stretched across a wooden box. The dough is pushed through, resulting in a mass of square spaghetti. Mine had a brilliant red chilli and tomato sauce which rendered me speechless for quite some time. It was followed by *scamorza*, a sack-shaped cheese made so well by the local shepherds, which is cut in half and grilled over hot embers to make *scamorza ai ferri*.

That night when we got home, I realised I'd left my shutters open – and what that meant. Quite soon, there were two large bats screeching around over the bed. I was transfixed by the sight of Elena, my hostess, being dive-bombed by the things until one got completely stuck in her long blonde hair. Then I got my scissors out. She doesn't wear her hair long any more. To cheer her up I took everyone out to lunch the following day. We went to Sulmona, an ancient town at the foot of the Maiella mountains famous for making aromatic liqueurs from herbs, and as being the birthplace of Ovid in 43 BC. We ate at *ITALIA DA NICOLA*, which offered us roast *abbacchio* suckling lamb, and kid, and casseroled rabbit and hare.

The National Park of the Abruzzi is in this province – a huge wooded and mountainous area which used to be the Royal Family's hunting ground. Still full of wonderful wildlife – including wildcats, wolves and bears – it is a marvellous place for a picnic with plenty of local *salumi*, bread and wine.

The other three provinces of the Abruzzi, Teramo, Pesaro and Chieti, all contain growing towns with restaurants providing traditional local food, and always the friendly Abruzzese atmosphere.

SALUMI

Salami, Sausages and Cured Meats

There is a prevailing strong, coarse and very highly flavoured taste and texture in all the local *salumi*. It is well worth trying the *salami* and *prosciutto* labelled *di montagna* from the mountains, as they are often hand cured. *Mortadella di Campotosto* is very much like that from Bologna, though a little drier, and a great deal spicier, with a strong flavour of garlic.

The *salsicce di fegato di maiale* are superb pork liver sausages, soft and fragrant, and perfect for cooking over an open fire.

PASTA

Pasta is obviously very important to under-developed regions. The town of Fara San Martino is the home of manufactured pasta. A hand-made

---

Local Specialities

- *Vermicelli in salsa Abruzzese* Vermicelli dressed with a sauce made with chopped courgette flowers, saffron, parsley, onions and *pecorino*.
- *Crespelle* are a kind of lasagne, with a filling of *mozzarella*, artichokes, spinach, parsley and chicken livers. It is served at weddings in a tall timbale, cut into portions.

Abruzzi offering is the delicious spaghetti or *maccheroni alla chitarra* made with the guitar-like wire-framed instrument I've already described. *Scripelle* are little pasta fritters, more like pancakes, which you'll find at the bottom of a bowl of broth. Or they can be cooked *in timballo* with layers of *mozzarella*, mince and spinach.

Strengozze or *maltagliate* are irregular-shaped pasta pieces, made of flour and water, which are always dressed with a mutton sauce.

PESCE E FRUTTI DI MARE

Fish and Seafood

Although the sea is so near, this is not a land of fishermen. Of course some fishing is carried out, and all the most common fish of the Adriatic will appear on the menu in seaside resorts. There are many wonderful fish specialities, but this is a region of shepherds and meat is always the priority. In Pescara they combine the ubiquitous

---

Local Specialities

- *Acciughe all'Abruzzese* Fresh anchovies split and stuffed with a salted anchovy, tossed in egg and flour and fried in olive oil.
- *Seppioline alla cetrullo* Small squid filled with parsley, capers, garlic and salted anchovies which are first fried, sautéed in wine, then boiled in water to finally tenderise them – they are very tasty and perfect in any climate.
- *Stoccafisso all'Abruzzese* Stew of stockfish with potatoes, tomatoes, dried *porcini*, chilli, and bay leaves.
- *Trotelle al pomodoro* Small trout cooked in a casserole with tomatoes.

peperoncino with an assortment of fish to produce *brodetto alla pescarese*, an extremely hot, peppery fish stew. Local white wine vinegar is used to preserve octopus or small squid, with *peperoncino* and garlic, too. The mountain streams also produce fresh fish, notably trout.

CARNE E CACCIA
Meat and Game

Without question mutton, lamb and kid are the most important meat. Lamb *agnello* is either roasted or grilled, or cooked in delicious stew, usually lightly flavoured with chilli. Mutton *pecora* is almost always casseroled. *Abbacchio* is a young unweaned lamb that is often cut into chunks and roasted. *Castrato* is a young castrated sheep or kid, often used to make roasts or minced

---

Local Specialities

- *Agnello a cutturo* Lamb cooked in a huge pot with plenty of fragrant herbs.
- *Agnello all'arrabbiata* Pieces of lamb cooked with plenty of *peperoncino*.
- *N'docca n'docca* A calorie-packed pork offal stew for cold winter days.
- *Tacchino alla canzanese* Boned and rolled turkey, boiled with plenty of herbs, then covered with a thick jelly made from the ground bones.

---

up to made a kind of meat loaf, *alenoto di castrato*. This is also used to make the delicious casserole with tomatoes, wine, herbs, celery and onions called *intingolo di castrato*.

Pork *maiale* is used a great deal to make sausages, *salami* and the local coarse *prosciutto*, leaving the odd bits like the trotters, ears, head and so on to be made into specialities like *n'docca n'docca* and *zampini in gelatina* a hot dish of pigs' trotters in their own jelly, coloured pink by the addition of tomato.

Poultry is very good quality, and they eat turkey for Christmas dinner. Hare *lepre*, rabbit *coniglio* and pigeon *piccione* are the only types of game I've come across here, and they are often in stews or turned into pasta sauces.

FORMAGGIO
Cheese

Scamorza, that sack-shaped cheese, takes pride of place. To my mind it is perfect in every way, both in flavour and texture – and it grills to perfection on the barbecue.

Various *caciotta* cheeses are also made from ewes' milk and are available throughout the region. *Pecorino Abruzzese* is similar to the Roman cheese and is used grated over pasta instead of *parmigiano*. It is worth shopping around for cheese in this region – most good cheese shops will let you have a taste before you part with your lire.

FRUTTA E VERDURA
Fruit and Vegetables

Overlooking the Adriatic is a stretch of land famous for its garden produce: carrots, potatoes, and beetroot are grown successfully. Delicious floury potatoes grow in the now drained bed of Lake Fucino. Cardoons *cardi*, celery *sedano* and peppers *peperoni* are excellent local products too, and wheat is grown in the sheltered basins inland. Much of this produce is of such good quality that it finds its way to the markets of Rome and Naples.

Two of the traditional products of the Abruzzi are saffron and licorice *zafferano e liquirizia*, which are used in confectionery and the pharmaceutical industry.

Figs *fichi* and *uva regina* grapes are particularly good here, and eaten fresh make a marvellous combination with local cheeses and *salumi* for picnics or light snacks.

PASTICCERIA
Cakes, Biscuits and Puddings

- *Cassata Abruzzese* Speciality of Sulmona, it is layers of sponge cake with 3 different custards between each layer, chocolate, caramel and nougat.
- *Parrozzo Abruzzese* Simple cake taking its name from *pan rozzo*, the old peasant cake of little round *focaccine* covered with chocolate. It has evolved into a light buttery almondy cake with bitter chocolate covering.

Auguri!

At all Italian weddings *confetti* of sugared almonds are given to the guests as a gift from the bride and groom. Either the almonds are handed out with a ladle or they are brought wrapped up in a tulle square with a small gift attached, and a card with the names of the happy pair inside. But at an Abruzzi wedding I went to recently they did something completely different and apparently traditional. After a 7-hour banquet the bride and groom walked through the village streets to their bedroom for the night with all the guests following on the opposite pavement – all throwing sugared almonds at the happy couple to hurry them on their way. Only once safely indoors did the pelting cease and the extremely loud crowd of guests disperse.

- *Nocci Attorrati* Toasted almonds with a sugar covering.
- *Sanguinaccio* Jam-like spread made with freshly-killed pig's blood, candied fruit, almonds, nuts and *mosto*. Traditionally made in the Chieti area in November and December when the *mosto* from the wine harvest and the blood from the recently-killed pig are readily available.
- *Pepatelli* Christmas speciality from Teramo of biscuits made with fine bran, flour, honey and white pepper.
- *Pizza di Ricotta* A tart with *ricotta*, candied peel, maraschino and cinnamon.
- *Torrone al Cioccolato* Soft nougat covered with chocolate – a famous product of Aquila.
- *Torrone di Fichi Secchi* A wonderful version of nougat with dried figs, from Chieti.

VINO
Wine

On these craggy rocks you won't find lush vineyards and fat shiny grapes for making wines like those that have made Piedmont, Lombardy and Tuscany famous. The vine has to cling to the little soil it has and drag what goodness it can out of it – the results are wines that have a somewhat sour, bitterish, almost home-made quality about them.

RED WINE
- *Marsicano Rosso* A good basic red table wine made in the province of Aquila. Sometimes available as a rosé.
- *Montepulciano d'Abruzzo* Considered one of the best wines of Central Italy, this is a D.O.C. wine, which complements the traditional rustic specialities of the region. There is a cherry red version called
- *Cerasuolo d'Abruzzi* which is sometimes considered better than the *Montepulciano* for its more elegant and refined characteristics.

There are 3 local wines which will usually only be available within the region, that vary from white to red to rosé depending on the year. They are *Pergolone*, *Roseolo* and *Rustico*.

WHITE WINE
- *Peligno Bianco* Produced with the white grapes of the Peligno valley in the province of Aquila. Excellent with fish.
- *Trebbiano d'Abruzzo* The best version comes from Chieti, where it is made using only Trebbiano grapes. Elsewhere it is mixed with other wines. An excellent table wine which goes extremely well with cheese and vegetable dishes. If aged at least a year it will be worth drinking with fish.

DESSERT WINE
- *Moscato Bianco* Delicious golden yellow wine with a bitterish aftertaste, perfect with *parozzo* or other local cakes.

BEVANDE
Drinks

- *Centerbe* The most famous of all the Abruzzi liqueurs, this is a bitter-sweet concoction made with 100 or more wild herbs gathered in the mountains. Once made (it can be prepared very easily at home) it can be drunk from one month after it's bottled.
- *Ratafia* A home-made and wonderfully warm-

ing liqueur made in June when *amarene* bitter cherries are at their best. It has to stand for 40 days in the sun before being bottled – the older it is the better it is. It was designed to be drunk during the freezing winter months to keep snow-bound households warm and cheerful.

WORTH TAKING HOME

Centerbe is a must. It usually comes in a lovely ornamental bottle, and if chilled makes a very pleasant after-dinner digestif.

Torrone keeps for months, and will make delicious gifts. *Pepatelli* is such an unusual combination of honey and pepper it's worth buying to let others taste it too! Any local cheeses – remember that *scamorza* barbecues brilliantly. Take home as many whole *pepedinie* chillies as you can and hang them up in your kitchen. Any of the local wines are worth taking home with you, too.

SAGRE E FESTE
Festivals

St Anthony's day, 17 January, is very well respected: Caramanico has fireworks and they eat boiled corn-on-the-cob to celebrate the day. In Villavallelonga they eat broad beans and *panette*, bread made with eggs and flour.

At L'Aquila they celebrate the day with *La Sagra della Porchetta* – a whole pig is roasted on the spit, eaten with bread and plenty of wine to the tune of the local band.

At Alfandena they have *La Sagra della Salsiccia*, where sausages are the theme of the day, grilled in the open air and eaten with bread and wine.

Aquilano di Tossicia celebrates the *Sagra del Timballo Aprutino* on 4 August. Local housewives prepare the traditional dish of stuffed fritters for visitors among singing and dancing.

At Giulianova around 9 August, a traditional port festival is held, with a procession of fishing boats in the sea, lots of fried fish and a marvellous firework display.

MOLISE – Sleeping Beauty

Whereas the Abruzzi seems to have always been relatively successful, Molise, a bit more remote, gives me the impression that it's still recovering from its past. Like Basilicata, this is a sort of sleeping region, waiting for a handsome prince to wake it up with a large cheque and a sensible plan to improve the situation. The rest of the country thinks of Molise as desperately lonely and poor – indeed it is, but it is also very beautiful. The people seem content with their simplicity and gentle farming existence. But there are problems: there is very little tourism because there are practically no major roads, there is no industrial development, and even agriculture is held back by the way in which the land is divided up into small fields, and by the extreme stoniness of the soil – all of which makes the use of modern farm machinery impossible. So, like parts of the Abruzzi, sheep-farming is the main resource.

The climate on the coastline is typically Mediterranean, and inland the snow sometimes lasts right into June. While summers are affected by drought, in November the rain never seems to stop.

CAMPOBASSO & PROVINCE

Contrary to its name, which means 'low field', Campobasso is a major market town built on a hill dominating the Biferno valley, an agricultural plain growing vegetables. Termoli is the only other major town, a seaside resort and port where ferries to the Tremiti Islands set sail.

ISERNIA & PROVINCE

Isernia dates from the 2nd century B.C., and has several well-kept Roman and medieval monuments. It is an important crossroads for communications with Campania, Lazio and the Abruzzi, and an agricultural market town. Agnone is an agricultural and holiday centre, favoured by Italians who believe holidays *in collina* in the hills to be very healthy. There is a marvellous old restaurant here called *RISTORANTE DEI BUONI AMICI*, where they serve excellent hand-made durum wheat pasta with delicious mutton and tomato sauce.

SALUMI
Salami, Sausages and Cured Meats

The *salumi* are coarse peasant-style standbys – designed to warm and satisfy during the winter months. *Pamparella* is delicious dried pork, preserved in *peperoncino*. It is a vital ingredient for many of the best pasta sauces. It is normally sold loose, and requires soaking in water to reconstitute it before use.

Prosciutto affumicato is smoked *prosciutto*, though there is also a non-smoked one. All kinds of delicious sausages *salsicce* in various sizes and all with a strong flavour, underlined with *peperoncino*.

PASTA

In a region that has known such despair and misery, where the ground seems to yield very little and cash is always short, pasta comes into its own. Dressed very simply with tomatoes and/or chilli, pasta in 100 different shapes is at the heart of the gastronomic scene in Molise. The locals are very good at making it at home, and one of the best commercial packet varieties throughout the country is called *La Molisana*. The very food that was created out of poverty, with the simplest ingredients, flour and water, continues to triumph in this area where poverty is still part of everyday life.

Tacconi are sheets of pasta, hand-made with flour and water, which are then cut into little pieces, boiled and dressed with a sauce.

PESCE E FRUTTI DI MARE
Fish and Seafood

Just about the only alternative to meat or pasta is the excellent trout caught in the Biferno river. Since by tradition this is a shepherding people, the locally-caught fish is exported to Rome's markets rather than be eaten in any quantity by the inhabitants. Fishing takes place round the Tremiti Islands. *Brodetto di pesce alla marinara* is made on board the boats with the very freshest haul of the morning. Various kinds of fish are cooked together, flavoured with plenty of chilli and olive oil and eaten with hunks of the delicious coarse bread.

Local Specialities
- *Capretto allo spiedo alla Molisana* Young kid, wrapped in sheets of lard and turned slowly over a fire on a spit. The lard is removed near the end of cooking to give a crisp golden skin.
- *Coniglio alla Molisana* Pieces of rabbit, cooked on sticks, each piece wrapped in a slice of ham and a small sausage. The rabbit pieces alternate on the sticks with leaves of sage and are cooked over a herb-scented fire.
- *Gniummeriddi* A common dish in all the southern regions of the country. Lamb's gut, stuffed with liver, heart and lung, and cooked over an open wood fire.
- *Pezzata* Mutton stew, which in spite of difficulties in cooking because of the almost overpowering flavour of the meat, is mild and delicious.

CARNE E CACCIA
Meat and Game

The meat in Molise is typical of the shepherds – lamb, mutton and kid – just like in the Abruzzi, with the addition of some rabbit and pork. And as in all poor regions, offal is popular.

FORMAGGIO
Cheese

Molise is famous for its excellent ewes' milk cheese – they've learnt by years of experience. *Pecorino*, a highly flavoured one, and *pecorino con la goccia*, which is a soft version, going gooey at the edges. *Provolone* is a huge oval cheese with a strong flavour, which is also available smoked. *Ricotta* is made with cows' milk whey.

FRUTTA E VERDURA
Fruit and Vegetables

The farming is mostly at subsistence level and there are only a few coastal areas where the methods of farming are sophisticated enough to allow produce to be sent to market. Dessert grapes are the main produce, with some peaches *pesche*, apricots *albicocche*, plums *susine* and apples *mele*. Most hardy vegetables are available, beans *fagioli*, potatoes *patate*, tomatoes *pomodori*, chickpeas *ceci* and wheat and some other cereals. Peppers *peperoni*, aubergines *melanzane*, and fiery chillies *peperoncini* are also grown.

PASTICCERIA
Cakes, Biscuits and Puddings

Not many cakes here, there's no time or money for frivolous eating. Most of these cakes are made for particular festivals.

• *Ostie Richiene* The famous Christmas speciality. Hosts (circles of rice paper) are filled with almonds and nuts.

• *Ferratelle* Special wafer-thin cakes made with a hot iron, rather like French *galettes*. Tradition has it that you must place the dough on the bottom plate of the iron, bring the top plate down to close it, and then cook for as long as it takes you to say a short prayer!

• *Fiadoni* Only just sweet pastries with a cheesy filling. Each pastry is finished off with an olive leaf stuck in the top.

• *Torta di Pasqua con perline* A very simple light cake, sprinkled with sugar. Usually eaten on Easter morning, after it has been blessed at Mass, with hard-boiled eggs and slices of *salame*.

VINO
Wine

The region has only two D.O.C. wines – allowed, so I'm told, more for encouragement than as an indication of the quality! They are *Biferno* and *Pentro*, both available in red, white and rosé. Other wines of the region include:

RED WINE
• *Montepulciano del Molise* A dry red wine. Certain to become a D.O.C. wine.
• *Ramitello Rosso* Dry and red, made with a combination of Montepulciano and Sangiovese grapes.

WHITE WINE
• *Ramitello Bianco* The white version of the above, made with Trebbiano and Malvasia grapes.

WORTH TAKING HOME

Bunches of *peperoncino* again, it grows so red and strong here. *Pecorino* and all kinds of local cheese, particularly if you can buy them from shepherds' stalls by the roadsides, or from farms. At Isernia, Michele Pulsone sells marvellous tiny *mozzarelle* called *latticini*.

11 CAMPANIA

Pompeii, Pizze e Pomi d'Oro

This is a region where Mamma Nature has worked overtime. The landscape is either stunningly beautiful or excitingly dangerous, but either way the whole world comes to admire it.

At least 10 different races have left their mark on Naples alone – Greek, Roman, Byzantine, Gothic, Saracen, Teutonic, Balkan, Castilian, Catalan and Gaul. The Phoenicians, Samnites and Longobards also set up home here. Yet, the specialities on offer in the average Neapolitan *trattoria*, spread out on market stalls or parked on the family balcony are neither Greek, nor Teutonic, nor Gallic – when it came to the kitchen, and eating, the Spaniards won hands down, leaving an all-embracing, warm, bright rich and filling array of dishes.

There is no land anywhere in the world where

vegetables and fruit grow so full of richness and flavour and perfume. Any local will tell you that what *he* needs to survive is bread, tomatoes, oil and wine – but they must have come from *his* Campania. There is a pride and a cheery make-the-best-of-it quality here which is completely charming. The air is filled with the scent of frying oil and tomato sauce, baking pizzas and freshly-caught fish. Happiness is the most important ingredient here – it's a region which thrives on exuberance, a playful corner of the world that is never content to be still – like a wide open smiling face.

Campania is a long, wide region, with a very varied landscape, stretching from Garigliano in the north right down to Sapri on the Gulf of Policastro in the south. Surrounding it are the regions of Lazio, Molise, Puglia and Basilicata.

The coastline, plains and islands all boast of an exceptionally pleasant climate, the sea breezes cool down the summer, and provide mild winters. Rain is scarce. Inland, winter is almost unknown – the only place it really gets cold and snows is very high in the mountains.

Magic and Miracles

In Campania, where the forces of nature, the weight of history and the strength of man have pulled together to make this the south's most prosperous and exciting region, there is yet another dimension which has its hold on the people – the supernatural. Divine intervention has acted as a counterpoint to the overwhelming belief in magic. There are thousands of miracles attributed to the Holy Virgin Mary and the saints, thousands of churches and sanctuaries built to commemorate the immense devotion of the faithful.

In a land where religious fervour and pagan beliefs are still so much the order of the day, there is the even deeper mystery of the earth's own disturbances – volcanic eruptions and earthquakes. The first dated testimonies of earthquakes go back 5,400 years. Pliny died in 70 AD because he stayed to attempt a written account of the vast eruption of Vesuvius which occurred that year. Nowadays scientists have the means to tell us why these natural catastrophes occur, but the sunshine and the sea are not enough to give the

region the optimism it deserves. Faces are still marked by the grief caused by the enormous loss of life following the earthquake of 1980.

In Campania man is only in charge of his destiny if the laws of nature see fit. So, religious belief and magic mix together to give hope and faith to the community at large.

Dare to eat the golden apple

And finally, to introduce you to this land of enchantment where the art of *arrangiarsi* (getting on with it, making the best of a bad job, inventing one's living) has its finest roots: It was the Neapolitans who were first daring enough to eat tomatoes. Having arrived in Europe from South America in the 16th century, these 'fruits' spent quite some time hanging about before the people of Naples, no doubt attracted by the brilliant red colour and shiny skin, finally gave in to temptation and married it off to what has become its perfect and eternal wife – pasta, or on the mistress – pizza.

So, the symbols of Campanian cooking must be the bright red, hardly cooked fresh tomato, on mounds of steaming maccheroni or spaghetti, so *al dente* that they're called *veddi veddi* ('green green' – like sour fruits), pizza, and mountains of sparkling fresh fish . . . to the tune of a mandolin.

NAPOLI & PROVINCE

Parts of Naples may be squalid, her slums are diabolical, but it's a city of theatre, music and the arts, situated in one of the most stunningly beautiful bays in the Mediterranean.

Thousand-year-old pizza

Pizza is Naples' most famous gastronomic contribution to the world. The Greeks and Romans were the first to have anything to do with pizza's ancestor: Roman *moretum* was none other than plain white pizza, baked in the oven and eaten with raw onion. Round about the year 1000 the word *picea* was used to describe the famous disc of bread dough coated with all her colourful toppings of herbs, fish or red onion. Soon after, *pizza* entered the Italian language as an official word. In the 17th century a Neapolitan operetta was written which contained the song *'Le due Pizzelle'*, but it wasn't until the 18th century that *'la Regina Pizza'* came into being, a pizza with tomato topping. In 1889, *Pizza Margherita*, the

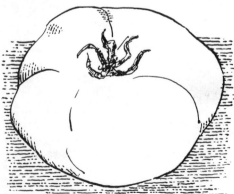

most famous and popular of them all was born. That summer, King Umberto and Queen Margherita of Italy decided to spend their summer holiday at Capodimonte.

The queen had heard so much about pizza, but had never eaten it. Finding herself in the kingdom of the pizza she demanded that it be prepared for her. Don Raffaele Esposito, the most famous of all pizza makers, was brought to the court. He made several kinds of pizze for his queen, among which was one representing the colours of the flag, red – tomato, white – *mozzarella*, and green – basil. This was her favourite, and from that day on has been called *Pizza alla Margherita*.

Any occasion is good enough for eating pizza to the Neapolitan – breakfast, mid-morning, lunch, tea or supper. For those of you who wish to keep pace with pizza's historical background, go to the *pizzerie* in Naples' historical centre, particularly the one at Port'Alba, considered by most to be Naples' best. Here d'Annunzio and di Giacomo have sat and eaten. For the younger generation, there are countless *pizzerie* with wooden tables and benches, brightly coloured lights and music – ideal meeting places. If you fancy a walk, at Vico Equense, on the Sorrento coast, you'll find the famous *pizza al metro*, baked in long oblong tins. It's sold by length – metres or centimetres – as required. All Naples' *pizzerie* have little windows

Pizza – The Full Story

Recently the pizza makers of Naples got to the stage where their traditional art form and internationally renowned dish was being so badly bastardised the world over, appearing with the most weird and unorthodox toppings, that it was decided that for a chef to be able to call a pizza a Pizza he had to conform to a series of rules and regulations, as drawn up by the pizza makers' confederation. This turns pizza almost into a D.O.C. element, with regular checks being carried out nationally to make sure the rules are being abided by.

For pizza to be Pizza, it has to be prepared in a specific way, be baked in a brick oven, and have only a proper traditional topping. Thank goodness somebody cares that much!

Here are some of the ways in which the world-famous Neapolitan speciality will be prepared:

- *Pizza ai Cicenielli* Tiny little fish like whitebait are spread all over the plain pizza. No tomato, just garlic, pepper and plenty of good olive oil.
- *Pizza ai Funghi* You should get just mushrooms, no tomatoes, with garlic, parsley and olive oil. However, more often than not, you will get the mushrooms *and* the tomato.
- *Pizza al Pomodoro* Topped with tomato, chopped parsley and basil. Seasoned with salt and pepper and olive oil. If a handful of *par-*

migiano is added, it's called *al pomodoro e formaggio*.
- *Pizza alla Marinara* Often causes confusion as people expect fish on it, but it is called this because the sailors love it so much. The oldest and simplest way of preparing pizza, it's oil, tomato, garlic, salt and pepper and a pinch of oregano.
- *Pizza alle Vongole* Cooked clams, spread over a pizza baked with tomato, oregano, salt and pepper.
- *Pizza Quattro Stagioni* All kinds of revolting messes have been served under this name. The original means a pizza with four sections, each one housing a different topping. These should be: clams, mussels, artichoke hearts and black olives. They can be laid directly on to the plain pizza base, or on top of a tomato, oil, salt and pepper topping.
- *Pizza alla Romana* This is what the Neapolitans call what the Romans call *Pizza alla Napoletana*! It is actually the only kind of pizza that should have *mozzarella* on it, but times have changed so much since the original recipes!
- *Calzone* Literally meaning trouser leg, this is a circle of pizza, filled with *salame, mozzarella*, hard-boiled egg, folded in half then baked or deep fried.

strategically placed to look on to the street, with the various pizze and *calzoni* on view, to be bought and eaten, wrapped in paper, as you walk, not to be tortured by knife and fork, so as not to lose any of the heat or flavour.

Coffee on your doorstep

The ritual of coffee drinking is another aspect of Naples which must not be forgotten. Once upon a time *O Caffettiere* was the early morning walking alarm clock. Unable to afford a shop, he would bring the coffee round the streets in a basket, piping hot and fragrant, so that even the poorest family would have a moment's luxury – home-delivered coffee – at the start of the day.

In the 18th and 19th centuries, cafés were important meeting places for writers, poets and artists, Neapolitan or not. The *CAFFÈ GAMBRINUS* (still a very 'in' joint) was where d'Annunzio wrote most of his poems; the *CAFFÈ NOTTE E GIORNO* is a twenty-four-hour spectacle of Neapolitan life. Here you can sit with the lorry driver having his breakfast at dawn before starting his long-haul trip, or watch the snobs trip in on their way back from a cabaret show (I saw Andy Warhol here), or watch the jealous husband gnash his teeth over a glass of something or other. Coffee always, but it must be real coffee – preferably made with the traditional Neapolitan coffee machine, which allows the water to trickle softly through the strong roasted grounds, so as not to 'burn' the coffee, and thus giving it full flavour.

Dopo la messa

Sunday lunch after Mass is a ritual for Neapolitans – a huge plate of pasta dressed with excellent *ragù*. This varies according to household, family traditions and family likes and dislikes, but *Il Mangiatore di Maccheroni* the Maccheroni eater is still a traditional image of Neapolitan life and theatre – the eating, selling and buying of the dish always crops up in Commedia dell'Arte scenes. For many, it's the only day of the week that meat is eaten, but *ragù* is always made with beef or pork, with sultanas, pinenuts and many other optional additions.

In the shadow of Vesuvius

Outside Naples, everything lies in the shadow of the volcano. Its volcanic soil makes crops grow rich and abundantly. Tomatoes, vines and vege-

Food Relics from the Ashes

From the digs at Pompeii it has been possible to establish that the common kitchen was very small, with an earth floor and no chimney. There was a sink, a bread oven and a few 'rings' on which to cook, situated in the brick wall. Knives, spatulas, wooden, metal and bone spoons, sieves, grills, spits, pestles and mortars and containers made of terracotta or bronze have all been found.

The food itself, amphorae containing wine, oil, must, fish sauce, olives, dried fruit and vegetables, and fresh fruit and vegetables, was all kept in a separate pantry. The fish sauces would have been bought pre-packed in terracotta pots in either Greece, Spain or the Black Sea.

Saucepans most commonly used for cooking were made of clay with a lid. There were several different spoons, each with its own purpose, one for oysters, one for eggs, and huge ladles for dishing out wine.

tables, whatever grows here is of superb quality. Here are the historical centres of Pompeii, Ercolano and Baia sul Golfo. Pompeii was perfectly preserved under its cover of ashes and lava until 1860, when it was first uncovered. To the visitor it now appears like magic, with tree-lined avenues, temples, *osterie*, the market, the gladiators' gymnasium, public buildings and private homes, mosaics, fountains, columns, amphorae that once contained wine. It's all there to see, casting a spell of its own on whoever comes.

At Ercolano, *LA STALLA* is a *trattoria* thick with pilgrims to the Basilica or tourists to the ruins, but providing excellent local food. There is local *salame, soppressata, fusilli al ragù, spaghetti alle vongole* with clams, *verdure sott 'olio* vegetables in oil, *carne e pesce alla brace* meat and fish over charcoal, and the local wine is the light and sparkling *Lettere*. Also in Ercolano *LE GINESTRE* has terraces overlooking the foot of Vesuvius. You can sit and admire the view over a variety of original antipasti, then move on to *linguine* with lobster, or the traditional *spaghetti alle vongole veraci* with fresh clams in their shells and follow that with superb grilled or roast fish.

The excellent wine is made with grapes from the vineyards you see before you.

Pearls in the Gulf

The islands of Capri and Ischia are inundated with tourists – Capri, made famous by Emperor Tiberius and his orgies, has given the *Insalata Caprese* to the world. Ideally suited to the climate, it is the original salad of *mozzarella*, tomatoes, basil and olive oil.

Ischia has less to see of historical interest, but instead this is the place to go for hot thermal spring swimming, or warm mud baths. The only covered spa, which includes mud baths, is at the Antiche Terme Comunali by the port. I guarantee a marvellous experience, particularly if you go when the air is chilly – to be cold and then swim in hot water is quite exceptionally wonderful.

Afterwards, go to *UGO, RISTORANTE GIARDINI DELL'EDEN*, for excellent island fare – beautiful *antipasti di mare*, spaghetti with sea urchin sauce, marvellous stuffed peppers and aubergines ... you'll be hungry after your swim. This is non-snob Ischia cuisine, not jet-setters' food.

CASERTA & PROVINCE

This town is best known for its magnificent Palazzo Reale of the Bourbons, behind which is the vast parkland, filled with statues, fountains and waterfalls. The province is mostly flat, and easy to cultivate, the rich volcanic soil yielding all manner of luscious and tasty fruit and vegetables, especially aubergines, tomatoes, peas, beans and salads, all of which take a high priority in the cuisine.

SALERNO & PROVINCE

The oldest part of Salerno scrambles round the central hill on top of which perches the Norman castle of Arechi. This is an industrial city, its port amongst the most important in southern Italy. The main towns of the region are Nocera Inferiore, Cavi dei Tirreni and Battipaglia, all of which are main agricultural markets selling the best of local produce – cherries, plums, melons, tomatoes and fish from the coast. Here look out for *friarelli*, the tender broccoli that grow only here. Along the coast lie Amalfi, Vietri sul Mare and Positano, package tour paradise.

BENEVENTO & PROVINCE

This is a city in a mountainous province, which has kept its name since 275 BC, when the Romans won their battle with Pyrrhus and renamed the town which had previously been called Maleventum, because of its centuries-old associations with pagan worship, witches and wizards. Today it is the home of the liqueur Strega.

The territory of the province is generally unpopulated and fairly lonely. In the high valley of the Fortore is San Bartolomeo in Galdo, an important market town. Sant'Agata dei Goti markets the cherries, plums, melons and figs and marvellous vegetables grown in the surrounding rich fertile fields.

AVELLINO & PROVINCE

This province suffered great loss from the earthquake of 1980. The main town of Avellino is extremely old, and of important historical value, yet with a lively modern atmosphere. I found lots of marvellous shops – if you're passing through and wanting picnic fare, the *TERMINIO* cheese shop is worth a visit for local *treccia*, *mozzarella*, *pecorino* and *caciocavallo*. Deliciously tasty local bread from *IERMANO* in viale Gramsci, and round off the shopping with pastries from *PASTICCERIA DIANA* in corso Vittorio Emanuele.

SALUMI
Salami, Sausages and Cured Meats

The most outstanding feature of the local *salumeria* is that it is blessed with a really good strong flavour – there is no delicate *prosciuttino* to be found down here. *Salame Napoletano* is highly flavoured and peppery. A bit too fatty for my taste, but delicious with good fresh bread. The *prosciutto Napoletano* also tends to be very highly flavoured with good thick fat round the edges, which can be used as the basis for many pasta sauces, and is often used instead of bacon. The *salsicce* are small and strong, particularly the tiny little brain sausage *cervellatino*. Very common is *strutto*, lard, which is used for frying, one of the most common cooking methods for the area – Neapolitan housewives are famous for being good *friggitrici* fryers.

Local Specialities

• *Laganelle e Ceci Laganelle* are slightly wider than *tagliatelle*, made with just flour and water, and are part of a dish called *Lampe e Tuone* Thunder and Lightning. This is a winter pasta soup with chickpeas, liberally sprinkled with oregano.

• *Lasagna di Carnevale* Wide strips of dry pasta arranged in layers with meatballs, sausages, hard-boiled eggs, *ricotta, mozzarella* and Parmesan cheese, all dressed with a rich *ragù*, pork or beef, and tomato sauce.

• *Pasta e Spolichini* A traditional dish from the island of Ischia. The secret lies in using three or four different kinds of pasta, so as to create a jumble of shapes. *Spolichini* are a kind of bean. The beans and pasta are cooked separately, and mixed just before serving.

• *Spaghetti aglio e 'oglio'* The simplest of all pasta dishes, very healthy and quick to make. A pan of olive oil with garlic fried into it, a small piece of red chilli, and a handful of chopped parsley, poured over *al dente* spaghetti and tossed.

• *Strangoloprieve* Home-made *maccheroni* – usually dressed with *ragù*, or a simple lard and tomato sauce.

PASTA

If Emilia Romagna is the home of fresh pasta, then Campania is the adoptive parent of dry durum wheat pasta – as bought in packets. In days gone by this area was famous for its wheatfields, producing excellent grain. Nowadays it is mostly imported from North America and Canada, but still the Neapolitan passion burns for his steaming plate of pasta dressed with a brilliant red sauce. There are many local factories making pasta which the Neapolitans collectively call *maccheroni* or *maccarune*. Under this name, the locally preferred pasta shapes are the following: *zite, zitone, mezze zite, paccheri, vermicelli, linguine, maltagliati, fusilli, perciatelli, farfalloni* and many many more. The last time I researched this, there were 652 shapes.

Local Specialities

• *Capitone Marinato* Traditional dish served on Christmas Eve. A huge fat eel is cooked in vinegar with bay leaves and garlic, then left to marinate in its sauce for several days. It is eaten cold as an *antipasto* with bread to mop up the marinade.

• *Impepata di Cozze* Open mussels coated with a great deal of freshly ground pepper and cooked with garlic and parsley.

• *Polpo alla Luciana* Reef-caught octopus, cooked with garlic, *peperoncino* and parsley, served with olive oil and lemon juice.

• *Zuppa di Pesce* Fish soup consisting of fresh fish and seafood cooked together very quickly in tomato, *peperoncino* and parsley and poured over slices of toasted bread.

PESCE E FRUTTI DI MARE

Fish and Seafood

The seafood and fish of the Gulf of Naples have been famous for centuries. These people adore their sea and are passionate about the fruits it yields for them. Market tables are covered with an astonishing array of fresh fish, blessed it is said with a superior flavour thanks to the presence of a particular weed in the sea – although recent pollution *inquinamento* has no doubt put paid to that. Great efforts are, in fact, being made to purify the sea. In some areas mini-purifiers are actually set up inside the restaurant dining rooms, and live seafood is purified before being cooked.

Pescato della Mattinata means 'what was caught this morning', so you will be offered a selection of the fresh haul of the day. The selection is always varied and depends entirely on weather conditions, luck and state of the sea. The better-quality fish like gilthead *orata* or sea bass *spigola* will be cooked most simply, while the cheaper the fish, the more it will be dressed up. Expensive fish will be priced on the menu according to weight.

There may be swordfish *pesce spada*, which

will be cut into hunky steaks and grilled or stewed. Very popular are octopus and squid *polpi e seppioline*, used in a wide variety of local dishes. *Cozze*, huge succulent orange mussels, and *vongole* little clams will turn up in seafood salads, on spaghetti or can be eaten in the shells. Lobster *aragosta* less impressive than the Sardinian variety, but nevertheless very tasty, and big juicy prawns *gamberoni* are grilled, baked or fried.

The local *Zuppa di pesce* is made with *scrofano*, *pesce rospo* and *soglioline*, scorpion fish, toadfish and tiny Adriatic soles, tomatoes and herbs.

Anchovies *acciughe* are the unmissable ingredient for Pizza Napoletana. *Capitone* is a huge eel, traditionally served on Christmas Eve.

Sea urchins *ricci* have become considerably more risky in recent years because of pollution, but are still very popular and can be bought from street sellers to be eaten as you sightsee, or will appear on pasta dishes.

Mussillo is the local version of *baccalà*, though why they should need dried fish with this wealth of fresh delights is quite beyond me.

CARNE E CACCIA

Meat and Game

On the plains, beef and milk cows are kept by many farmers. Higher up on the mountain slopes, sheep farming is still widely practised. Sheep and goat farming were once a much more widely popular method of earning one's living, but today such a hard life is no longer attractive and most people prefer to look for a job in the factories. Beef *manzo* and veal *vitello* are therefore the two most common types of meat on the menu, followed by pork and chicken, with some kid and lamb at Easter time.

In the provinces tucked further inland, local mountain game such as wild boar *cinghiale* and venison *capriolo* are often 'dish of the day'.

FORMAGGIO

Cheese

Lazio, the Abruzzi and other regions just play at making *mozzarella*. Here they take it very seriously indeed, and once you have tasted the local version, no other will ever taste the same! The Piana del Sele is the main buffalo-rearing area, and from the buffalo milk, fat, round, perfect *mozzarella* is produced, *Mozzarella di Bufala*. It tastes slightly fattier, more cheesy than the milky cow's variety.

Treccia is another version, strips of cows' milk *mozzarella* which are plaited into a braid about 7 inches long.

Smaller, juicy *mozzarelle* are called *latticini* or *bocconcini*, and *cigliegine* are even smaller round ones!

Pecorino is very good here – hard local ewes' milk cheese for grating on certain pasta dishes.

Provolone is one of the largest Italian cheeses and like *pecorino* is available *dolce* mild or *piccante* peppery. It has quite a hard texture and a pale colour. *Provola* is a smaller version of the same thing – you buy a whole one to feed about six people.

FRUTTA E VERDURA

Fruit and Vegetables

Most of the region's territory is either mountainous or so badly irrigated that the production of fruit and vegetables is limited to the coastal plains in the provinces of Naples, Caserta and Salerno. But the rich volcanic soil produces fruit and vegetables of such exceptional quality and quantity that many fields destined for wheat and

---

Local Specialities

- *Genovese* A dish of meat cooked with a great deal of onion, carrots and celery – obviously an import from Liguria, now part of Neapolitan cuisine. The addition of tomato is considered almost against the law, but many do put it in! The sauce of this dish is often used to dress pasta, usually *mezzi ziti*.
- *Sartu di Riso* Complicated dish of rice with meatballs, sausages, *mozzarella*, tomato, mushrooms, hard-boiled eggs and more, baked in the oven.
- *Zuppa di Soffritto* Also known as *Zuppa Forte*, it consists of offal, cooked with tomato, rosemary, peppers, oil and bay leaves. With the addition of water, it becomes a kind of soup, poured over slices of bread, or it can be used as a sauce to dress pasta, usually *perciatelli*. Dates back to the Spanish occupation as a dish prepared by soldiers over camp fires.

Local Specialities

- **Gattò di Patate** From the French word *gâteau* comes the name of this savoury potato mould with *mozzarella, salame, provola* cheese and hard-boiled eggs. Excellent either hot or cold so good picnic fare.
- **Minestra Maritata** A winter soup of Spanish origin, with all the fattiest parts of the pig, and all the vegetables available boiled together in a big pot.
- **Parmigiana di Melanzane** Layers of fried aubergine, *mozzarella* in slices, grated Parmesan and basil. One of my all-time favourite dishes. Courgettes are also delicious prepared in this way.
- **Pasta Cresciuta** Superb dish of deep-fried courgette flowers. All Neapolitan housewives are good at frying, and this dish shows off their expertise.
- **Peperoni Ripieni** Stuffed peppers, containing breadcrumbs, black olives, capers, sultanas, anchovies and parsley, which turn into a delicious combination of flavours in the baking.
- **Zucchine a Scapece** Fried courgettes, marinated in vinegar with fresh mint and chopped garlic. An old Spanish dish, can also be used with aubergines or small fish.

grain have instead been converted to fruit and vegetable areas.

Campania produces the nation's best cherries *ciliege*, plums *susine*, apricots *albicocche*, hazelnuts *nocciole* and figs *fichi*. Lemon and orange groves are everywhere, and peaches *pesche*, melons *meloni* and watermelons *cocomeri* thrive, and the *fichi d'India* prickly pears are ubiquitous. Beware when you eat these – peel with gloves on, cut in half and eat with a spoon and fork.

Best vegetables of course are the tomatoes *pomodori*, then potatoes *patate*, aubergines *melanzane*, peppers *peperoni*, beans *fagioli* and peas *piselli*. Artichokes *carciofi* are very popular too.

PASTICCERIA
Cakes, Biscuits and Puddings

Neapolitan pastries and sweets are famous for intricacy and lightness. Here are a few from the huge variety you might encounter.

- **Amarene al Liquore** Bitter-sweet cherries, preserved in sugar, alcohol and rum, used for decorating sweets or as a digestif at the end of a big meal.
- **Coviglie al Caffè/Cioccolato** Cream and coffee or cream and chocolate pudding served with whipped cream in small bowls.
- **Divino Amore** Traditional Christmas cake with pink almond paste.
- **Pastiera** Very famous Easter pie with a filling of ricotta, eggs, milk and rice, barley or corn, with candied peel, cinnamon and sugar.
- **Pizza Dolce** As the name suggests, a sweet pizza. A very plain pastry case with a filling of *ricotta*, almonds, jam and/or custard.
- **Sfogliatelle** Very complicated to make properly, these are extremely light and crisp pastries with a delicious filling of *ricotta* and candied fruit.
- **Struffoli** This has to have Greek origins! A mass of deep-fried little pastries, mixed into a bowl of honey and candied peel, then shaped into a cake with wet hands. Very sweet, but very good, it's a traditional Christmas cake.
- **Zuppa Inglese alla Napoletana** Neapolitan version of trifle – layers of sponge soaked in liqueur, with custard in between and the odd chocolate chip here and there.

Ice Cream Takes the Biscuit

Neapolitans are almost as good, but not quite as good, as the Sicilians at making ice cream. The first Neapolitan café to be opened in Paris was the Café Napolitaine, run by Tortoni, who created the memorable ice cream *Bisquit Tortoni* – layers of cream, ice cream and biscuits soaked in liqueur.

VINO
Wine

The best Campanian wines are those from the inland districts like those round Irpinia and in the Benevento province. In other areas wines tend to be very similar to those which will crop up in neighbouring Basilicata – good but not special. Very good red and white wines are available on Ischia and Capri.

RED WINE
• *Aglianico d'Irpinia* Excellent ruby red, smooth dry table wine.
• *Taurasi* Nicknamed the *Barbaresco del Sud*, this is a very aromatic wine which is best drunk with the more refined meat dishes, game and strong cheeses.

WHITE WINE
• *Greco di Tufo* An ancient wine, produced here for several hundred years with more or less the same grapes. A very decided flavour, and being extremely dry, it makes a good aperitif too.
• *Solopaca* A very good dry white, which is perfect for drinking with antipasti or egg dishes. Also available as a red or rosé wine.
• *Vesuvio* A very pale yellow wine with a slightly fizzy taste. Excellent with fish.
• *Lacryma Christi* The name means 'Christ's Tears'. The most common version is a white, slightly fruity straw yellow. Sometimes available totally sweet, then it's a dessert wine. A rarer red version is produced – a delicate ruby with a harmonious flavour.
• *Gran Furore della Divina Costiera* I had to put this one in just because of its name. Completely over the top – typically Neapolitan! It means 'Great Frenzy of the Divine Coast' (whatever that means!). It's white, dry and delicious.

BEVANDE
Drinks

• *Strega* Named after the witches of Benevento, it is a bright yellow sweet concoction made with a wide variety of herbs and is reminiscent of Chartreuse. The best is made by Giuseppe Alberti.

WORTH TAKING HOME

Local coffee is superb, deeply toasted with plenty of body and flavour – you won't taste coffee like it anywhere else.

If you can work out a way of transporting it, you should take at least one *mozzarella*. Remember it must be kept in its whey until used. *Provola* is much easier to transport, coming in a secure rind, held together by a bit of string.

Local lemons are juicier and more full of flavour than anywhere else on the mainland. Easy to carry, take a dozen home with you. Garlic and *peperoncino* too, as the sun's heat has made them full of flavour.

There are so many kinds of pasta that just don't find their way to other parts of the country; you should spend some time checking out all the different shapes, and take home some of the more unusual ones.

Go for the D.O.C. wines if you want wine to keep, otherwise take home a bottle of wine you like the taste of – almost all restaurants and *trattorie* will sell you a bottle of their house wine.

SAGRE E FESTE
Festivals

All over the region, to celebrate Sant'Antonio, 17 January, the little street urchins known as *scugnizzi* run through the streets shouting and playing pranks. This all leads up to the fireside festivities in honour of the saint with local pastries and wine galore.

Heady Wines and Golden Beaches

P Foggia

PUGLIA

BASILICATA

Potenza

Matera

Adriatic Sea

Bari

Brindisi

Miele

Taranto

Lecce

Golfo Taranto

Tyrrhenian Sea

CALABRIA

Cosenza

Catanzaro

Ionian Sea

Reggio di Calabria

Once past Bari, so they say, and you're in a different world.

The 3 southern regions which make up the toe, sole and heel of the boot have all got the hot summer months in common – the sun gives them an equality which is easily recognisable. But there the real similarity ends, as each one emerges with its own character and customs, regional specialities, wines and problems, though some do overlap.

The mountainous landscape and sheer size of Calabria and Puglia, and the sparseness of Basilicata make it difficult and extremely expensive to create a proper road or rail system to link the 3, and although appeals have been made, the funds have not been forthcoming. So, these regions continue to live separate lives from each other, with little intercommunication between them.

Of the 3 Puglia is the most well-off, with a fast-expanding tourist industry, fairly good road and rail systems, and a very efficient irrigation system planned by Caesar but not introduced until 1906, which permits crops to grow healthily. The historical naval link with Greece through its rapidly expanding ports also helps to keep this region's economy buoyant.

PUGLIA –
The heel digs in
Puglia is the heel of the boot, the hottest and driest of all the regions, with a long and very beautiful coastline, clear blue waters, sandy coves, rocky bays or long white sanded beaches. Inland is the *Tavoliere*, Italy's largest peninsular plain, bordered by Puglia's only 2 rivers, the Fortone and the Ofanto. This is florid countryside, producing a glorious abundance: Italy's best wheat, providing the pasta which reigns supreme; the huge black and green olives, which seem to find their way into every dish; almonds, hazelnuts, walnuts, chestnuts and all manner of vegetables; olive oil, wine, fruit – all these spill off the colourful market stalls in the streets and piazzas of the towns of San Severo, Cerignola, Lucera or Trinitapoli. It is a timeless place, reeking of pagan history, where old, very old, habits are not dead, nor are they dying easily.

The *Tavoliere's* sea port is Manfredonia, which sits at the feet of the Gargano, the 'spur' of Italy's boot, a promontory of rounded hills topped by the Foresta Umbra, a thick shady forest of pines, oaks, beeches and elms.

The *Murghe* is the arid bleak strip of land snaking down the centre of the region. Its chalky surface yields little, apart from the peculiar phenomenon of water springing up out of the ground and then disappearing, to reappear in the fertile green strip, the *Terra di Bari*, on the eastern coast.

The southernmost tip of the region, the Penisola Salentina, stretches down into the sea towards Greece. Here you can feel the deep-rooted influence of centuries long ago, when it was the gods of Olympus who were worshipped here, not the Vatican. They call it *le Terre Greche* – the Greek lands.

With the rich agriculture in this area, everything is good. Pasta is at the centre of the picture, epitomised by *orecchiette*, little ears, cooked with flair and in many different ways. Meat, usually lamb or kid, fish, seafood and vegetables complete the scene. And fruit is especially delicious here – figs, melons, watermelons and grapes. Herbs are used a lot, and in general the impression given is one of a joyful and healthy gastronomic scene combining flavours expertly to produce a table which is a delight to look at.

BARI & PROVINCE
Bari, being central, has always contributed to the dynamism of the area. Commercially she has always been important, and she is an increasingly well-organised port with excellent trade exchanges with Greece, Yugoslavia and the Middle East. The old town is much as it was, with narrow cobbled streets and tiny piazzas.

To the north, the port towns of Barletta, Trani, Bisceglie and Molfetta are active market towns, specialising in excellent olive oil and wine, and developing as resorts.

Almonds and olives
Just outside Bari is Bitonto, which has always been a centre for growing and processing almonds. This was the ancient Greek colony of Bytonton and amongst the blossom-covered trees and olive groves it is hard to believe this is still Italy – even more confusing when you visit the cathedral, which strangely has a peculiarly Anglo-Saxon feel about it. Here the olive oil has a fabulous reputation, to the point where various of

my recipes collected from the area call for *olio d'oliva di Bitonto*.

At a restaurant called *TABERNA MEDIOEVALE* in Carbonara di Puglia I had some excellent and very orthodox Pugliese dishes. As everywhere, the meal was simple and earthy, with plenty of fresh vegetables and some preserved in oil, *salame, orecchiette con cime di rapa, orecchiette* with turnip tops, lamb stew, and excellent cakes made with the freshest *ricotta, pastiera di crema e frutta*.

Alberobello is a place to visit to see the *trulli*, little conical stone buildings grouped together like white-painted beehives. There are hundreds of them dotted about in the fields. The *TRULLO D'ORO* in via Cavallotti is just what one always imagines an Italian restaurant should be like – open all year, informal and relaxed. The owner, Pietro Mongardi, takes obvious pleasure in serving good peasant cooking, which after all is what the local cuisine is all about. A selection of crunchy raw vegetables was served *in pinzimonio* – with a little bowl of superb lightly salted olive oil to dip into. This is popular all over southern Italy, but only worth having if the vegetables are really fresh and the olive oil of best quality.

BRINDISI & PROVINCE

The last time I went to this port, favoured by the Romans as an excellent harbour for cargoes to and from Greece, I was a rucksacked teenager, heading off for adventures in the Aegean islands. I was enchanted then by its gardens, the whiteness of the buildings and the dozens of handsome sailors strolling along the hot pavements. More recently I returned to see the ugly industrial explosion surrounding it – the pier has grown to accommodate huge ships bearing crude oil, and refineries pour out smoke into the sunny skies. I realise this means employment for the desperate southerners, who would otherwise head north, but the result is a chaos which seems so out of place with the holiday atmosphere of passenger ships heading to Corfu, Patras, Piraeus ...

I found an oasis of peace at *LA BOTTE* in Corso Garibaldi, where the excellent range of local specialities includes herby charcoal-grilled lamb and the delicious *fave e cicoria alla Brindisina con uva Malvasia*, broad beans with chicory and Malvasia grapes.

Away from the city the fields are thick with vines and healthy vegetables, gnarled olive and proud almond trees. There is an excellent market for all this local produce at Mesagne.

FOGGIA & PROVINCE

Sitting smack in the middle of the *Tavoliere*, Foggia was one of the most important livestock markets of the South, but it was appallingly badly bombed in the last war, and the programme of reconstruction seems yet to end. Shepherds and cowherds used to come from Campania and the Abruzzi to gather at the Foggia market. Now it is mainly an agricultural market town.

At a restaurant with an amazingly long name, *CICOLELLA IN FIERA, AL SIGILLO DI FEDERICO II*, I ate dishes with their roots embedded in ancient history indeed: *Tiella d'interiora d'agnello con verdure e funghi* was lamb's innards with vegetables and mushrooms, *Peperoncini e pomodori in padella*, a stew of tiny hard round tomatoes and chillies, and *crostata di mostarda di frutta* was a pastry tart filled with pickled fruit.

Foggia is surrounded by a prairie-like landscape which is dotted with wild pear and apple trees.

LECCE & PROVINCE

In the myriad olive groves surrounding this lovely city, the harvest is still mostly picked by hand – peasants bend low to the ground to fill their baskets. It has a Roman theatre, amphitheatre and a medieval castle, but its golden era was the 16th and 17th centuries, which have left splendid baroque palaces and churches. The lovely warm yellow stone, *pietra Leccese*, is used extensively, giving a delicious ochre tinge to the light.

Historical experience

The best known of the local restaurants is *GINO E GIANNI* in via 4 Finite. I was delighted to see on the menu a dish I have only ever read or written about. It dates from deepest Roman history. *Ciceri et Triia* is one of the earliest recorded pasta recipes, consisting of wide strips of pasta like *lasagne*, fried with chickpeas. The Romans were among the first to introduce pasta into their diet. They did so by making a gruel mixture with flour and water, then frying it in tiny quantities to make thin pancakes which would be cut into

Retaining the Flavour

The sun is used to dry out all manner of vegetables – everywhere you see tables covered in tomatoes, peppers, aubergines, *lampascioni*, olives, and many more, all drying in the sun. Then they are preserved in jars of the wonderful olive oil, smelling pungently of oregano and other herbs.

It's not only vegetables that are preserved like this. Little cheeses are permeated with completely different flavours after a good soak in oil.

Octopus is preserved in jars *sott'aceto* in vinegar. The freshly caught fish is pounded with a mallet to tenderise it, then it's boiled in water, but not before it's been bounced in a basket to make the tentacles curl up. Then it's put in jars with fresh mint, garlic, vinegar and plenty of olive oil. Served as antipasto, it's called *Polpi sott'aceto*.

---

strips and mixed with the other ingredients. These modern ones were made differently, of course, boiled then fried with the chickpeas. One mouthful and I understood why and how they have stood the test of time. In Puglia I was lulled into a stupor by the heat, was thrilled by the views and refreshed by the clear blue water. I saw history, touched and smelled history and now I was eating history!

TARANTO & PROVINCE

Taranto sits on a sort of bridge between two lagoons, the Mar Grande and the Mar Piccolo. The original Greek settlement was here on this narrow peninsular strip of land. Now oysters, mussels, scallops and other seafood are cultivated in these seas.

Taranto has a serious pollution problem, following an even more violent industrial explosion than that of Brindisi. There is a disordered look to the modern sections of the town, where the sky has lost its brightness. On the Mar Piccolo the views are less disturbing and I lunched at *IL GAMBERO* on *scaloppina di cernia* perch, *frittura di pesce dei due Mari*, fried fish from the two seas, and *pappardelle scivolose all'aragosta* slippery *pappardelle* with lobster.

Golden grapes

The surrounding countryside is as fertile and thriving as everywhere else. Here *uva regina* is grown profusely. It means queen of the grapes and that's what it is – the sweetest, crunchiest most juicy and golden of them all, famous because it's the best, even better than its main rival *uva Italia*.

Heading out towards the area called Rocce di Massafra, I stopped amongst flowers and palm trees for a meal at *LE ROCCE* in Massafra. The menu here depends on what's good at market that morning, and there were that day an endless supply of antipasti, superb fresh fish grilled over a pungent fire, then a walk in the orchard and vegetable garden, admiring the view. Nearby at Villa di Massafra I lingered over a wickedly delicious ice cream at the *PICCOLO BAR DI VITO ANTONIO LATERZA*.

SALUMI
Salami, Sausages and Cured Meats

Since there's little pork in this region there's not much variety here. Small, fat, hard *salamini* with dark red meat and very little fat. Plenty of *soppressata*, cooked sausage made with diced pork meat. Very little *prosciutto*, which is lean and dry.

PASTA

Puglia's pasta, for the most part hand-made, is left quite thick and coarse, all the better to soak up the hearty rich sauces permeated with the distinctive flavours of local herbs they are so fond of using – rue, sage, thyme, oregano, rosemary and others I can't even find a translation for.

The most important and famous of Puglia's pasta are *orecchiette* little ears, which you can

Local Specialities

- *Panzarotti alla barese* Little circles of pasta folded in half and deep fried in olive oil with a filling tucked inside the fold. In the city of Bari I came across three fillings, a rich tomato and meat sauce, egg and cheese, and *ricotta* with *prosciutto*.
- *Lanache di Casa* Also a speciality from Bari, pasta dressed with stuffed mussels in a tomato sauce, with plenty of herbs and garlic.

still see being made by hand by black-clad peasant women patiently scraping across the rough table tops to give them the traditional grooves in order to soak up the sauce. They are on sale all over the country ready made, but locally you will find better quality and more choice. They are usually served with lamb chops and tomato sauce, turnip tops and olive oil or potatoes with rue.

The other local hand-made pasta are *cavatieddi* which look like little shells and are served with similar sauces.

Other specialities using any kind of short stubby pasta include *pasta ai peperoni*, peppers, *pasta al cavolfiore*, cauliflower, *pasta alla catalogna*.

PESCE E FRUTTI DI MARE
Fish and Seafood

Puglia gives Italy most of her fish, as all along the coast and out to sea this is an important local industry. Mussels *cozze* and oysters *ostriche* are cultivated in the two seas at Taranto. Lobster *aragosta*, scampi, prawns *gamberetti* and squill

Local Specialities

- *Ostriche alla Tarantina* Oysters opened and coated with garlic, parsley, breadcrumbs and a dribble of oil – placed in a hot oven to brown.
- *Zuppa di pesce* Fish soup, more like a stew, excellent all over the region thanks to the quality and variety of fish. In Gallipoli it has a light vinegary flavour and onions, and one in Brindisi contains a lot of eel.

cicale are all caught off the beaches. Gilthead *dorada*, mackerel *sgombro*, sea bass *branzino* and many many others are caught off the reefs, beaches and out to sea. Many of them have names in dialect that change from province to province. When choosing what to eat or buy, just go for what seems freshest and best suits your appetite and you won't be disappointed. Most restaurants will offer you 'fish' *pesce* on the menu, so you know that will just be whatever the boat has brought in that day. And let me not forget the delicious sea urchins *ricci*, yellow as egg yolk and tender squid and octopus *seppie e polpi*, including the marvellous *polpi sott'aceto*, octopus pickled in vinegar.

CARNE E CACCIA
Meat and Game

Beef and pork are in short supply, as is poultry. Game is practically non-existent. Instead, lots of lamb and kid. Horsemeat *cavallo* is also fairly popular, particularly in the Salento area. There's not a great variety of meat in the Puglia, but this doesn't really matter considering the amount of superb seafood and vegetables there are.

Local Specialities

- *Agnello al Quero* or *allo Spiedo* Roast lamb cooked on a spit over a fire of branches of rosemary, thyme and other herbs.
- *Braciole di Cavallo* Horse-meat steaks, cooked in a rich tomato sauce and used to dress pasta dishes.
- *Gnummerieddi* or *coratella* Sounds disgusting but tastes delicious. As in the Abruzzi and Molise, lamb gut is filled with minced offal, herbs and garlic. Very good stewed in a sauce, but best grilled over an open fire, preferably made with olive branches.

FORMAGGIO
Cheese

In infinite number, all delicious, all over the region. *Mozzarella di bufala* pure white *mozzarella* made with buffalo milk, and *bocconcini*, small *mozzarelle* made with cows' milk, and *latticini*, the same thing. *Ricotta*, in various forms, fresh for making cakes and puddings, or dried to grate on to pasta, or salted, preserved in olive oil. *Caprini* are goat's cheeses also preserved in oil, or soft and fresh. In Foggia and its province look out for *fagottini*, little smoked cheeses tied up with a piece of straw, their rind dark and hard. In Andria, don't miss *burrata*, a snow-white, soft, creamy and totally addictive cow cheese.

Everywhere there's a slightly sour-tasting *pecorino*, made of sheep's milk, in varying degrees of strength as elsewhere. And there are hundreds of *cacciotine*, small whole cheeses made to individual recipes, and all the fresh cheeses, known simply as *formaggio fresco*, that float in bowls of translucent whey, or sit coolly on a bed of vine leaves.

FRUTTA E VERDURA
Fruit and Vegetables

This is one of Italy's leading regions. Needing a minimum amount of water, vines and olives grow well here. Since the development of the irrigation system wheat is also grown extensively on the *Tavoliere*, so is barley and other cereals. Grapes, both for eating and wine, are by far the most important fruit. Almonds *mandorle* too are available everywhere. Olives come in all sizes, both green and black. They are grown both for eating and for oil. The huge, almost erotic *fichi fioroni* figs from Terra di Bari are famous, as are the golden melons from Brindisi called *poponi*, and the incredibly sweet pink-fleshed watermelons *cocomeri* available all over the region.

But it's in the vegetable kingdom that Puglia really shows us what she can produce. Most important is the bitter wild onion called *lampasciuoli*, or *lampascioni*, which grows all over the southern regions of Italy under different names. On the Daunia mountains grow mushrooms known simply as *funghi della Daunia*, which can be bought at market stalls. Puglia produces artichokes *carciofi*, bright green cauliflower *cavolfiore pugliese*, juicy peppers *peperoni*, fat and shiny aubergines *melanzane*, huge heads of chicory *cicoria*, vast quantities of marvellous broad beans *fave*, turnips *rapa* and turnip tops *cime di rapa*. But the symbol of the region has to be her very special tomato *pomodoro*. It's a plum-shaped, firm-fleshed com-

Local Speciality

● *Fave e cicoria* (*n'capriata* in dialect) An ancient dish of marvellous simplicity. Purée of peeled dried broad beans, laid with a mound of boiled chicory, dressed with olive oil from Bitonto. Best in the southern *paesi greci*, of Salentino, where the broad beans are so tender they don't need peeling.

pact little tomato, dark red, juicy and sweet, just perfect for making sauces. They keep so well you will see them everywhere strung up between bamboos. Here and there you will also see fields of sugar beet. Living as I do in East Anglia, I recognised it instantly and was astonished to see it sweltering in this sun – I always associated it with ice, mud, snow and tractors taking up the whole road.

PASTICCERIA
Cakes, Biscuits and Puddings

All the important days of the calendar, Christmas, Easter and all the saints' days, are respected and honoured around the table in Puglia – and each special day has its special cake, pastry or pudding. And around these are platters loaded with all manner of plump dried fruit, often stuffed with nuts and almonds for a contrast in flavour. And always those enormous juicy figs.

● *Carteddate* Delicious and very intricate honey pastries made with nimble fingers. With the same basic dough they also make *purcidizzu*. The light pastry, once shaped as required, is deep-fried in oil, drained and then soaked completely in honey. They are then arranged into a pyramid and decorated with tiny sugared almonds or cinnamon and sugar. Mainly a Christmas speciality.

● *Mustazzeuli* Fabulous almond biscuits that seem hard, but crumble in your mouth.

● *Cupete* or *Copate* Blond crisp almond nougat confection. Small quantities are sandwiched between rice paper and sold in stacks like pancakes.

There are lots of different cakes and puddings which use *ricotta* as a main ingredient.

● *Cassata di ricotta* A famous early ancestor of ice cream, a little heavy and very rich, but simply delicious – especially if washed down with plenty of cold white wine.

• *Dita di apostoli* Apostles' fingers. Deep-fried egg white with a filling of *ricotta* and chocolate. Very good hot or cold.

• *Zuppa Inglese* The Pugliese version of trifle. Layers of the lightest sponge cake with creamy custard, *Alchermes* and candied fruit between the layers, coated with a final layer of meringue.

• *Bocconotti* or *taralli* Biscuits with which to end a meal over a glass of dessert wine, from Martina Franca.

Pasta dough is used to make pastries, filled with *ricotta*, jam, honey or *cotognata*, a superb quince confection, made in and around Lecce. The pastries are then either baked or deep fried.

The ice creams of Puglia are all hand-made with a passion and artistry to rival that of Sicily. They are rich, smooth and bursting with flavour.

Local Specialities

• *Cialledda* A simple peasant dish typical of Bari and Foggia. Slices of good bread from Altamura or Gravina are laid in a bowl. A selection of fresh herbs are boiled in a little water which is then strained over the bread. A sprinkling of *peperoncino* and a couple of tablespoons of good olive oil complete the dish.

• *Friselle* The *frisella* is a little bread roll made with durum wheat which is placed in the oven to harden. It is then soaked in a little cold water, dressed with olive oil, *peperoncino* and fresh sliced tomatoes.

VINO
Wine

I don't know whether it's the incredible heat that causes the wine of Puglia to be so alcoholic, but it certainly does 'cut your legs' as they say! The vines here have no hillsides to scramble up, so they grow thick and sturdy, close to the ground, entwined on intricate trellises like Bacchic festoons. Famous throughout history for its potency and headiness, Pugliese wine is now used as a *vino da taglio*, to add strength to other wines. D.O.C. wines used to be rather thin on the off-licence shelves in Puglia, but in recent years efforts have been made to improve their image.

Only about 2 per cent of the wine produced in this region is actually bottled and labelled. The rest is either left *sfuso* – in barrels to be drunk by the carafe, or is used as *vino da taglio*.

It's not only the heat that give these wines their potency and excellence. There is experience in the vineyards, the super efficient *ente regionale* for the development of local agriculture, the co-operatives, the huge cellars shared by several vineyards, and not least the ability to work together in harmony so as to produce wine that the region is immensely proud of.

As for me, I found it hard to stand up after lunch, so I sat and admire the view over cupfuls of the strong aromatic coffee they make so well ...

These are some of the wines presented at the recent Fiera del Levante, southern Italy's most important trade fair. They are all wines with a D.O.C. label.

SPECIAL RED WINE
• *Cacc'e mitte di Lucera* (meaning 'put it away and let's have some more') from Lucera, Troia and Biccari.

RED WINE
• *Orta Nova*, both red and rosé, from parts of Foggia, Manfredonia, Cappelle, Orta Nova and Cerdone. Drink them young.
• *Rosso Canosa* from Canosa di Puglia. One of the better-known Pugliese wines, it's a refreshing, unsophisticated wine when young that ages well.

WHITE WINE
• *Ostuni* A very special white wine made exclusively from Ottavianello grapes. From Ostuni and surroundings.
• *Leverano* from Leverano and Arnesano, a sharp, clean-tasting wine with a distinctive bouquet.

ROSÉ WINE
• *Copertino* from Carmiano, Copertino, Arnesano, Monteroni and Galatina. A delicately-flavoured wine with a heady effect. Its pretty colour belies its vigour.

SPUMANTI
• *Gravina* from Gravina di Puglia, Poggiorsini and Spinazzola.
• *San Severo* from Torremaggiore, San Paolo

Civitale, San Severo and parts of Apricena, Rignano, Lucera, Poggio Imperiale, Castel Nuovo di Dauni and Lesina. Both these are delicious sparkling wines to enjoy with fruit or desserts.

If you can't get hold of any of the above, enjoy the excellent wines available in carafe everywhere – just don't try to drive after more than three glasses!

DESSERT WINE
• *Moscato di Trani* a sweet golden liqueurish wine, available in Trani, Bisceglie, Corato, Andria, Canosa and Ruvo.

BEVANDE
Drinks

In a region where tomatoes and almonds vie for prime position in order of importance as the gastronomic symbol, the almond has ended up in a drinkable form as *latte di mandorle*, almond milk, which is popular all over southern Italy. It's made by soaking almonds thoroughly in water, then squeezing them through a muslin cloth to strain out the milk. Drunk sweetened and ice cold its a marvellously refreshing drink. When it's sold in a bottle it's called *Orzata*, and you have to dilute it.

WORTH TAKING HOME

Plenty of the marvellous deep green olive oil, good everywhere, but if you want the best you should buy the varieties (in order of importance) from Bitonto, Molfetta, Andria and Barletta.

All kinds of vegetables preserved in the oil too, especially *lampascioni* if you really want to relive the flavour of Puglia. Dried white broad beans *fave secche* that will keep for ever – the best ones are from Zollino. Soak them overnight and use them as any other pulses.

Marvellous nuts from the town of Noci – walnuts in particular. Almonds, almond milk, almond pastries – all fabulous.

Take home any of the local cheeses, especially dry *ricotta* and *pecorino* as they keep best. Bunches of bright red *peperoncino*, jars of olives,

black and green. And plenty of the wonderful wine.

Go to Lecce and province for *cotognata*, thick quince jelly eaten in squares like chocolate.

SAGRE E FESTE
Festivals

On the first weekend in November, Lecce holds a fair for All Souls' Day. It centres round the ceremony performed in the courtyard of the Vescovado, the Bishop's Palace, as it has done for 500 years.

Called *Lu Panieri*, the Baskets, it is an evocation of the time when local peasants brought gifts of walnuts and chestnuts to the bishop, as a request for tax exemption.

Also on All Souls' Day you may find brightly coloured sticks of rock, *fanfullicchie*, on sale at the cemetery gates, though this is a dying tradition.

11–20 August (approx.). At San Giovanni Rotondo in the province of Foggia, every year they celebrate the charming custom of having a *Festa dell'Ospite* Guest's Festival. For a week or more the town resounds to the sounds and colours of the lively local folklore exhibitions with plenty of the local gastronomic specialities on offer, all washed down with local wines.

At Novoli in the province of Lecce, to celebrate St. Anthony's day on 17 January they have the country's biggest bonfire. It takes a month to construct it out of branches and trees gathered locally, after which it is lit on the evening of the 16th. It stands 30 metres (90 feet) high, taller than the cathedral façade opposite. Around it, blessing of animals and local produce takes place, along with processions, games and fairground-type stalls and events. When the fire has burned down to embers, these are then gathered up and distributed amongst the local homes to be added to the already lit home fires for good luck and the blessing of the saint enters the home. The traditional dish with which all these festivities are marked is the stuffed lamb gut called *turcinieddi*, cooked over an open fire and washed down with the local *moscato*.

FORGOTTEN BASILICATA

While Puglia, in spite of knowing the misery of being part of the impoverished south, has managed to emerge as an increasingly popular holiday location, Basilicata has somehow failed to attract the tourists who would do so much to boost the economy.

This region has always been poor – poverty has driven itself deep into the way of life, like a stake driven into the ground. *'E terra dimenticata da Dio'* they say – the land God has forgotten, and indeed there are signs that somebody somewhere forgot to provide the region with the basics for survival. Water is a constant problem – though there are plenty of streams, they need taming to provide much-needed irrigation. The soil is arid, thin and stony, with little woodland to prevent soil erosion caused by the wind that blows hot and dry.

Bleak Banishment

During the Fascist regime, Jews and 'undesirables' were banished to the further reaches of this region. Although places like Eboli are a little bleak, and with a certain amount of obscure pagan culture in the air, I can think of a lot worse places that Mussolini could have posted them off to. Read Carlo Levi's *Christ Stopped at Eboli* for an idea of what it must have been like to be an exile here.

More so than in Puglia, or Calabria on its other side, the people here seem locked into some kind of time-warp, unable or unwilling to move into the 20th century and adopt better and more efficient farming methods. Here you will still see horse-drawn ploughs tilling small fields divided by stone walls, women dressed in the same traditional costume their mothers wore before them. Not even the discovery of methane gas, the newfound hope for regional prosperity, seems to have woken them.

All this makes for a very relaxing and lovely place for a holiday, but for the local population life is hard, and many head north for a better life.

From Basilicata to Lucania and back

Taking its name from its earliest inhabitants, the Lucani, the region was first called Lucania. Under the Byzantines it was renamed Basilicata (from the Greek work *basilikos*, which indicated the governor's standing). This name stuck through the period of Norman rule when the boundaries were the same as today, and up to 1932, when, till 1947, it became Lucania again. Today it is Basilicata, although its people are called Lucani!

This is a small region, squeezed between Campania, Puglia and Calabria. It has a tiny bit of Tyrrhenian coastline on the west, and the Gulf of Taranto as its southern limit. It is almost entirely mountainous or hilly, with deep valleys through which run torrents and rivers wending their way across the narrow plains towards the sea. It's a bitter landscape, arid and brown, scorched by the sun. The ancient forests have gone, leaving only the odd lonely tree, and the ground is scarred by landslides. Here and there a patch of green, but for the most part it reminds me of North Africa or parts of the Middle East.

Villages huddle at the feet of ruined castles on hillsides – isolated houses are a rare feature of this countryside. There are neither important ports, towns nor commercial centres of any note here. Only in the north, where the ashes of the now extinct volcano, Monte Vulturo, have given the region what it most requires, fertile soil, is there any real success. Here vineyards, fruit groves and olives flourish, with dense woodlands higher up the mountains.

The climate is typical of the southern mountainous areas, with bitterly cold windswept snowy winters, and steaming hot dry summers. Along the Gulf of Taranto there are very mild winters, and very hot summers.

There is a captivating charm about this region. The harshness of the light and the dust-filled gusts of wind are not without their attraction, and there are vast cool vineyards and olive groves through which you can meander. This is unspoilt countryside, for a large part undiscovered. If you're looking for a lonely, naturally beautiful and untouristy Italy, come to Basilicata.

The flavours of the sun

As for the food, this has to be a vegetarian's paradise – never have I come across such a wealth of deliciously imaginative ways to cook vegetables – and what vegetables! Fat and juicy and distinctively perfumed with fresh herbs – you will get enormous helpings of them, as they are taking the place of fish or meat. There's marvellous cheese too, and very good heavy and rich olive oil. The chilli rules here too, and everything is touched by the sting of sun-warmed *peperoncino*, colourful, bright and full of flavour – laughing in the face of misery and hunger.

POTENZA & PROVINCE

Whenever you watch the weather forecast on TV in Italy, Potenza invariably has the lowest or the highest temperatures, the strongest winds – and generally the worst weather going. It's an agricultural city, basing its economy on the surrounding countryside.

The entire province is mountainous. I enjoyed being here very much. I spent more time than I had intended just exploring – it was so great to be somewhere uncrowded, easygoing (perhaps too much so, hence the lack of any significant progress), and where the old traditions of shepherding, picking olives off the ground by hand, drying chillies by the thousands in the warm winds are carried out as they were centuries ago.

To the north, near Monte Vulture, is the ancient Norman city of Melfi. The land here is fertile, yielding vines, olives and grain, some processed in the small market towns like Lavello and Venosa. Lauria is a sheep-farming centre, with many delicious ewe's milk cheeses available. Avigliano is the most important wine centre. Local wine here is strong and slightly sour, with a few notable exceptions.

The town of Maratea is situated on what has to be the most beautiful and atmospheric bay on Italy's coastline. Surrounded by mountains, looking out over the Golfo di Policastro, this is a wonderful holiday haunt, with a resort called Marina di Maratea. At the wonderful seafood *trattoria* called ZIA MARIUCCIA you can sample the delights of this poor land with so little to offer and feast your eyes on the fabulous view. It has become chic to eat here, just as Maratea, relatively unknown, has become an 'in' place for holidays. The *trattoria* is run by the grandchildren of the original Mariuccia, who must be turning in her grave at the sight of all these 'foreign' holidaymakers flocking to her tables.

In Ferrandina I discovered a restaurant called DEGLI ULIVI and could have stayed there for ever. In the middle of a huge olive grove, this is an elegant but comfortable restaurant, where you can linger for hours over platefuls of hot black olives, coarsely cut home-made pasta and superb locally shot game.

MATERA & PROVINCE

The mountain on which Matera stands is a maze of tunnels, caves and grottoes in which up to only a few years ago thousands of people were still living. This horrendous human anthill was home to local people for hundreds, maybe even thousands of years, and only recently have they been moved into new suburbs.

AL BOCCONCINO is a delightful family-run *trattoria* with mum and dad in the kitchen and their offspring in charge of service. Local specialities included the superb purée of chicory and broad beans, *'n capriata di fave e cicoria*, similar to that of Puglia, and a delicious local *soppressata*, a squashy, soft blood sausage. There were marvellous views over the valley, and very good wine.

Within the province lies the ancient Greek settlement of Metaponto, which is now a fashionable resort. Methane gas has been discovered in this impoverished soil, bringing salvation to the area called the Valle del Basento.

Part of this province is a fertile reclaimed marsh, where the lively market towns of Bernalda, Tricarico and Stigliano are making the best of all the local fruit, vegetables, wine, olive oil and cheese. Bernalda is a very pretty little town perched on the cliff top overlooking the beach at Metaponto below. Here I ate at *FIFINA*, a tiny *trattoria* with only five tables, but where every dish was absolutely authentic and in tune with the surroundings. There was *Pancia di capretto e salsicce saltate in padella* – goat belly and sausages sautéed with wine and covered with a kid and tomato sauce, *pasta con fagioli* – pasta with fresh beans, *pecora stufata alla pastora* – casserole of ewe with a rich tomato and onion sauce, and the house wine was particularly good.

SALUMI
Salami, Sausages and Cured Meats

First and foremost comes *lucanica*, that marvellous soft sausage copied all over Italy but whose birthplace is right here. In ancient times, Horace, Martial and Cicero all wrote about it in

Local Specialities

- *Lucanica* Long continuously coiled pork sausage flavoured with black pepper and sweet red chilli. It can be eaten fresh, fried, grilled or in a sauce, or can be smoked and cured.
- *Pezzente salame* made for the *pezzente*, beggars. Consists of all the bits normally thrown away by the butcher – lung, liver, and ground-up nerve endings, seasoned with garlic and pepper.
- *Sugna piccante* Lard mixed carefully with salt and chopped *peperoncino*, kept in glass or terracotta jars. Used in cooking or spread on slices of toasted bread.

almost poetic terms. It's a long, pink sausage in a continuous coil which is sold by the length or weight. It's used a great deal in pasta sauces, or fried or grilled and eaten on its own. The dialect name is *luganiga* or *laganega*, and the versions in other regions all have similar variations of that name.

As in other places where winters are harsh, there are many recipes for *salame* and sausages to see the family through the winter months. *Salame* and sausages are very lean, with a very fine grain, and are preserved in jars of olive oil to keep them soft and very chewy. *Prosciutto* is also much leaner here, with a very fibrous, dry texture, and a good strong flavour. *Soppressata*, blood sausage, is very popular, and is used to make a peculiar local pie with shortcrust pastry called *Torta di pastafrolla col sanguinaccio*.

PASTA

In a region where so little grows or survives, an amazing number of pasta shapes emerge from the tabletops of the black-shrouded women. Homemade pasta is the basis of all the local cooking – it is coarse, dried durum wheat dough, poor but nourishing, rolled into a hundred imaginative shapes: *strascinati*, *fusilli*, sort of *tagliatelle* called *lagane*, and *strangulapreuti* – you know

Eat And Shut Up

Fascism had a very close relationship with food. '*Mangia e Taci*' ('Eat and Shut Up') was the punchline of a joke about Fascism, and it is still the most concise expression of the thinking behind the regime. Real eating, as opposed to metaphoric eating, was one of Mussolini's great passions in life until stomach problems forced him to give up his gluttony.

One of the most extraordinary figures to come out of that Fascist period was the weird Doctor Marinetti, who advised Mussolini on what Italians should be eating to make them the world's greatest power. Pasta was out of the question, as were most things Italians were used to eating. My grandfather was working for the

Italian government at the time, and my mother tells stories of him coming home, roaring with laughter at the extraordinary ideas that Mussolini had put to the Senate that day – like feeding the entire population on pills rather than letting them eat anything, so as to save the country a lot of hard work in farming.

Strongly patriotic advertising campaigns raged, events like *La Battaglia del Grano*, and loaves of bread sold with *Pane del Duce* printed on the loaf tin so as to stand out clearly on the crust – these are all images of those years that are hard to forget and impossible to repeat. Just as unforgettable are the years of misery suffered by those banished to Lucania.

they're cooked by the way they sink to the bottom of the pan. All these are dressed with a generous helping of *peperoncino*, which, before the introduction of quinine, was the local cure for malaria.

PESCE E FRUTTI DI MARE

Fish and Seafood

Fishing as such is not a local event – and on the whole fish and seafood do not figure much in the local cuisine. At seaside restaurants and trattorie you will find fish on the menu – squid *seppie*, octopus *polpo*, prawns *gamberi*, shrimps *gam-*

beretti, mackerel *sgombro*, bass *branzino*, cod *merluzzo* and so on, just as everywhere in the Adriatic or Tyrrhenian. You'll also find swordfish *pesce spada*, served as steaks.

CARNE E CACCIA

Meat and Game

In Lucanian cooking, a meat or fish course is almost non-existent. It has always been a large and generous helping of the delicious local vegetables which has followed the first course of pasta.

Lamb *agnello* is the meat which seems to

figure most prominently on the local menu. It can be simply grilled, or cooked in fiery stews. Kid is prepared in much the same way. Pork appears quite frequently but the pig is mostly preserved as *salumi* for the cold winter. As all over the south, *gnummerieddi* lamb's gut, stuffed and rolled, is the most typical of the local meat dishes.

In season a certain amount of local game is eaten, snipe *beccaccino*, being especially popular.

FORMAGGIO

Cheese

Butter is completely ignored in local recipes, but the cheese of this region deserves special emphasis. Local *caciocavallo*, *buttirro*, *scamorza* and *mozzarella* are all exceptional here, and are sought after in other parts of the country. *Pecorino* and all kinds of ewe's milk cheeses are a very important part of the food scene. Everywhere you can see the cheese rounds hanging from the rafters of houses and barns, golden and plump, occasionally dripping of their juice, and exuding that pungent unmistakable smell of good freshly-made cheese.

FRUTTA E VERDURA

Fruit and Vegetables

Grain of all sorts seems to be what survives best in this inhospitable land. Oats, barley and mostly durum wheat are of very high quality. Yet, despite all this, this is the one region where vegetables are used most thoroughly.

Local Specialities

- *Calzone di verdura* An envelope of bread is stuffed with chard, olives or sultanas, dressed with olive oil and baked. Eaten hot or cold – good for picnics.
- *Cappelle di funghi al forno* Locally picked *porcini* mushrooms baked with chilli and herbs and eaten as an accompaniment to or in place of grilled steaks.
- *Ciammotta* A combination of fried vegetables.
- *Ciaudedda* Stewed artichokes, onions, broad beans and potatoes, cooked with olive oil and bacon.
- *Insalata di lampasciuoli* Bitter wild onions boiled and dressed with a simple combination of white wine vinegar, chilli, oil, salt and parsley.
- *Funghi a fungitello, Cardoncelli* Mushrooms cooked with tomatoes, herbs and chilli powder.

- *Mandorlata di peperoni* A stew of peppers, cooked with thin strips of almonds – at least one must be a bitter one to give the dish its special flavour. Sugar and a good dose of the much used *diavolicchio* (*peperoncino* – dried red chilli) finishes it off. Best in the Seise area.
- *Melanzane al forno* Aubergines baked in the oven with anchovies, olives, capers, breadcrumbs and herbs, with a covering of excellent local olive oil.
- *Patate lessate con diavolicchio* Plain boiled potatoes generously dressed with olive oil in which a couple of chopped chillies have been fried.
- *Piatto d'erbe alla Lucana* Vegetable stew made with a variety of the locally grown vegetables.

Aubergines *melanzane*, peppers *peperoni*, tomatoes *pomodori* (particularly local wild tomatoes), *lampasciuoli* (bitter wild onions, also popular in Calabria and Puglia), the delicious little tasty lentils from Potenza, *lenticche di Potenza*, onions *cipolle*, marvellous mushrooms *funghi* from Matera, broad beans *fave* from Lavello, asparagus *asparagi*, parsley *prezzemolo* and *peperoncino*. All these grow extensively and are eaten all the time. Figs *fichi*, strawberries *fragole*, almonds *mandorle*, walnuts *noci* and eating grapes *uva* all grow well too, and of course there are the olives and vines. Oranges *aranci*, lemons *limoni* and the enormous local limes *cedri* thrive here in the heat.

PASTICCERIA

Cakes, Biscuits and Puddings

Cake-making is a luxury few can afford to indulge in, so there are not many.
- *Cuccia* Dry, hard grain, soaked in water then mixed with sugar, chocolate and pomegranate seeds.
- *Frittelle alla Lucana* Plain but delicious little fritters made with eggs, flour, semolina and bay leaves.
- *Copete* Crunchy almond paste sandwiched between two hosts of rice paper.

- *Strangolapreti fritti* Priest stranglers (home-made pasta) made with eggs, flour and lemons, fried in olive oil and dusted with icing sugar.
- *Torta di Latticini alla Lucana* Pastry tart filled with grated *pecorino*, *ricotta*, eggs, *prosciutto* and fresh *latticini* (small *mozzarelle*).
- *Focaccia al miele* Absolutely delicious local pizza dough soaked in honey.

VINO

Wine

There is only one D.O.C. wine in this region, but it is so marvellous that it should be famous throughout Europe, let alone Italy:

RED WINE
- *Aglianico del Vulture* Made with Aglianico grapes grown on the eastern side of Monte Vulture, and in the hilly area between Venosa and Genzano. It has a decisive delicious flavour.
- *Aglianico dei Colli Lucani* Cousin of the above, and is decidedly inferior, but it improves with age.

WHITE WINE
- *Asprino* A rather odd but not unpleasant wine, with a slightly fizzy quality and a very sharp flavour. Generally considered a 'thirst-quenching' wine.

• *Malvasia delle Lucania* The dry version is yellow and bright, with a delicious lingering flavour, best drunk young. The sweet version, which ages well, changes to an amber colour and is syrupy and smooth – a perfect way to end a meal in splendour.

SPUMANTI

Two delightful, if rather sweetish, *Spumanti* are produced here.

• *Malvasia del Vulture* and *Moscato del Vulture* are both very unusual and well worth trying.

WORTH TAKING HOME

Bunches of dried chillies, strings of dried *porcini* wild boletus mushrooms – just soak them in water for half an hour before you want to cook them (use the water in cooking) – a deliciously powerful flavour.

The olive oil is rich and heavy, with a very strong flavour, so taste before you buy, you may prefer something milder from another region.

Try to find *sugna piccante* – it's very good added to soups and stews for extra flavouring – just add half a teaspoonful.

Take some Malvasia, and some of the soft and delicious cheeses.

SAGRE E FESTE

Festivals

One of the most heartfelt religious festivities of this region is that of San Giuseppe (St. Joseph) on 19 March. Various local *festas* take place to mark this day and the traditional cooking of huge quantities of *lagane e fagioli* with beans is still carried out in many parts of the region. The pasta dish is then distributed amongst the local poor.

In the autumn, when the *cardoncelli* mushrooms are in season, various villages and towns in the inland areas throw a *festa* to celebrate this time of year. Look out for a *festa del fungo* sign or a poster telling you about a *sagra del cardoncello*. There you will be able to taste this delicious mushroom cooked *a Fungitiello* in a casserole with tomatoes, herbs and the inevitable *peperoncino*; or cook and eat them simply grilled over an open fire.

CALABRIA – Kicking Into Touch

Though Basilicata and Calabria share a similar sort of mountain landscape, Basilicata has been thoroughly stripped of its woodland, while Calabria has preserved hers. Masses of flowers, trees, wildlife and greenery are what separates arid rocky Basilicata from the beauty of Calabria.

In neither region is there any tendency towards large towns or cities, and the population is mainly scattered in small villages and isolated houses.

Tourism is just beginning to make major advances, and in Calabria, being the richer of the 2 with more scope for tourist appeal (woodland, lakes, mountains and a long coastline), it is all happening much more quickly – often with disastrously untidy and even downright abhorrent results of unplanned development.

Calabria is the southernmost region of the country – it's the toe of the boot, traditionally said to be kicking Sicily away. Only 3 kilometres (just over 2 miles) separate the mainland from Sicily, but it might as well be 3 million, the regions are so different. The landscape changes at every turn – an endless contrast of sea and mountain views. The slopes descend almost to the water's edge, leaving just a brief tract of plain along the coastline, surrounding the mouths of the rivers, where land has been reclaimed and holds flourishing agricultural fields, rich in vegetables, fruit, vineyards and olive groves.

All the mountain ranges are rich in woodland and spring water. The layout of the land isolates towns and villages, while the long coastline has no natural harbours – this is a big region and it is not without its problems.

The heart of Calabria is the *Sila*, a wide, flat plateau of rolling hills covered in woodland of oaks, beeches and chestnuts, known as *Il grande bosco d'Italia* – Italy's great wood. A paradise for animals (or it would be if it weren't for the hunters) – hare, quails, pheasant, partridge, woodcock, wolves and boar all live here in a scene of stunning beauty; they are hunted savagely. Three lovely lakes have been constructed to provide electricity and are filled with huge and delicious trout. This is an area with a marvellously healthy climate, and to miss seeing it would be to miss the whole point of Calabria.

The coastline is the longest of all Italy's regions

and was for centuries pillaged by the Saracens and ravaged by malaria, pushing the population further and further inland, where they thrived at higher and healthier altitudes. They are beginning to return to the coast now, setting up new towns with the name Marina, corresponding with the original inland settlement: Marina di Belvedere, Marina di Catanzaro and so on.

The general climate of the region is inevitably influenced by the sea, giving hot summers cooled by the breezes and fairly mild winters. In the mountains, however, particularly the high peaks like the Pollino and Aspromonte, the winters are very cold with snow and rain. All over the mountains the danger of landslides is a constant and terrifying reality.

The Calabrian economy is based on farming fruit and vegetables. Farming communities live in villages isolated from the rest of society, often far away from the fields where their crops grow. The region is desperately poor, with many far-

mers emigrating north to the abandoned farms in central Italy where conditions are easier. Others abandon farming altogether, travelling north to factories to obtain a living wage. Many men leave their wives and children behind, returning south in their thousands for holidays.

Mountain cooking dominates the cuisine. Wonderful cheeses eaten at any time, with rough local bread and wine, or any of the delicious sausages, salame or ham. In a land with little room for stock, the pig reigns supreme.

CATANZARO & PROVINCE

The agricultural and commercial city of Catanzaro is not far from the sea, perched on a stony peak with deep gorges either side. Founded in the 10th century by the Byzantines, its location was chosen for its ease of defence, but now, to facilitate access, a long viaduct has been built over the Fiumarella river.

Along the gulf of Santa Eufemia are two major agricultural centres, Lamezia Terme, and the ancient settlement of Vibo Valentia, with its remarkable collection of Greek, Roman and medieval ruins. The two main holiday centres are Tropea and Pizzo on the Tyrrhenian coast – Pizzo is where the tuna fishermen bring in their haul.

COSENZA & PROVINCE

Cosenza is at the point where the Busento and Crati rivers cross, in the middle of one of the most fertile areas of the region. It is a thriving market town with a few minor industries springing up. I dined at *LA CALAVRISELLA* in via Girolamo de Rada in central Cosenza. It is a well-positioned restaurant on a corner, so you can watch the activities of the lively world outside as you eat. There was an interesting selection of ultra-local dishes – apparently even more specialised than just Calabrian – this is Cosentina cuisine! *Ciambotta milleprofumi* was a pie stuffed to bursting point with all kinds of superb fresh vegetables including aubergines, peppers and courgettes. *Bauletto di vitello farcito con burrino* a slice of veal stuffed with Sila cheese, and *crucetta cosentina*, stuffed figs. It was simple food cooked with flair and passion and a strict hold on traditions. The old cooking methods are favoured everywhere here – the spit, the griddle, the grill placed over an open fire, the brick oven – all is cooked with simplicity and the kind of austerity born of longtime poverty.

REGGIO DI CALABRIA & PROVINCE

Reggio di Calabria (always just known as Reggio Calabria) is the most densely populated city in the region, and has often violently demonstrated its desire to become its capital. It sits at the feet of the Aspromonte (Bitter mountain) on the Straits of Messina, isolated from the rest of the region, and tied to Messina for commercial reasons. Almost completely destroyed by two earthquakes in 1783 and 1908, it has both times overcome its hardships and has emerged a modern, earthquake-proof city. It is the main passenger port, with ships leaving regularly for Sicily, while the nearby port of Villa San Giovanni carries the cargo and vehicle ferries.

Friends directed me to a restaurant in Reggio

Calabria itself, which is supposed to be the very best in Calabria. It is called *BAYLIK* which is Turkish for fish, and is in via Leone 1. It deserves to be returned to again and again and again. The proprietor is practically a caricature of the typical southerner, but his fanatical obsession with his local cuisine is almost arrogant, yet, to me, very touching. If only others were so brave! The result is a menu which reflects the fabulous seaside views you can enjoy from the tables. *Pasta col pesce spada*, pasta with swordfish, *pasticciata di vongole e cozze* a kind of *lasagne* with clams and mussels, *grigliata dello stretto*, a vast platter of fresh grilled fish caught in the Straits, *fracaglia* a dish of tiny fried red mullet, *involtini di pesce spada* stuffed swordfish steaks – all deliciously fresh. And, if you don't like fish, there's *nzideddi* stuffed kid gut, or *salsicce al carbone* charcoal grilled sausages, beans, lentils, chickpeas, or the wonderful *parmigiana di zucchine* courgettes with Parmesan. There really is something for everyone here, and you can be absolutely certain that every single item on the menu is authentically regional.

The province contains most of the centres where Calabrian produce is processed for use – mostly olives, bergamot and pasta. Roarno, Palmi, Gioia Tauro and Nurianova are all market towns, situated in richly cultivated areas covered with vineyards, olive groves and citrus trees. Siderno, Locri, Scilla and Bagnara are all seaside resorts and fishing ports.

SALUMI
Salami, Sausages and Cured Meats

Entire families live off what they have managed to make out of one pig for the entire duration of the winter months. They are experts in the preserving of pork and all kinds of wonderful *salumi* emerge from years of patient tradition. Very little *prosciutto*, but countless kinds of sausages and *salami* – you are really spoiled for choice.

Many many different *salsicce* – one which is half minced meat and half liver *salsiccia di carne e fegato*, another, even richer is *salsiccia di fegato* liver sausage, which is skewered on to a stick of bay and grilled on an open fire. The other most popular *salumi* are *soppressata* and a rich, greasy sausage which has to weep a drop of fat as you cut it, called *salsiccia che piange*.

PASTA

Calabrian women are rightfully proud of their wide variety of superb home-made pastas. Many traditional versions are produced from long hours of hard work on the flour and water dough. *Fusilli*, long spaghetti twisted round a tool called a *firriettu* so they look like corkscrew curls, *paternoster, filatieddi, ricci di donna, canneroni* and many others – the customs and methods are handed down from generation to generation along with the expertise.

For special occasions there are *sagne chine*, home-made lasagne stuffed with all manner of 'gifts from God', ranging from artichokes, hard-boiled eggs, fresh cheese and meatballs to mushrooms and other seasonal wonders.

PESCE E FRUTTI DI MARE
Fish and seafood

Oddly enough for a region with such a long coastline, very little fishing is carried out locally. Swordfish *pesce spada* is caught off the Bagnara coast between Palmi and Scilla, and appears frequently on menus, the most delectable dish being steamed swordfish dressed with capers, parsley, lemon juice, oregano and garlic. *Neonata* is the

Local Specialities

- *Alici in Tortiera* Fresh anchovies baked with herbs, garlic and breadcrumbs.
- *Alici a Beccafico* Stuffed and fried anchovies served with a tomato sauce.
- *Baccala alla Verbicarese* Dried salt cod stewed with potatoes, dried *peperoni*, olive oil and salt.
- *Mustica* A dish of Arab origin. Tiny new-born anchovies are preserved with salt and pepper in terracotta pots under a layer or six of olive oil. With the addition of a great deal of *peperoncino* they turn this into a kind of mousse, called *Caviale Calabrese* which is incredibly hot but very delicious.
- *Tonno o alalonga in agrodolce* Chunks of tuna fried, mixed with fried onions that are covered with vinegar and sugar.

term which refers to newly-born very small fish, which are fried like whitebait or served in a variety of other ways, pickled, in a tomato sauce and so on. Squid or cuttlefish *calamari*, octopus *polpi* and prawns *gamberi* appear fairly regularly, as do all types of larger fish that are either grilled or roasted. Oysters *ostriche*, mussels *cozze* and other shellfish crop up occasionally, but generally speaking fish and seafood are served less than you'd expect. From the lakes of the Sila come perfect, fleshy, juicy trout *trota*, which are very fresh and usually cooked very simply on a hot-plate with just a sprinkling of olive oil and lemon juice.

Alalonga (Thunus allalunga) is also caught and eaten. This is a small tuna with very white and juicy meat and a delicious flavour. Tuna *tonno* is also served often. Freshly caught anchovies *alici* are prepared in various ways, too, as are *baccalà* and *pesce stocco*.

CARNE E CACCIA

Meat and game

Down here they should build a monument to the glory of their favourite animal – the pig. Pork turns up wherever you go, and every single bit of it is used. It's a lean, angry, stubborn animal with a black skin which is allowed to roam freely through winding village streets and lush fields all year until October, when it meets its end in a ceremonious killing. This is followed by a day of festivity in which the best parts of the pig are

Local Specialities

• *Murseddu* A plain pizza *focaccia*, stuffed with pork offal or lamb offal and fried with *peperoncino*. The name derives from the idea that it must be consumed in huge bites. It's delicious, but you need the constitution of a horse to digest it successfully!

• *Pitta* The Calabresi are very good at making this king of *focaccia* (bread dough flattened out as for *pizza* and covered in oil and salt before baking until golden. This version is fairly thick, and can be stuffed with anything from *salame* to *peperoni* or sardines to tomatoes.

eaten with mountains of aubergines, peppers, olives and onions, washed down with rivers of wine. Then they get to work turning the remaining meat into food for the winter. All manner of sausages and *salumi* are prepared, but you can be certain that as far as fresh meat goes, you will find pork on the menu at every turn. *Cicciole*, pork crackling, is used to stuff *pitta*, the local version of *focaccia* or *pizza bianca*.

Kid, lamb and mutton are also used a great deal, and beef and veal come far behind. Poultry is virtually ignored, but game when in season is eaten a lot, especially in the mountains. Rich and strong-tasting wild boar is cooked very simply, either roasted in the oven or on the spit, dressed with garlic, parsley and bay.

FORMAGGIO

Cheese

The cheeses produced on the Sila are famous throughout Italy. They are mountain cheeses which retain an inimitable flavour of lush fresh grass and sunlight. *Caciocavallo* is the largest, a hardish, peppery cheese used all over the country in various dishes, originally from Calabria, but then there are many more – each one better than the last. Make a point of tasting each and every one. If you like cheese as much as I do you'll be in heaven. The most common are *tumu, rinusu, impanata* and *butirro* and *burrino*. The amazing *butirro* has a hard, fibrous crust and a soft and buttery interior, fresh, creamy and tender. Also as in other parts of the country where you find sheep, excellent *pecorino*.

All this cheese can be served for breakfast, lunch, tea or dinner, and they'll come with great hunks of *pane casareccio* – round blackened bread baked in a wood oven, with a very thick hard crust and a soft and fluffy middle.

FRUTTA E VERDURA

Fruit and Vegetables

There is little land that can be used to grow crops, but the narrow fields are put to good use. Calabria is the producer of one third of the national output of olive oil – which gives you an idea of the number of olive trees there are!

It is second after Sicily in the production of

Local Specialities

- *Licurdia* A vegetable soup with a vast amount of onions, cooked separately, poured over slices of toasted bread, covered with ground black pepper.
- *Macco di fave* A superb and very thick broad bean soup, which is dressed with olive oil, *pecorino* and masses of black pepper just before serving.

oranges, figs and *cedri* limes. They are yellow, about as big as a grapefruit, but very knobbly. They aren't very nice to eat, but their peel is used to make candied peel, which appears in so many cakes, and their juice is used to make a syrup to dilute with water for a refreshing drink.

Bergamot is a crop exclusive to this region. It is a citrus fruit, so I'll include it here, though it's impossible to eat, being terribly bitter. Its peel yields an essence which, once distilled, is used in perfume manufacture. It's a perfume in itself and has the ability to 'fix' other perfumes, and is therefore very valuable to the trade. It is exported all over the world. The fruit pickers are instantly recognisable by the indelible brown staining of their skin.

Other traditional crops include rosemary, used generously to flavour the pork dishes, licorice and jasmine. Potatoes, pulses and vines, which produce very little but excellent wine, and many eating grapes.

Boney's beet blockade

The development of sugar beet began here when Napoleon refused access to English ships bringing sugar cane to the rest of Europe, and so it became necessary to introduce another sugar source. It was first used in Calabria, and the sugar beet industry has helped keep the region alive.

Peppers *peperoni* from Calabria are considered the best in the country. They are rich sweet and juicy like none other and come in enormous sizes.

Aubergines *melanzane* are the most ubiquitous regional vegetable. Courgettes *zucchine* are also used a lot, as are onions, in particular those wild ones like the Pugliese *lampasciuoli*, which here are called *cipollizza* or *cipuddizza*. Mushrooms which grow on the mountains are

also very popular, especially the fabulous *rossito* with its big red hat. And, of course, tomatoes of all shapes and sizes from juicy round salad tomatoes to the little plum-shaped ones used to dress the local hand-made pasta.

Every year the papers are filled with stories of people dying from eating wild mushrooms. Unless you know what you are doing, PLEASE don't be tempted to try mushrooms growing wild.

Salad *insalata* is very popular, and many combinations of all these vegetables are put together imaginatively to create some lovely dishes. There are all kinds of vegetable stews, fried, baked, grilled and stuffed vegetables – all delicious and extremely healthy.

Fichi Ripieni alla Sibarita

These wonderfully rich stuffed figs last for a very long time in an airtight container. The dry figs have to be fat and soft, and then they are opened up and filled with chopped almonds and walnuts and cocoa, then baked in the oven. They are then laid in terracotta pots in layers with a good dousing of *mosto cotto*, cooked wine must – cooked to reduce it and make it syrupy – over each layer. Also a sprinkling of sugar, ground cloves and cinnamon is added to each layer. Finally they are covered in the must and used as needed. They are utterly delicious, and a very good way of using up the dried figs left over from Christmas time.

PASTICCERIA

Cakes, Biscuits and Puddings

There's a delightful array of simple pastries here – no fancy puddings like the Sicilians will show you. These are very basic, easy-to-make cakes and puddings with a long tradition.

- *Bocconotti Calabresi* From Mormanno, little golden pastry cases with a lovely jammy filling. These locally made jams translate all the evocative floral scents of Calabria into tastes you'll always remember.
- *Cannariculi* Traditional Christmas cakes made of pastry fingers, fried in oil and soaked in honey, decorated with tiny sugar spangles *diavolicchi*.
- *Chinullie* Christmas sweet *ravioli*, whose

dough contains vermouth, olive oil and lemons, filled with cocoa, chestnuts, chocolate, candied fruit, cloves and cinnamon, chopped *torrone*, crushed vanilla sweets, sugar and honey! They can also be filled with aniseed-flavoured *ricotta* or with cinnamon and jam. They are deep fried in oil and are served dusted with clove powder, cinnamon and sugar, and are then smothered with liquefied honey.

- *Cicirata* Another Christmas speciality. Little lumps of rich dough are fried in boiling oil, dipped in honey and shaped into a single large cake with a hole in the middle, traditionally served on orange leaves.
- *Pignolata* Very like the above, but the pieces of dough are bigger and mixed with honey into which pieces of orange peel have been added, and are shaped according to taste. The cake is dusted with icing sugar and *diavolicchi*.
- *Mostaccioli* Also known as *nzudda*, these biscuits have a strong Arab link. They are sold everywhere and are delicious if a little bit sweet. A honey and liqueur dough is cut into letters of the alphabet, fishes, flowers, etc., and are baked.
- *Mostarda* Traditionally prepared during harvest time – *vendemmia*. It's a mixture of boiled wine must, flour, cocoa and cinnamon, cooked until it forms a smooth cream, then sprinkled with toasted chopped almonds.
- *Panzarotte* Envelopes of fine pastry, richly filled with *ricotta*, chocolate, candied fruit and sugar.
- *Passulate* From the village of Ardore, a traditional Christmas cake. The dough is made with honey, flour, raisins, almonds, walnuts, lemon and spices, rolled out and cut into squares, each of which is laid on a lemon leaf and baked.
- *Piccillato di Pasqua* Easter cake made with yeast and flavoured with orange. Sometimes it is baked with whole eggs in the dough.
- *Scalille* or *scaledde* Christmas treat. Biscuits rolled into sausage shapes and wound round a stick to give them a shape just like *fusilli*. Fried and soaked in honey or sugar syrup.
- *Turtiddi* Sweet *gnocchi* containing Moscato wine, honey, cinnamon and oranges. Fried and smothered in melted honey and orange juice. They're served piping hot, and are very popular with children.
- *Uova alla monacella* Castrovillari speciality. Deep-fried hard-boiled eggs stuffed with sugar, cinnamon and cocoa. There's a savoury dish with

the same name where the eggs are cut in half and smothered with a piquant tomato sauce and parsley.
- *Fichi al cioccolato* Figs stuffed with chocolate chips and candied fruit, and rolled in fine cocoa.

VINO
Wine

There are very few wines produced in this region, but they have ancient traditions to make up for that.

RED WINE
- *Ciro* The oldest of all the southern wines, it was drunk during the original Olympic Games! Produced in the area of Ciro and Ciro Marina with Gaglioppo, Greco Bianco and Trebbiano vines, it is a dry, superior table wine in the red and rosé versions, with characteristic bouquet and a fragrant full flavour.
- *Pollino* An excellent and well-known table wine, perfect with grilled meat. A light-coloured ruby red wine with a pleasantly winey bouquet and a full-bodied dry flavour. The best one is the *Lacrima di Castrovillari Pollino*.
- *Savuto* Also known as *Succo di Pietra* (stone juice), this is a fine ruby red wine with bright glints of light. A lovely rounded, dry, velvety wine. Ages well and marries best with roasts and game dishes.

WHITE WINE
- *Ciro* The white version of the above is slightly fruity.

DESSERT WINE
- *Greco di Gerace* Another very old wine, produced in Gerace and surroundings for many centuries. A golden wine with a smooth sweet flavour and a bouquet of orange blossom. An excellent dessert wine which is also good as an aperitif.
- *Moscato di Calabria* Produced in very small quantities, making it a valuable rarity, a golden and smooth dessert wine. Can be aged for many many years – is much sought after and will be expensive if it's the real thing.

There are a few other local wines worth mentioning: *Vini di Palmi* and *Greco di Ponte Grande* (reds), *Bianco di Squillace* and *Bianco di Nicastro* (whites).

BEVANDE
Drinks

Apart from rather nasty home-made liqueurs with unpronounceable names I haven't come across a single real 'drink' as such down this far south. Plenty of imported stuff from the rest of the country or the world but nothing which I can honestly say was born here. If anybody can enlighten me please write and tell me – others can enjoy the delicious wines and as an after-dinner drink I suggest a glass of Moscato or Malvasia.

WORTH TAKING HOME

Take jars of vegetables, aubergines, tomatoes, peppers in olive oil. The olive oil itself is very strong, with a persistent flavour and smell, so if you prefer delicate oil you can buy *olio d'oliva fino*, which is less hefty but more expensive. As with all these southern regions, take dried *peperoncini* to recreate the burning flavours of the southern heat.

Butirro has a hard outer skin so could easily be taken home, and above all the delicious stuffed dried figs *fichi ripieni* which can be bought in packets or loose.

Any of the wines mentioned, and the *Sciroppo di Cedro*, for a different soft drink.

If you are tempted to buy some pure bergamot scent, take care, as it can stain your skin in the sun. Put it on clothes instead.

To serve all your home-made Calabrian dishes, take the beautiful olive green painted and glazed earthenware bowls, plates and pots.

SAGRE E FESTE
Festivals

24 August 1987 saw the reinstatement after a 20-year absence of the *Festa della Varia* at Palmi in the province of Reggio Calabria. At this festa a very high cart is drawn along by about 500 bearers. On the cart, about 50 local people are dressed up to represent a pageant of the Virgin's ascent to heaven. The event is completed with much music and dancing and local specialities sold from kiosks as well as lots of the local wines.

If you are visiting this region in the early part of the autumn, look out for signs directing you to one of the small local *Festa del Porco* or *Sagra del Maiale*, where the slaughtering of the pig for winter provisions will be marked by traditional festivities of some kind or another – certainly there will be plenty of delicious local fare to eat and drink.

Most of the food you eat at these events will be cooked over an open fire as tradition dictates. Look out for the wonderful special bread baked to mark this occasion in the Reggio Calabria province, where the hot, freshly baked loaves are split open and filled with tomatoes cooked over the open fire and doused with olive oil, salt and pepper to make the most amazing sandwiches.

Culinary Eruptions and Elaborate Executions

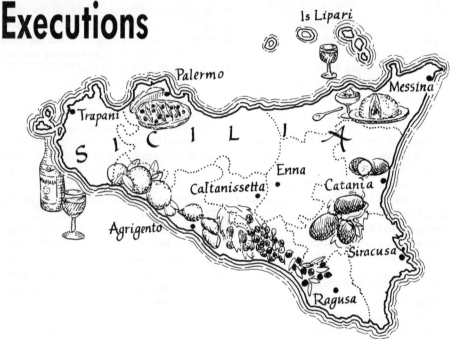

Sicilia – fields of lusty grain as far as the eye can see, and vast dry areas of cracked soil, where nothing can grow. Villages and towns where time stands still, yet other parts where it is racing past the inhabitants at top speed. But the natural differences, weather differences and the cultural differences are not enough to explain the contrasts that are so alive on the island.

To understand why Sicily is the way she is, it is necessary to find out a little about her history.

From her position in the middle of the Mediterranean, the island has been open to influences and invasions from various fronts. The Phoenicians left little imprint, the Greeks, who farmed the land, and controlled maritime commerce, eventually conflicted with each other so much

that the Romans intervened and conquered the island in 247 BC. For the Romans, however, Sicily was no more than *Il Granaio*, the Granary. The soil was put under strain, its wheat, sowed and reaped by imported slaves, feeding the whole empire, and by 827, at the end of the Roman domination, Sicily was reduced to tiny rural communities, linked by common despair.

The Arabs conquered in 827 and cities were reborn. Palermo became the Mediterranean's most important port. The Arabs introduced new crops which have become the island's way of life: jasmine, cotton, oranges, lemons, palms, aubergines. They invented irrigation systems to get the most out of the land. They divided the land into small sections that were easy to control.

Their influence is still strongly felt – in the cuisine, and methods of agriculture – intense, specialised and cleverly divided between citrus fruits and vegetables, directly derived from ancient Arab gardens. And they introduced ice cream.

The Normans took over and introduced a Golden Age until the 13th century, and then the Spanish abandoned the island to a free-for-all feudal system – and with absentee landlords, whether Spanish Bourbons or later the Savoy royal family, the peasants lost out. Eventually, by the beginning of this century, the hope of finding a better life elsewhere led to thousands of people packing up all they owned in a couple of suitcases and abandoning Sicily.

The island fared no better under Fascism – as in Roman times, the soil was weakened by the *battaglia del grano* the battle for grain, and a feeling of independence was felt throughout the land, helped along by the Mafia and Cosa Nostra. Finally she was given special status in 1946 as an autonomous region of Italy.

A government fund, the *Cassa per il Mezzogiorno*, was set up to help the poverty-stricken south, and it did give some relief. Sicily is very different today, but many of her social, physical, psychological and economic characteristics have roots that go back to times that will never be forgotten.

If you can't take the heat ...

It's not just hot here, this is boiling, asphyxiating, dry African heat. Headlines in the papers read '2,000 chickens die of heart attacks as a result of scorching heat!', 'Violent fires throughout Sicily, the temperature is over 40°C. During the day, the streets in small villages and towns are deserted – everyone is indoors, waiting for the cool of the evening to venture out for a breath of air and a cool drink. In all small towns and villages there are kiosks at the centre of the square selling drinks with odd names, *limone al limone, mandarino al limone* lemon lemon or mandarin lemon to the overheated population. This tradition goes back a long way, and although today the drinks are made with fruit juice, soda water and sugar, once there was only water on offer – it was rare and precious enough to sell by the glassful.

But it isn't always so hot – spring is the best time to go, when the temperatures are bearable, and the citrus groves and almond trees are in blossom, or autumn when the sea is warm, and everything feels ripe and mature.

Worship the guest

In the land where in true Arabic tradition the guest is sacred, tourism as an industry seems to find difficulties in getting off the ground. Communications are a problem, roads and public transport often appalling and many hotels leave much to be desired – and there is little help from the government. Things are beginning to improve, and some holiday companies have managed to break through the net, but the island is still full of potential that goes unused. From some points of view his is a good thing, and there is plenty of scope for the visitor seeking unspoilt beaches and small undiscovered secrets.

Women's toil

We first visited Sicily with a friend who ran a Birmingham restaurant, known as Jo. He invited us to spend a holiday with his family in his home village of Resuttano. I had an idea that life in the inland areas of Sicily would be far removed from the rest of Italy, but nothing could have prepared me for the experiences in store. Jo, now Giuseppe, had left behind his adopted English ways. The warm jovial man had become cunning, severe, mysterious and old fashioned within a day. Because I'm a woman I wasn't allowed to walk alone outside the house, and none of us went for a walk after dark. But my worst experience came about in the kitchen.

Jo's mother did all the cooking for the vast household of sisters, brothers, aunts, cousins and grandchildren – we were never less than twenty for a meal – aided by other similarly clad, black-shrouded women in long skirts. Fascinated by the constant activity – drying fruit, bottling tomato sauce, decanting wine from huge barrels, making tough coarse bread and pasta, I would spend hours just watching them. One day I asked if I could help. Their reaction was unexpected. After much rapid discussion, raised voices, arguing and waving of hands, none of which I could understand, the dialect was too thick, Jo was summoned. He explained that they wanted to know whether I was menstruating. 'If so, you can't join in – the bread won't rise, the pasta will crumble and the tomato sauce will go sour – no woman can cook while in that condition.'

It looks funny now, but on that day I was as

embarrassed as I have ever been. Still, when I replied that I was all right, within minutes I was wrapped in a huge apron, being taught how to peel the rock hard, juicy tomatoes for the sauce, completely accepted by the sisterhood of the kitchen.

Shortly before the end of the holiday we went riding through the local woods – more like a thicket, and I saw my very first dead body. He hung from a tree, legs and arms dangling, a buzz of wasps and flies all around him. We, 'the English', were horrified. 'Call the police' I screamed, 'for God's sake DO something!' I was hysterical, filled with an inexplicable terror and grief at the sight of this dead person, swinging so silently from the tree. The Sicilians had other ideas: 'Non è Roba Nostra,' they said quietly, and rode on calmly. (It's not Our Business). The man hung there until the people involved in the hanging saw fit to call in the authorities – nobody else did or would have done so, however much we insisted.

I felt totally overwhelmed by the power of this island and its powers that be and those that have been. So much here is unspoken, lurking dangerously, a sinister presence in the background. If you are afraid, you *will* conform to the rules, and only the very foolhardy are not scared. Everything here, either directly or indirectly, is controlled by the Mafia – the crops mysteriously fail overnight if the payments are not received on time, the tourist industry – which could be the making of the island – is sadly under-developed – it is obviously against somebody's best interests to have too many visitors here, but there are instead plenty of petrol refineries to shatter the landscape and mess up the crystal clear blue waters. One thing for sure, it may be Italy's other large island, but if you discount the fact that they're both surrounded by water, there the similarity with Sardegna comes to a full stop.

Baroque cuisine and peasant fare

To me Sicilian cuisine divides up into two separate categories. There is the rich baroque cuisine of the sumptuous homes of island princes, Norman and Spanish noblemen and Arab conquerors, and then there is the simple peasant food of the working classes. I can't say which is the most typical or traditional. They are equally important in catching the spirit of the island's

eating habits, and you cannot really separate them either, as there are so many dishes that overlap. With the variety of religious festivities to celebrate, and so many customs of hospitality, added to the 'over the top' nature that is the nature of the people, many specialities have emerged.

PALERMO & PROVINCE

Founded by the Phoenicians, taken over by the Romans and Arabs, Palermo has always been the most densely populated and active port on the island. There are many interesting old monuments to see, but as an abrupt and painful contrast, the city is also filled with squalid neighbourhoods, with people living in unbelievable conditions.

The Chickpea Massacre

On Easter Sunday 1282 the horrendous Vespers Massacre took place when the long-suffering population of Palermo cruelly butchered their Norman rulers. This furious tide of rage erupted in Palermo like lava from Etna itself following the alleged insult of a young girl praying at vespers in the Church of Santo Spirito. Every Norman found incapable of pronouncing *cicero* (the word for chickpea, nowadays called *ceci*) was savagely killed. Suddenly the tolling bells took on a new meaning.

Within the province are several interesting towns. Mondello, an old fishing village, is now a lively seaside resort. Monreale, on a hill dominating a fertile plain, the Conca d'Oro or Golden Conch, where orange groves abound, is famous for its artistic masterpieces. Piana degli Albanesi has a colony of Albanian immigrants who settled here in the 15th century and have retained their costume and language – and no doubt the food, of their homeland.

Bagheria is a large market town for the local citrus groves and vineyards. Cefalù is a fishing port that is fast becoming popular as a holiday resort, and moving inland are Corleone and Partinico, both excellent market towns, the first immortalised by Mario Puzo in *The Godfather*.

MESSINA & PROVINCE

Once a Greek colony, Messina is at the feet of the Peloritani mountains and gives its name to the brief strip of water that separates Sicily from Calabria.

Within the province is the wonderful resort of Taormina, built on a terrace 200m above the sea, providing marvellous views along the coastline, with Etna smouldering in the background. There are plenty of good hotels and restaurants here offering an enormous variety of superb fresh fish. It is one place where the importance of developing the tourist industry has taken root and flourished. I enjoyed a delightful meal at *ANGELO A MARE-DELFINO* in via Nazionale, sitting on a terrace full of flowers overlooking Mazzaro Bay – the mussels were fantastic, and the atmosphere welcoming.

Of the Aeolian Islands, two are still active volcanoes, Stromboli and Vulcano. These islands don't just give the visitor clean sea, perfect hospitality and fresh fish – they also have an important agricultural contribution to make – their Malvasia grapes, that make the wine that Guy de Maupassant called 'the wine of the devil'.

CATANIA & PROVINCE

On the southern slopes of Mount Etna, Catania is the second largest city in spite of repeated damage by volcanic eruptions and earthquakes. The fertility of the soil on the volcanic slopes, growing vines, oranges, lemons and olives, encourages people to go on living there in spite of the constant threat. Recently Catania has undergone something of an industrial revolution, gaining her the name of Milan of the South.

This stretch of coastline is where the last few fishermen's traditional homes can be seen, squashed between discotheques and restaurants. At Aci Trezza, a seaside resort, you can see the famous Cyclops Rocks sticking out black and threatening from the sea. They are, according to legend, the rocks that Polyphemus threw at Ulysses as he tried to escape.

SIRACUSA & PROVINCE

Siracusa was the first and most important of the island's settlements, a vast archaeological park, filled with evidence of her glorious past – the amphitheatre, Greek theatre and many other relics. Here is the most joyful restaurant I have ever encountered, the *JONICO A RUTTA E CIAULI*, which is on the Riviera Dionisio il Grande. Run by the 5 merry Giudice brothers, it is a beautiful restaurant with wide open terraces with terrific views over the sea. The pasta is superb, the wine makes you giggle and the whole atmosphere is fun.

Steer clear of Augusta, it's a horrifying complex of factories and refineries. Better to head for Floridia, Noto, Avola or Pachino, all centres for local olives, almonds and citrus fruits, lovely markets.

RAGUSA & PROVINCE

Ragusa is a city of two separate nuclei. Ragusa Ibla is the old city, with irregular narrow streets, some shabby houses, some fabulous palazzi. Modern Ragusa has looked on life differently since the discovery of natural gas and petroleum. This is an agricultural area producing wine, cereals and olive oil. The surrounding countryside is rich and fertile with all the aubergines, courgettes, tomatoes, peppers, citrus fruits and peaches pouring into the market towns of Vittoria, Modica, Comiso and Scicli.

CALTANISSETTA & PROVINCE

The ancient city of Caltanissetta is situated in a hilly district in the centre of the island. It's an agricultural centre, and rich in mineral deposits like sulphur, salt and potassium.

The province is mountainous and hilly, sloping down to the sea at the port of Gela.

AGRIGENTO & PROVINCE

Agrigento rises up on a hill facing the sea, and at the feet of the hill stretches the Valle dei Tempii, the Valley of Temples, a huge archaeological complex of interest to historians and tourists alike. Agrigento's port is Porto Empedocle, and is just a few kilometres from the city centre.

Like Caltanissetta, this province is rich in mineral deposits. The town of Canicatti is one of the richest towns in the island, thanks to the production of *uva regina* (regina grapes) which has brought enormous prosperity to the town and its surroundings. Canicatti used to be a poor town

– a few donkeys still take their place in the traffic jams of BMWs and Porsches. Almonds grew here, but were snubbed by the sweet industry. Then, somebody asked a scientist to analyse a lump of earth, and the grape industry exploded in earnest. This was land where vines could grow high, helped up by trellises, high and wide enough for tractors to be driven under and between them. Vines took over from orchards, vegetable patches, chicken runs, and were planted in every available space – including flower pots! Suddenly people were earning more than 20 million lire a year! Emigrants have returned, here a vine surgeon earns more than a bank clerk.

Unfortunately, drunk on its overnight success, the town doesn't know how to channel its money, and there are no new schools, hotels, or roads here. Old traditions die hard though – All Souls' Day is still celebrated rather than Christmas, mourning is still governed by strict rules, and gossip rules the day in this ultimately provincial town.

The Pelagie Islands are part of this province. Lampedusa and Linosa are African in origin, appearance and feel. Linosa is where the mother turtles come and lay their eggs. Both islands produce much of Sicily's fresh fish, though locally the illegal method of bombing fish out of the water is also used. There are some sharks round the islands, and shark steak *pescecane* is often available.

TRAPANI & PROVINCE

Trapani is a lively active port, with cargo boats, ferries and fishing smacks.

The province is rich and fertile with vines, grain and olives growing abundantly, and the old traditions are respected and put into practice as a daily part of life.

In Trapani, authentic Trapanese cuisine can be enjoyed at P & G, in via Spalti. I had huge, superb scampi and lobster as delicious kebabs, and wonderful *cuscus alla Trapanese* couscous, a remnant of the Arab domination here. This restaurant boasts a special wine list, with many valuable Marsala wines.

Marsala is a beautiful ancient Arab port (*Mars-Allah* – port of Allah) and gives its name to the world-famous wine produced here. This wine is obviously the town's main speciality and it is interesting to note that it was an Englishman, John Woodhouse, who first introduced the strong wine to the rest of the world.

I also found in the town wonderful ice cream at the *GELATERIA CAITO*, where they make the ice

Aja Mola! Aja Mola!

Tuna fish used to be caught in great shoals off Sicilian shores. The ports of Trapani, Mazara del Vallo and Aci Trezza have all seen the gangs of fishermen descend to the harbour at dawn, with the leader, the *rais*, leading the chanting: '*Aja Mola! Aja Mola! Aja Mola e iemunnini!*' he calls, his men all answering '*Aja Mola! Aja Mola!*' The shoals of fish will have found their route blocked by a series of nets, arranged in such a way as to lead the tuna into the final closed-off net. When the *rais* declares enough fish are trapped in the last net (called the death room), the *mattanza* begins. This is a word derived from the Spanish *matar*, to kill. '*Spara a tunnina,*' calls the *rais*, and with harpoon and hooks the men try to spear the fish, which sometimes weigh up to 300 kg each, and heave them on to the boats. The fish lash about with fear, and mostly end up killing each other with great sweeps of their tails. The sea becomes blood red, but the ritual is carried out with great speed and efficiency. Very soon the boats regain the shore, and the tuna is taken off to the factories to be processed.

These days only two places – Castiglione and the island of Favignana – still practise this method of fishing, though twenty years ago it was a way of life in fifteen places round the island. The old *rais* will tell you it's because there aren't so many tuna in the sea, but it's also because there has been no attempt to modernise the task, and the skilled craftsmen required for the job are not available. Since Vincenzo Florio first thought of preserving tuna in olive oil in the last century, things have not progressed much. This tuna is the best in the world – the Japanese say so, and they come here to buy it and transport it back to Japan to be eaten raw – at extortionate prices, while Europe eats tuna imported from Japan and the South Pacific!

cream that the island is so rightly famous for, with fresh produce and no chemicals.

ENNA & PROVINCE

The only landlocked province on the island, and its provincial capital is the highest main city in Italy. Enna sits on a vast plateau with marvellous views. This is a typically agricultural province, with local markets at Nicosia, Leonforte and Piazza Armerina, where there is also a Roman villa.

SALUMI

Salami, Sausages and Cured Meats

I haven't come across a single traditional island speciality in this category, although copies of *salumi* made elsewhere on the mainland are eaten, and in true Sicilian fashion they are turned into colourful, imaginative and exciting elements that have little in common with the original. Lard is used a great deal in the preparation of meat dishes, and certain kinds of *salame* appear filled with crunchy pistachio nuts for a note of colour and extra flavour.

PASTA

Many people think that the original pasta shapes came from this island, when the huge Muslim

---

Local Specialities

- *Pasta con le sarde* A timbale of pasta with sardines, pinenuts, raisins and fresh wild fennel. Alphonse Daudet exclaimed, on eating this, that Sicilian cooking is an extension of Spanish Baroque art.
- *Pasta di vruoccoli arriminata* Pasta with cauliflower. The pasta is cooked, tossed in a pan with the cauliflower, anchovies, tomato purée, pinenuts, raisins, saffron and garlic. The end result is brilliantly coloured and looks rather Indian.
- *Pasta alla Norma* Though in existence long before composer Bellini discovered it, it was named after his opera *Norma*. Spaghetti with aubergines.

---

contingent began to make *Ittryia* in the 10th century. These were a kind of very rough fusilli, made with flour and water. Nowadays *maccaruni di casa* are similar, usually dressed with a pork and tomato ragù.

Today pasta is very popular, often covered with wonderful fish.

PESCE E FRUTTI DI MARE

Fish and Seafood

Apart from the dwindling tuna fish catch, Sicily is surrounded by productive clear blue waters yielding anchovies *alici*, sardines *sardine*, mackerel

---

Local Specialities

- *Pescespada alla ghiotta* One of the many ways of preparing swordfish, this is with oil, tomato, capers, onions, celery and potatoes.
- *Pescestocco a ghiotta* In 1070 Roger the Norman arrived in Palermo, bringing with him salted herrings and dried salt cod from the cold north. Here *Baccalà* is called *pescestocco* and is cooked like the swordfish above, but with pears instead of potatoes.
- *Sarde a beccaficu* The *beccafico* is a plump little bird, and the sardines in this dish are named after it, all round and plump with their filling of raisins, pinenuts, breadcrumbs, garlic and herbs. (The filling will vary according to where you are.) The fish's tail is left sticking up just like a bird's tail.

---

sgombro, swordfish *pesce spada*, lobsters *aragosta*, huge succulent octopus *polpo* and plenty of brilliant orange, juicy mussels *cozze*. Nobody knows exactly why, but the fish caught around the remarkable island of Pantelleria reach vast proportions never seen elsewhere. Octopus and *dentice* have been caught here measuring up to a metre in length. Certain kinds of local shark *pesce cane* are considered a great delicacy and will be cooked as steaks.

CARNE E CACCIA
Meat and Game

Since livestock needs green grass and water to survive, and there is not much of either, this is almost completely a non-meat cuisine. With such bounty from the sea, vegetables, fruit and pasta, the islanders have no need to eat meat, nor apparently any desire. And although some meat does permeate the menus, it is unlikely that very much of it will be produced on the island.

There may be some lamb, usually cooked in a stew, with the resulting juices poured over pasta, and veal, which is usually rolled and stuffed. Kid is usually cooked whole, in the oven, with rosemary, garlic and sliced potatoes. Mutton appears with a huge selection of herbs, including mint, to hide the unpleasant smell, and lots of green olives.

Chicken can be served in a casserole with aubergines, or boiled, chilled and covered with *salsa al tonno*, sauce made with tuna fish, mayonnaise, capers, anchovies and lemon juice. Pork is not very popular. Perhaps it is generally too hot and unhealthy a climate for it to be eaten safely, or perhaps the old Muslim taboos put people off the idea, but I have eaten it as escalopes with Marsala, and it was delicious.

All the national offal dishes reappear on the island even though they are under different names. Just in case you find yourself in a situation where you're not sure of what's on your menu and you aren't mad about offal, here is a guide: *stig-ghiole* or *turcinuna* are little kebabs made with kid's gut. *Sanceli* is like *sanguinaccio* – a kind of sausage made with fresh pig's blood, either sweet with sultanas and pinenuts, or savoury with cheese and walnuts. *Testina di vitello* is a calf's head, which will usually be cooked in a rich tomato sauce with herbs and spices. *Turtiduzza* is a collection of various kinds of offal from a kid or lamb, including lung, heart, spleen and so on, cooked in a tomato sauce.

Inland, various kinds of game are available, but rabbit and the plump little birds called *beccaficu*, garden warblers, are the most traditional, and most likely to be served.

FORMAGGIO
Cheese

Little cheese is produced on the island, although the strong *pecorino* ewes' milk cheese is a vital ingredient for many dishes. As elsewhere, it can be *dolce*, a sweet bland cheese, used in many dishes, but can also be eaten on its own, or *piccante* a strong peppery version, with a lingering aftertaste. *Ricotta* also crops up, as does *caciocavallo*.

Canestrato is a firm, sliceable cheese which is sold in its little basket *canestro* and is used to make a fabulous dish called *caciu all'argintera*, fried cheese with herbs and oil and vinegar, which takes its name from its inventor. He was a failed silversmith (*Argentiere*) who became unable to afford meat any more, and decided to eat cheese instead.

FRUTTA E VERDURA
Fruit and Vegetables

Grapes, in particular *uva regina*, the variety exported all over the world from little towns like Canicatti, are rivalling the production of citrus fruits, although every effort is being made to keep this most Sicilian of cultures. Lemons are grown all year round, and oranges and various kinds of tangerines are also grown at different times to try to keep them flowing into the European markets all year round. This is an attempt to withstand the competition from Spain, Israel, Algeria and Morocco, who flood the markets with citrus fruits at cheaper prices. Olives, almonds, figs, pistachio

---

Local Specialities

- *Babbalucci du festinu* Pieces of pork crackling, fried in olive oil and chopped garlic, pepper and parsley. Eaten on June 24 in Aci Trezza for San Giovanni and around 13 July for Santa Rosalia.
- *Farsumagru* Literally means False Lean, because you'd never know that it was meat lurking under all that tomato sauce. It's actually a roll of veal or beef, with a filling of chopped eggs, minced meat, herbs and *prosciutto*.

Aulivi cunsati is actually a sauce, the traditional accompaniment to mutton. It is squashed green olives and sliced celery, with mint for extra flavour, dressed with oil and vinegar.

Local Specialities

• *Cassata alla Siciliana* The original recipe calls for ice cream made with *ricotta*, candied fruit, pistachios, sugar and chocolate, placed inside a bowl lined with sponge cake soaked in liqueur, iced with a thin layer of pale green pistachio, the traditional colour of classical Sicilian pastry making.

nuts and carob are also widely produced. Melons and watermelons are sweeter and juicier on the island than just about anywhere on the mainland.

Among the vegetables, peas, artichokes, tomatoes, peppers, aubergines, courgettes, capers, *peperoncino* and various kinds of salads are the ones which grow best and most profitably here. Aubergines *melanzane* arrived on the island during the long Arab reign, and since then have become an integral part of the cuisine – there are literally thousands of recipes for cooking them.

PASTICCERIA

Cakes, Biscuits and Puddings

Sicily is famous the world over for her marvellous selection of pastries, ice creams, cakes and sweets. All over Italy the best *pasticcerie* have a Sicilian in the kitchen. They are passionate and artistic about their ice cream making, which has its origins back in the times when the Arabs brought their sorbet to the island along with citrus fruits and palms. Do not be surprised if you get lemon sorbet in your *cornetto* at breakfast time, with cappuccino – they are *mad* about the stuff.

• *Cassata alla Siciliana* used to be the traditional Easter dessert, and is now a world-renowned ice cream speciality. The name comes from the Arab word *quas'at*, which literally means large round bowl. It was nuns who perfected its preparation, and they became so intent on perfection, that at the end of the 16th century, the religious authorities of Mazzara del Vallo prohibited the Holy Orders from making *Cassata* any more, as they were neglecting their other duties during Easter week.

• *Cassarulata di gelato* is different from *cassata* in that there is no sponge cake. Instead, the bowl is lined with pistachio ice cream and the inside filled with whipped cream and egg whites, mixed with candied fruit, nuts and sugar. As with *cassata*, once the 'cake' is frozen, it is turned out on to a dish and sliced.

Other *gelati* include delicious jasmine-flavoured sorbets, and orange blossom concoctions, *zagara*, bright pink watermelon *cocomero* ice cream, and scooped-out melons filled with delicious lemon ice cream.

The pastries and cakes of Sicily are just as famous and delectable.

• *Frutta alla Martotana* is almond paste, made into tiny fruit shapes – apricots, pears, apples, figs and so on, coloured with vegetable dye and elegantly presented on a dish. It takes its name from one of Palermo's convents, where the nuns used to make the fruit many centuries ago. The technique of using almond paste in this way, modelling it like clay, is a great Sicilian speciality, and is used to make other very realistic shapes, sandwiches, cakes or *salame*, for example. Once they were made for special saints' days, now they are available all the year round.

• *Scorzette di arance candite* Crisp sweets made with orange peel sliced into thin strips, boiled and covered in melted sugar.

• *Sospiri di monaca* (Nun's sigh) little light soufflés made with egg whites and hazelnuts.

Local Specialities

• *Caponata* Deep-fried aubergines, octopus, olives, toasted almonds and chocolate.
• *Arancini di riso* A rare use of rice in Sicilian cooking. Little rissoles with peas and meat, and a little cheese, dipped in egg and fried in boiling oil. They are meant to look like little oranges *arancini*.

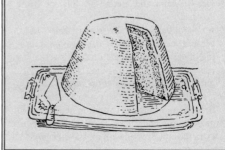

VINO
Wine

In the past, the wine of the island was so strong and alcoholic that it was mainly used as a *vino da taglio* to add to other wines. Nowadays there is a move towards developing a whole section of very drinkable table wines, made exclusively in Sicilian vineyards. The new Sicilian wines are tending to be light and fruity, but there is still much to be done to develop the wine of the island fully.

SPECIAL RED WINE
• *Eloro Rosso* This is a garnet-coloured wine with a fresh dry flavour, generally considered an élite wine. (Also available as white.)
• *Cerasuolo di Vittoria* A delicious D.O.C. wine with a very decisive flavour. It has a characteristic light surface foam when poured. Ages extremely well.

RED WINE
• *Corvo de Casteldaccia* A well-known table wine, whose better vintages are for special occasions. A marvellous colour, very bright ruby red.
• *Etna* A delicious rounded wine with a warming undertone. Perfect for drinking with strong cheese or roast meats.

WHITE WINE
• *Alcamo* Marvellous dry D.O.C. wine, light and airy with a most unusual mother-of-pearl colouring. Hard work has made it into a D.O.C. wine, though previously its decisive bouquet and aromatic flavour were used for the making of vermouths.
• *Rapitala* Another superb dry D.O.C. white, less aromatic and strongly flavoured than the above but perfect for drinking with all Sicilian fish dishes.

ROSÉ WINE
• *Eloro Rosato* A much sought-after delicate rosé, produced in very small quantities. A fine, elegant table wine with a cherry colour.

SPUMANTE
• *Solimano* A natural, light champagne, made with semi-dried grapes, giving it a sweet and raisiny flavour.

• *Gran Spumante Corvo* Fruity demi-sec or dry, light and golden, made in champenois method. Excellent as an aperitif, or with a special meal.

BEVANDE
Drinks

I have put all the island's sweet dessert wines into this section because they're not really dessert wines at all – they are what you are likely to be served as a drink when visiting, or what is drunk over a game of cards or a political discussion down at the village café.
• *Malvasia di Lipari* Produced on the islands of Salina and Stromboli. The Romans called it 'The Ambrosia of the Gods', which will give you a fair idea of how long it's been around. Made with Malvasia grapes, with a small addition of currant grapes. This is a really exceptional wine, and comes in three forms: *naturale*, *passito* or *liquoroso* – naturally sweet, slightly sweeter and liqueurish.

Marsala

As much a part of the island as orange groves and *mafiosi*, this is a wine which varies in flavour and intensity depending very much on how much you spend for a bottle. It can be as dry as a dry sherry, or as sweet as a sticky liqueur. To make Marsala, the wine has *calamich* (cooked must) added to it. It is then treated to make it more, or less, robust, depending on which kind of Marsala it will be, and then aged in casks. The longer it's aged, the more expensive it will be.
• *Marsala Vergine* Dry, amber, and served as an aperitif.
• *Marsala Speciale* is Marsala to which other ingredients have been added, such as cream, raisins, or coffee. *Marsala all'Uovo* is mixed with egg.
• *Marsala Fine* is a fairly medium-priced wine, coming in varying degrees of sweetness – dry, *amabile* or sweet.
• *Marsala Superiore* The top of the range, also dry, *amabile* or sweet. A word of advice – if you drink this wine with desserts, avoid chocolate. The two flavours clash horribly!
• *Moscato* Another sweet wine to be drunk at the end of a meal or simply as an aperitif.
• *Moscato di Pantelleria* comes from the island of the same name and can be bought *naturale*

naturally sparkling, or *liquoroso* like a liqueur.

• *Passito* This is a wine made from grapes that have been allowed to wilt and dry out slightly. The grapes used will be wrinkled and soft, and would naturally produce a much sweeter wine than if fresh firm grapes were used. It is made in four variations: *dolce* sweet, *liquoroso* like a liqueur, *extra* more alcoholic, and *Tanit*, after the Phoenician goddess of fertility – very popular with couples trying for a male heir to add to their family!

WORTH TAKING HOME

Every time I've returned from Sicily I've brought home a basket of oranges, lemons and tangerines, all with a bunch of deep green leaves attached – perfect for cheering up dull days of English weather.

Bring back a few bottles of *moscato*, Malvasia and Marsala with you, and keep them till the cold becomes unbearable – then crack one open, sit back, glare at the snow and dream about the sunshine and sparkle that have gone into each bottle.

The marzipan sweets and cakes make marvellous presents. This is in fact sweetie heaven, and presents for all your sweet-toothed friends and relations you'll find no problem.

If sweet wines are not your scene, slide in a couple of bottles of the dry reds and whites of the island. The Corvo wines are excellent (as served on all Alitalia flights I've ever been on). Do remember that quite a lot of the local coarser wines will be very alcoholic.

If you can, take a tray of Sicilian pastries – the *PASTICCERIA RUSSOTTI* in Corso Umberto in Taormina is famous – but only if your journey is imminent, and shortish.

Sicilian cheeses travel well, but tend to smell rather strong, so wrap them well.

The Island Rediscovers the Sea

Sardinia is unlike the rest of Italy. It's even totally different from that other great Italian island, Sicily. Sardinia has 100 contrasting faces: one moment you think you're in the Dolomites, the next you could be in the Sahara, a moment later you could be in a grubby oriental backstreet market, only to turn the corner and find yourself in a neat white Spanish town. There are vast areas of rocks and grass covered with myrtle and juniper, where sheep graze peacefully. There are cork trees, olive groves, palms of all sizes. There are marshes where the bright pink flamingoes fly clattering up into the air as you approach, wild ponies that play on the grassy slopes of Giarra di Gesturi, wild boar and deer that flash past you suddenly as you drive through ancient forests.

Completely forested in Roman times, the mostly mountainous island is now bare, the flat tops whipped by wild winds. Huge masses of rock and scraggy little bushes, open heathland and wide green valleys glow in the sun. Then there are the stunning beaches of white or coral pink sand bordered by imposing blocks of gnarled rock. This land has not been easy to tame, but where the battle has been won and crops and animals provided with water, splendid, profitable farmland has evolved.

The main activities of the islanders are farming and stockraising, both of which have always been difficult given the nature of the land and the lack of water. Frequent droughts have caused great loss of animal life. In the rainy season the rivers are torrential, in summer they're dry. Winter is tough in the mountains, though gentle along the coast. Summers are long, hot and dry, and in every season the cruel Mistral wind blows across from the west.

Sardinians are proud, noble people, the hardest working of all Italians – and they hardly consider themselves Italian at all. Their ancient civilisation is still clear in their dress and customs.

Malaria, pirates and many enemies have caused them over the centuries to move away from the coast, so despite the fact that this is an island (even its name indicates a link with fish), the culture is not marine, and they are not traditionally a fishing people. Shepherds and farmers, they are concentrated in villages and towns, leaving vast unpopulated spaces. Yet even here, social patterns are changing as new towns and holiday villages spring up, particularly on the coast.

The island is divided up into 4 official provinces, Cagliari, Sassari, Nuoro and Oristano, but ancient local regions with strange names, defying the rules of topography and politics, need to be mentioned too. In the northern corner are *Gallura Montana*, rich in cork trees and weirdly-shaped granite rock formations, and *Gallura Marittima*, with marvellous beaches and sharp reefs. *La Barbagia* in the centre is completely wooded and mountainous, home of the *muflone*, a protected sheep native only to this island and Corsica, living on the higher peaks. The *Campidano*, like a corridor between high plateaux, represents the region's most fertile area, and in the south are *L'Inglesiente* and *Sulcis*, like Tuscan mountain ranges, and rich in minerals.

In many dominating positions are the *nuraghi*, stone watchtowers which were built 12 or so centuries before Christ by the first mysterious inhabitants of the island.

Lobsters and suckling pig

Sardinian cooking is quite a separate issue from southern Italian fare. Culminating in the lobsters grilled over an open fire, or the succulent suckling pig roasted on the spit, it is permanently infused with the tingling scent of burning myrtle, a simple homely way of preparing delicious raw materials, with an explosion of tiny, delicate pastries to round off the meal. Perhaps it's the clear, unpolluted sea and clean fresh air which makes it so, but whatever one eats on this island always tastes perfect. And unsurprisingly, they are immensely proud of their specialities.

CAGLIARI & PROVINCE

The Phoenicians were the first to realise what a splendid situation the sheltered bay in the south of the island was for them, and founded a colony around the bay called Caralis. Cagliari is today the most important cultural, economic and political centre of Sardinia, but has always been a trade centre for merchants from all over the Mediterranean.

This province includes the agricultural area of Campidano.

SASSARI & PROVINCE

Sassari stands not far from the sea, on a plateau sloping gently down towards the Golfo dell'Asinara. It's an old town with a modern atmosphere, its ancient city walls now tree-lined avenues. I found a typical Sardinian *osteria* in *L'ASSASSINO*, providing traditional meat dishes – *piedine e testine d'agnello* stewed lamb's feet and head, *porcello al mirto* pork cooked with myrtle, and *coratella allo spiedino* grilled pork offal. In nearby via Rosello I bought some of the enormous variety of Sardinian pastries displayed in the *PASTICCERIA PIANA*.

Spanish atmosphere

Along the coast are many important port towns like Alghero, renowned for its lobster fishing and all the marvellous tourist resorts. Olbia is for arriving and departing from the airport or by ferry to Livorno, Genova or Civitavecchia. Then there is the Costa Smeralda, as chic and elegant and exclusive as you'll get anywhere in Italy. With its stunning beaches, it is completely unspoilt, the water like glass and the people here are helpful and content.

Also within the province are the islands of Caprera, where lies the remains of Garibaldi, La Maddalena, L'Asinara and other small islands. The whole area has a Catalan mood about it, the dialect tinged with Spanish and the old buildings look like leftovers from the long period of Aragonese domination. Even the food has a Spanish feel.

At Santa Teresa di Gallura is a restaurant called *CANNE AL VENTO*, owned by an ex-*contadino* known as Brancaccio. The place and the man are

Staff of Life

Sardinia is famous for its bread – there are so many different kinds ranging from the wafer-thin *carta da musica*, so called because it resembles the paper music is written on, its cracks representing the lines of music, to much more substantial frugal loaves to fill the shepherds during their days on the hills.

As you move from one town or village to another – the shape, method of baking and kneading bread will change completely. Look out for *pane carasau (carta da musica)* with which other delicacies are created: *pane fratau*, with eggs, tomatoes, *pecorino* and vinegar, and *pane guttiau*, which is sprinkled with olive oil and then served hot.

typical of what happened along this coastline when the millionaires came from the sea to transform the mood and the needs of an erstwhile debilitated sour land, where centuries of deforestation had eroded the surface soil. Everything on his menu was fishy, with lots of pasta and lobster.

In Alghero I ate in two completely different restaurants. *AI TUGURI*, via Majorca 57 is situated in a lovely 15th-century house with the most amazing range of Sardinian dishes at a very modest price. I had *tortino di asparagi selvatici* wild asparagus cake, *formaggio arrosto* roast cheese, and the delicious *maloreddus* pasta. At *LA LEPANTO* the mood was somewhat different, it's Algherese cuisine in a Catalan style.

NUORO & PROVINCE

Just half a century ago Nuoro was still a little shepherds' settlement with tumbledown rustic houses and tin alleys, lost in a rocky plain just north of Gennartu. Now it's a large modern town, a market for all the local melons, peaches, tomatoes, cheeses and fish. It's also the centre for traditional folklore studies.

The whole province is mountainous and stretches right across the island from coast to coast. Sheep are predominant. At Macomer, they make excellent *pecorino Sardo*. Sardinians adore this smooth tasty ewe's milk cheese with a hint of myrtle about its flavour.

In the Gulf of Orosei, backed by vineyards, olive groves and gardens, seaside resorts are plentiful – at Cala Gonone I discovered the famous 3-floored

restaurant called *SUCCOLOCONE* which had also been found by dozens of German tourists with whom I enjoyed some of the best lobster, roast piglet, *sebadas* and *culigiones*.

Rising up behind Orgosolo, where the older women still wear traditional heavy black clothes and head-coverings, is the thick forest famous as a hiding place for bandits. The mourning clothes are probably a result of the continual vendettas. Macomer, in the centre of the island, is very much a crossroads, where all the cultures of the various provinces come together and form a classic Sardinian mood. This is reflected in the kitchen, with all the best traditional dishes coming together too. At the *AGIPMOTEL* I had excellent spaghetti with *bottarga* of mullet, and there was also *spaghetti al cartoccio* (when it is wrapped in paper and cooks in its own steam) with fresh mountain mushrooms.

ORISTANO & PROVINCE

On the western coast is Oristano, a town full of good food shops. In via Campania I discovered *CREMERIA CODA*, a pasticceria selling delicious *sospiri*, *amaretti* and other almond-based pastries. I also bought fabulous cheese *ravioli* and *sebadas* made by Signora Cuozzo. At Riola, a nearby village, there's a lady called Michela Secchi who makes the most fantastic Sardinian bread. The Sardinians are enormously imaginative with bread – it comes in all shapes and textures, from the most brittle *carta da musica* to the huge soft heart-shaped loaves called *pane cuore*.

This province is intensively cultivated, with vineyards, fruit groves, tobacco, sugar beet and vegetables. Eucalyptus and pine trees have been planted along the coastline to protect the crops from the strong north-eastern winds. Cabras is a seaport on the edge of one of the largest seashore lagoons of the island.

SALUMI

Salami, Sausages and Cured Meats

As most of the pigs are roasted, little is left for making into *salumi*. An important one to mention though is *prosciutto di cinghiale*, thinly sliced, brittle wild boar ham. It tastes very gamey, with a rough texture. Once tasted never forgotten. *Salsiccie di cinghiale* is a kind of boar salame and is also superb.

PASTA

The pasta names sound Spanish. Ravioli are called *culurzones* or *culingionis*, and are stuffed with cheese, spinach, eggs and saffron. The home-made pasta that looks very much like *gnocchi* is called *malloreddus* or *macarones*. They are very very hard, so if you take some home (and they are available all over Italy), do remember they take a long time to cook.

Local Specialities

• *Culigiones* Huge *ravioli* filled with Swiss chard, and cheese, or eggs, nutmeg and *pecorino*, or even with a sweet filling.
• *Impanadas* Little pasta moulds with a meat filling that are baked in the oven. A speciality of Nuoro.
• *Maloreddus* Like very small *gnocchi*, made with saffron in the dough to give them a bright colour, usually dressed with tomato sauce with or without meat, and a good grating of *pecorino*.
• *Sa Fregula* There's an old Sardinian folk song in which the girl says 'Marry me, I know how to make Fregula too'. It's a kind of couscous, made with grains of wheat, often dressed with onions fried in lard, grated *pecorino* and black pepper.

PESCE E FRUTTI DI MARE

Fish and Seafood

Aragosta lobster, lobster and yet more lobster. And as this is for ever right at the top of the list of my favourite things to eat, I am in paradise. It is usually served simply split open and grilled, though it can be turned into a pasta sauce, or made into a salad.

In the lagoons and seaponds just inside the seashore eel *anguille* and *cefali* mullet thrive very happily. The other chief speciality is the incredibly expensive and totally delicious Sardinian version of caviar, *bottarga*. These fish eggs can be tuna, mullet or just about any other locally caught variety, but the most valued is *cefalo*. There are two kinds of mullet in Italy – *muggine*,

---

Local Specialities

• *Aragosta in insalata* While it's usually simply split open and grilled, or boiled whole, lobster is sometimes finely sliced and dressed with olive oil, lemon juice, salt and pepper and the lobster's own eggs.
• *Bottarga* Tuna fish eggs, or the more expensive variety, grey mullet eggs, soaked in salt water, then shaped into a slightly flattened sausage, sliced thinly and served as an antipasto with oil and lemon juice – or grated as a dressing on pasta.
• *Sa Burrida* The speciality of Cagliari, it's an offshoot of the Ligurian fish dish. It consists of catfish, skinned and filleted, covered with a sauce of walnuts, mixed with the minced liver of the fish and cooked with olive oil, white wine vinegar, parsley and garlic. The dish is then left for half a day before serving.
• *Sa cassola* Originally a Spanish dish, this is a rich fish stew with lots of different fish and seafood.

---

which stays nearer the beach, and *cefalo*, which tends to swim further out at sea.

Vongole baby clams fished and cooked in Sardinia tend to be much larger than those on the mainland.

CARNE E CACCIA

Meat and Game

Suckling pig, lamb and kid, all cooked very simply on the spit or *a carragiu*, a traditional Sardinian method, which is to dig a deep hole and build a fire at the bottom, then lay stones on the fire, put the pig on the stones, cover with a branch of myrtle and more stones, and then earth. The result is absolutely incredible, miles better than any roasted meat coming out of an oven. There are also excellent stews and casseroles.

Little thrushes *grive* are stewed with myrtle. Partridge *pernice*, and wild boar *cinghiale* are both cooked in the same way as the suckling pig. Cooking meat, usually whole calves, kids, lambs or boars, means a huge open fire scented with herbs and using wood from the thickets, with the meat on a spit made out of a pole of the most aromatic wood, over glowing embers.

Various kinds of offal are also very popular –

tripe *corda*, lamb's head *testina*, and heart, lung and spleen cooked together, *coratella*.

FORMAGGIO

Cheese

In Sardinia, cheese is fresh and herby, with a predominant flavour of myrtle and thyme. *Latticini* are small mozzarellas, and there are two distinct varieties. One is made with cows' milk and comes from the green valleys, and the other with ewes' milk, from the rocky hills. *Fiore Sardo* is eaten with thick slices of coarse bread when it's fresh, or grated over pasta once matured.

Pecorino Sardo is similar, but slightly more salty and mature. *Provolette (su casizzolu)* are strong aromatic little cheeses made with cows' milk, with all the flavour of the herby grass. *Fresa* is a flat, soft rather greasy cheese, but very buttery. The one that seems to be exported to the mainland most is *dolce Sardo* – it's sweet and creamy, and very delicious.

FRUTTA E VERDURA

Fruit and Vegetables

The land reclamation projects helped the island to increase its output in this field, but the lean nature of the soil does not permit a very wide or varied cultivation of any note.

Beetroot *barbabietole*, artichokes *carciofi*, barley and other grain take first place. Oranges, apples, pears, nectarines, plums, melons, figs and watermelons are grown here, but the most interesting oddity is the Japanese peach *pesca del giappone*, which is small, flat and green with a completely un-peachy and very unusual taste and texture.

PASTICCERIA

Cakes, Biscuits and Puddings

Like Sicily, Sardinia produces lots of delicious *pasticceria*. They are light and airy, and seem to have their origins in the Arab domination of the island.

- *Amarettus* Golden brown biscuits like macaroons.
- *Anicini* Crisp and crunchy aniseed-flavoured biscuits to eat with a glassful of sweet *Vernaccia*.
- *Aranciata nuorese* Honey-flavoured candied orange peel with almonds.
- *Blanchittus* or *bianchini* Light almond- and lemon-flavoured meringues.
- *Biscotti Sardi* Yeast biscuits.
- *Bugnoletti di patate* Sweet potato fritters dusted with sugar.
- *Caefus* Hand-made chocolates.
- *Candelaus* Tiny little tarts with an almond filling.
- *Culigionis* Fried *ravioli* with a sweet almond filling. (Also refers to the savoury one served as a first course.)
- *Gatto* A lemon-flavoured crunchy caramel.
- *Gesminus* Lightly scented golden meringues, once made with essence of jasmine, today usually orange flower water.
- *Gueffus* Sweet made with ground almonds, lemon and orange flower water with sugar.
- *Pabassinas di Cagliari* Cone-shaped biscuits made with raisins, walnuts, caraway seeds, orange peel and almonds and flour, bound together with *sapa*, made with wine must.

- *Pane di sapa* Tiny rolls, flavoured with spices, nuts and *sapa*, and decorated with *traggera*, tiny coloured sweets.
- *Papassinas Nuoresi* Iced biscuits containing almonds and raisins, made for all holy days.
- *Pardulas* Pastries made of coarse flour, olive oil and butter, then filled with a savoury or sweet filling.
- *Pirinchittus* Rich egg biscuits covered in icing.
- *Quaglio dolce* Quaglio is rennet, and this is a delicious cold junket.
- *Sebada* or *seada* Sweet cheese fritters smothered in bitter honey.
- *Suspirus* These are called 'sighs' because they are so very light and airy. Little almond meringues flavoured with vanilla and made with egg yolks. They are available all over the island, but are the speciality of the town of Ozieri.
- *Torta al formaggio* A hot sweet cheese cake, made with *pecorino Sardo*.
- *Turronis* or *torroncini* Wonderful almond nougat made with sugar, egg yolks, toasted almonds and lemon juice.

VINO

Wine

The stronger the sun gets, the headier the wine becomes. The most famous of Sardinian wines is *Vernaccia*, produced by vines of the same name which grow in the area round Oristano, and all over the lower Tirso valley. It is very similar to the Jerez de la Frontera wines from Spain, and is reminiscent of a very dry sherry, although it can also be syrupy and sweet.

It varies between 14 and 18 degrees, and the dry version is drunk as an aperitif, with seafood or with soup. The sweet version is a fine end to a meal accompanied by delicious Sardinian biscuits like *papassinas* or *amarettus*.

Other excellent wines include:

RED WINE
- *Ogliastra* A young wine, intensely red, from the Nuoro area. A good table wine.
- *Mandrolisai* As lovely as its name, with a bright ruby red colour, and less alcoholic than other Sardinian wines. A good everyday table wine.
- *Anghelu Ruju* A very special wine, aromatic and aristocratic. Produced with grapes from the Spanish Alicante vines, which are left to dry out in the sun. Rivals the best ports for flavour and intensity. Not really a wine to drink with meals.
- *Cannonau di Sardegna* The Sardinians' favourite wine. The colour ranges from ruby to apple red to orange. It's a strong wine, heady and rounded. Perfect to finish a meal with or to drink as an aperitif.

WHITE WINE
- *Nuragus* A fine dry wine, combining perfectly with roast fish, cheese and pasta.
- *Torbato* The dry version is the very best wine to drink with local fresh fish, whereas the sweet one, like Malaga wine, is drunk as a dessert wine or as an aperitif.
- *Trebbiano Sardo* Made with Trebbiano grapes, to which a little Vernaccia, Bombino and Nuragus are added. It has a very well-defined flavour, perfect for drinking with fish.
- *Vermentino* When young, this dry wine is for serving with fish. It becomes sweeter with age, and turns into an excellent dessert wine.

BEVANDE

Drinks

- *Sapa* A syrup of wine very similar to the one produced in Emilia Romagna, and can be diluted with water and ice to make a cooling drink, or used in cooking. It is made with *mosto*, the cloudy new wine made from Nuragus grapes, which must be made on the same day as you begin to make the *sapa*. Ten litres of *mosto* are boiled all day, then left to rest all night, strained through linen into a dark bottle, which is kept in the pantry; you end up with one litre of *Sapa*.

WORTH TAKING HOME

It is unusual to find some of the local wines anywhere outside the island, so it's worth taking a bottle or two of your favourite. But see whether they keep or not, as many Sardinian wines are designed to be drunk young.

Bottarga would make a very upmarket present (I think it's much better than caviar) – take some home to impress!

Take home *maloreddus, pecorino Sardo, fiore Sardo*, and lots of the delicious cakes and biscuits and sweets if you have a sweet tooth.

INDEX

INDEX

INDEX

INDEX

INDEX

INDEX